Bion's Sources

There are an increasing number of publications concerned with the work of Wilfred Bion (1897–1979). Many have sought new ideas from his writing; however, little attention has been paid to the intellectual context in which Bion wrote.

Bion's Sources traces where Bion's new ideas came from, what job he required of them, how successfully he used his context and how that has fertilised psychoanalysis. Expert contributors provide chapters on areas of the intellectual context separate from or adjacent to clinical psychoanalysis in Britain which have clearly influenced the texts Bion left (those published in his lifetime, or subsequently). Chapters explore the influences deriving from Wilfred Trotter, Henri Bergson and process philosophy, Kurt Lewin and group dynamics, Immanuel Kant, R.B. Braithwaite and the philosophy of science, the mathematics of notation and transformation, as well as the work of psychoanalysts who have applied their theories to social science, psychosomatics, and literature and the humanities.

By contextualising Bion in the wider culture of ideas, and removing him from the exclusive world of psychoanalysis, *Bion's Sources* aims to moderate his 'genius' by showing how it was shaped by very wide influences. This book will be of interest to psychoanalysts, clinicians and those interested in the history of psychoanalytic ideas.

Nuno Torres is a clinical psychologist, researcher and lecturer at ISPA-IU in Lisbon, Portugal. He is a fellow of the Research Training Program of the International Psychoanalytic Association, a member of the Society for Psychotherapy Research and a Visiting Fellow of the Centre for Psychoanalytic Studies at the University of Essex.

R.D. Hinshelwood is Professor in the Centre for Psychoanalytic Studies, University of Essex. He is a Fellow of the British Psychoanalytical Society, and a Fellow of the Royal College of Psychiatrists. He has authored numerous books and articles. *Observing Organisations* (2000) was edited with Wilhelm Skogstad and is among a number of texts he has written on psychoanalytic applications to social science.

Bion's Sources

The shaping of his paradigms

Edited by Nuno Torres and R.D. Hinshelwood

Routledge
Taylor & Francis Group
LONDON AND NEW YORK

First published 2013
by Routledge
4 Park Square, Milton Park, Abingdon, Oxon OX14 4RN
605 Third Avenue, New York, NY 10017

Routledge is an imprint of the Taylor & Francis Group, an informa business

British Library Cataloguing in Publication Data
A catalogue record for this book is available from the British Library

Library of Congress Cataloging in Publication Data
Bion's sources : the shaping of his paradigms / edited by Nuno Torres and Robert Hinshelwood.
pages cm
Includes index.
1. Bion, Wilfred R. |q (Wilfred Ruprecht), 1897–1979–Criticism and interpretation. 2. Psychoanalysis. I. Torres, Nuno, editor of compilation. II. Hinshelwood, R. D., editor of compilation.
RC438.6.B54B56 2013
616.89'17–dc23 2012038683

ISBN: 978-0-415-53208-2 (hbk)
ISBN: 978-0-415-53209-9 (pbk)
ISBN: 978-0-203-55606-1 (ebk)

Typeset in Garamond
by Wearset Ltd, Boldon, Tyne and Wear

Contents

Contributors

Matt ffytche is a Lecturer in Psychoanalytic Studies at the Centre for Psychoanalytic Studies at the University of Essex. He has written on the relationship between psychoanalysis and literature, with a particular attention to modernism, and to poetry, including (2010) 'Objects and How to Survive Them: Several Views of John Wilkinson's "Saccades" ', *Journal of British and Irish Innovative Poetry*, 2 (1), 7–34, and (2010) 'The Modernist Road to the Unconscious', in Peter Brooker, Andrzej Gasiorek, Deborah Longworth and Andrew Thacker (eds), *The Oxford Handbook of Modernisms*, Oxford, Oxford University Press, pp. 410–428. His most recent publication, *Foundation of the Unconscious: Schelling, Freud and the Birth of the Modern Psyche* (Cambridge University Press, 2011) is a work of intellectual history examining the emergence of a concept of the unconscious in German philosophy and psychology in the early nineteenth century.

Bob Harris is an Independent Consultant Psychotherapist and group analyst. He supervises clinical staff in a variety of contexts and teaches psychotherapy in the UK and abroad. He is a musician, and has special interest in the arts. He is formerly Director of Programmes at the Institute of Group Analysis, a regular conference speaker, the author of many journal articles and 'Working with Distressed Young People', Learning Matters/SAGE 2011.

R.D. Hinshelwood is Professor in the Centre for Psychoanalytic Studies, University of Essex, and previously Clinical Director, The Cassel Hospital, London. He is a Fellow of the British Psychoanalytical Society, and a Fellow of the Royal College of Psychiatrists. He has authored *A Dictionary of Kleinian Thought* (1989) and other books and articles on Kleinian psychoanalysis. *Observing Organisations* (2000) was edited with Wilhelm Skogstad and is among a number of texts on psychoanalytic applications to social science. He founded the *British Journal of Psychotherapy*, and *Psychoanalysis and History*. He has recently completed *Research on the Couch: Single Case Studies, Subjectivity and Psychoanalytic Knowledge* (Routledge 2013).

William J. Massicotte is a member of the Canadian Psychoanalytic Society and is engaged in full-time private practice in Montreal. His McGill PhD was done on psychoanalysis with a special emphasis on Bion. He is a philosopher who developed an interest in aspects of mathematics while doing his MA on Husserl (a mathematician turned philosopher). He has held many administrative positions and is currently the Co-Chair for North America of the IPA's Public Information Committee. He also teaches at the Montreal and Ottawa psychoanalytic institutes.

Kelly Noel-Smith combines a career in law with an academic interest in psychoanalysis. A partner in a London law firm, she is currently completing her PhD at Birkbeck College, University of London, on Freud's theory of time and the ancient Greek influence. Her publications include: 'Harry Potter's Oedipal Issues' (*Psychoanalytic Studies* 3: 199–207, 2001); and 'Time and Space as "Necessary Forms of Thought"' (*Free Associations* Vol. 9 Part 3 (no. 51): 394–442).

Malcolm Pines FRCP, FRCPsych, DPM[dist]. Past positions: consultant at The Cassel Hospital, St George's Hospital, The Maudsley Hospital, The Tavistock Clinic. Past president, The International Association of Group Psychotherapy; founder member, The Institute of Group Analysis London; former member British Psychoanalytical Society, and chair of its Publications Committee. Until recently, editor, *Group Analysis*. Collected papers: *Circular Reflections* [Jessica Kingsley, London, 1998]. Current interests: evolution of social psychology, history of psychoanalytic psychology, and cultural and social history.

Layla Redway-Harris graduated with a First Class BSc degree in the History, Philosophy and Social Studies of Science from University College London in 2010. Later that year she gave a talk in St Petersberg on the scientific endeavours to study collective consciousness. She has a keen interest in sustainable development and currently works as a technical advisor for the Energy Saving Trust.

Nuno Torres is a postdoctoral researcher at ISPA-IU (University Institute of Applied Psychology) in Lisbon. Fellow of the Research Training Program of the International Psychoanalytic Association, Visiting Fellow of the Centre for Psychoanalytic Studies at the University of Essex, member of the Society for Psychotherapy Research. Founding member of *DevelopMind*, an Association for Mental Health in Youth. His PhD focused on W.R. Bion's concept of proto-mental matrix as a bio-psycho-social model of emotional–containment disorders and bodily symptoms (addictions, psycho-dermatology and self-harm). Recently he has been researching on socio-emotional development: attachment, social competence and father involvement in children, adult close relationships, and patient–therapist relational factors – countertransference and therapeutic ingredients – in psychotherapy.

Dimitris Vonofakos is a Research Fellow at the Nottingham University Business School and a Fellow at the Centre for Psychoanalytic Studies, University of Essex. He is currently involved in the independent evaluation of public health policy and organisational change in NHS institutions in the North West of England, while academically his background is in psychology and psychoanalytic theory and methods. Some of his research interests include the psychoanalytic study of social and organisational dynamics, the historical development of psychoanalytic theory and the applications of psychoanalytic methods in the social sciences.

Christina Wieland is a psychoanalytic psychotherapist in private practice and a Fellow of the University of Essex. She has a special interest in Bion's work and has taught Bion at the University of Essex for many years. She also teaches in many psychoanalytic training institutions. Her book *The Undead Mother: Psychoanalytic Explorations of Masculinity, Femininity and Matricide* was first published by Rebus in 2000 and later reprinted by Karnac (2002). She is currently writing a book with the working title *Pact with the Devil: The Fascist State of Mind and the Manufacturing of Masculinity*, based on her doctoral thesis. The book is due to be published by Routledge in 2014.

Foreword

The new millennium has occasioned a bursting forth of new studies on all aspects of Bion's psychoanalytic thinking and intellectual development. The last twenty years have seen a proliferation of generalist studies (Bléandonu, Symington and Vermote) and dictionaries of his concepts (López-Corvo and P. Sandler) as well as his *Collected Works* (Mawson) that will appear presently. While these works have an important expository function, setting out in detail exactly what Bion's psychoanalytic thought was, books like *Bion's Sources* represent a new wave of specialist studies, where the questions involving Bion's corpus can now be expanded and provide the raw materials for lively debate amongst clinicians and academicians alike.

In their *Preface*, Torres and Hinshelwood discuss the need for interdisciplinary studies of Bion, making the current volume a matter of personal choice of academicians over a "practitioners only" model in terms of contributors. Perhaps to paraphrase Georges Clemenceau's famous aphorism from World War I, the editors thought that Bion studies have now become too serious a matter to be left to clinicians alone. I find myself in agreement with Torres and Hinshelwood's culturalist assumptions, insofar as analysts like Freud and Bion both held themselves to reading broadly – and reflecting the fruits of the journeys into philosophy, literature and physical sciences in their psychological writings. But the clinician might also ask: of what practical use is the immersion in Bion's cultural sources, to which one answer might be: allow yourself the experience of discovery by reading about the influences that permeated Bion's intellectual development, so that you might formulate some of your own answers to a growing conversation that is present at numerous conferences around the world. There is a growing climate of opinion that we stand to feel enriched by retracing some of the roads that Bion took in his analytic odyssey.

It is quite touching that Parthenope Bion was on the brink of making a full-length study of her father's life and work, a project that was cut short by her tragic and untimely death. She left us a poignant evocation of his personal library, most of which consisted of non-psychoanalytic books. This bibliographic "selected fact" tells us much about the intellectual proclivities of its owner. While other renowned analysts, like D.W. Winnicott, claimed an incapacity to read any analytic paper without simultaneously transforming its contents, *Bion's Sources* tells us much about the kinds of reading practices Bion cultivated – and more importantly, what he harvested from doing so.

So here is a list of questions that piqued my curiosity as I made my way through these chapters – and the reader will no doubt form his or her own questions that may guide their further reading – or most importantly, returning to Bion' writings themselves. Nothing can substitute for going back to the original texts. *Ad fontes!*

To the questions: how would one assess the relative contributions – all from different decades – of Wilfred Trotter, J.R. Hadfield, Kurt Lewin and John Rickman on Bion's (1955d, 1962) mature views of group dynamics? What were the relative contributions of Bion's Oxford education vis-à-vis the medical training culture in which he was immersed at University College London in 1920s – or the group culture under Hugh Crichton-Miller at the Tavistock Clinic during the 1930s? How was it that Bion evolved a "suspension of leadership" approach that formed a counterpoint to traditional educational and class-oriented methods of officer selection during World War II? How was it that Bion's relationship with his first analyst, John Rickman, transformed itself into a creative collaboration, all without falling into the more ordinary experience of a collusive "boundary crossing"? Is it, as Hinshelwood suggests, a matter of elective affinities between the two men: "The commonality of it bears the traces of Rickman's Quaker egalitarianism, and Bion's despair, learned in the First World War over the dependency of soldiers on an inadequate leadership"? What does the Rickman and Bion correspondence (1939–1951) tell us about analyst-patient mores of the pre-World War II generation?

Did Bion's group work and psychoanalytic training "bi-directionally" influence one another? It is also well known that Bion's analysis with Klein led to a reformulation of the "Group Dynamics" paper in 1955, but might one also debate how his group work influenced how he assessed his participation in what became known as the "Klein group" in the 1950s? How did Rickman's egalitarian, non-managerial style compare with Bion's experience with Melanie Klein, his second analyst (one whom he affectionately and privately nicknamed the "Boss"), and someone with a distinctly "top-down" managerial style, especially with members of her own group? To what extent did Bion's decision to leave an administratively loaded life as Director of the Tavistock Clinic (1956–1962), President of the British Psychoanalytical Society (1962–1965) as well as the head of the Melanie Klein Trust result from feeling he had too little time to do any research and writing? Is this one of the motives that led to Bion's relocation to Los Angeles in 1968, where he was left free to practice and write?

Another important set of crucial questions relate to the question of how Bion transmitted and transformed the work of Freud and Klein. While Bion derived many of his ideas about the "mental apparatus" from Freud, how was he able to embed this unitary model of mind into Klein's object relations paradigm, so that he was able to evolve a more complex interactional model based on his notion of "container/contained"? Was it again a matter of how Bion "Kleinianized" Freud's model of mind, while "Freudianizing" Klein's object relations model? And yet, how did Bion also arrive at his own distinctive view, where now on the basis of normal projective identification, the infant could make its sensory experience known to a mother who could deploy "alpha-function" in the form of reverie, and thereby contain and help metabolize the infant's distress? How was it – as one of the contributors notes – that Bion evolved a normal developmental model of the infant with its mother without ever citing the well-known work of his colleague, D.W. Winnicott?

What can be said of Bion's reading of Western philosophy – from Plato and Aristotle down to the Continental and English philosophers, such as Hume, Kant and Bergson? What occasioned Bion's apparently sudden turn to how philosophy and the physical/mathematical sciences could inform the workaday habits of the practicing psychoanalyst after Melanie Klein's death in 1960? To what extent did Bion render accurately or transform the philosophy of Immanual Kant, with whose work he came in contact while reading in History at Queen's College, Oxford? If as one of the contributors maintained, that Bion misread Kant while accurately depicting the work of Hume and Plato, what does this act of "textual transformation" tell us? Is Bion's reading of Kant a meaningful transformation, one necessary for the growth and development of psychoanalytic theory? How worthwhile was it for Bion to do an epistemological critique of the psychoanalytic situation, when in effect he now questioned how the analyst establishes what he or she learns in the consulting room – and how he conveys these findings to his colleagues? How does one evaluate the different forms of psychoanalytic "knowing," epitomized by those, like the contemporary Kleinian analysts in London, who tend to lean more favorably in the direction of Bion's work on the "K-link" vis-à-vis those like Grotstein, Ferro and Vermote, who emphasize intuitive ways of understanding the clinical situation – as symbolized by Bion's postulation of "O"?

Still another way Bion attempted to tackle problems posed by the philosophy of science, epitomized by his interest in Braithwaite, was to address how the "jobbing analyst" could obtain reliable knowledge and assessing what kind of knowledge we could trust – as he did when he constructed the grid. Since so few workaday analysts today spend much time writing about its numerous categories for how thoughts evolve – and to what uses they can put, what sense can we make of Bion's reading of Braithwaite, and his attempts to address the necessary and sufficient conditions of psychoanalytic knowledge? In the last analysis, was the grid a grand but ultimately doomed enterprise, one that Bion thought would aid the workaday analyst in communicating objectively the results of his analytic sessions with fellow analysts? Or has the knowledge garnered by the grid been deployed yet simultaneously transformed by succeeding generations of analysts?

Last but not least, especially from someone writing from Los Angeles, there is the "late Bion" of the post-epistemological or "literary/aesthetic" period in California after 1968. What are we to make of the psychoanalytic knowledge that Bion aimed to attain in his fictional writing? Was this an attempt at a "poetic model of the unconscious"? In what way can Bion's novels be regarded as a reworking of the ideas from his three previous periods of work? Was the quest for an objectivist or "scientifically" communicable form of psychoanalysis ultimately sacrificed on the altar of such an ephemeral concept as "O"? Or was the search for ultimate truth eventually going to lead to intuitive leaps beyond what the sensory apparatus could grasp? How are we to reconcile the claims of analysts who lean more heavily on Bion's emphasis of the "K-link" vis-à-vis those who emphasize the quality of *being* in O?

No doubt that other readers of the current volume will form their own personal queries. In the last analysis, *Bion's Sources* goes a long ways to whet our intellectual appetites to know more and debate the relative influences of Bion's wide-ranging reading and life experiences. He bequeathed psychoanalysis a powerful set of conceptual tools, the raw materials, especially in the shadow of the Controversial Discussions, in which the three-tiered training track system at the British Psychoanalytical Society was established. In light of the heated differences between Kleinians, Freudians and Independents to which Bion was privy, in my view, he gave us the means to both study and reconcile differences amongst different psychoanalytic schools. I trust that the current volume will contribute to passionate discussion amongst clinicians and academics alike.

We can honor Bion's legacy to psychoanalysis in no better way than to continue this interdisciplinary debate.

Joseph Aguayo
Los Angeles, August 2012

Preface

We met when one of us, Nuno, came to Essex University for doctoral studies with a project on Bion's proto-mental system, which was supervised by Bob. Then long after that, Nuno suggested a book on some of the sources, such as Trotter, from which Bion drew for his own ideas. Bob immediately thought of a remark Bion's daughter, Parthenope, once made to him. She studied her father's library and said although there were several thousand books, only about two to three metres of shelves were psychoanalytic books. And of course, this prompted the question: what were all those others?

After Parthenope's death, her husband, Luigi Talamo, published on the internet some very brief notes that Parthenope had left. We have copied them below from the website, www.sicap.it/merciai/parthenope/parthenope.htm, dated 1 February 2001, and accessed July 2010 (active from 2001 to 2010, the site has now been taken down).

She had set out her plan to capture her father's intellectual formation, a project sadly annulled by her very untimely death.

We cannot claim to have the close knowledge that Parthenope had of her father and his ideas, but we decided to have a go at something like the project that she was unable to do. This is not in any way a substitute, but a first effort to broaden the scope of 'Bion studies', by exploring Bion's reading, his restless search for ideas to help solve the problems he found in working as a psychoanalyst, and in communicating with colleagues. Too many different theories now make up psychoanalysis, and give rise to all sorts of conceptual and technical innovations that can all be lumped together as psychoanalysis. The study of how psychoanalytical theories and concepts come into being and are used by theoreticians and psychotherapists has always been present, but have recently become more salient under the umbrella term of conceptual research.

The people we found to write about the ideas that Bion used in association with his clinical work and his reflections on it are authors with academic knowledge rather than experienced psychoanalytic clinicians. We wanted people with a respect for where ideas came from, rather than people with the experience of the effective use of the ideas in practice – both in clinical practice and in their application to other fields of investigation. In that sense this book contains chapters that address the 'biographies' of concepts, not of people and patients. It is about the history of ideas, and by authors interested in the origins of Bion's ideas, the conceptual not clinical problems for which they are put to use, what happens to the ideas in the course of their new employment, and what consequences to their meanings come about.

One of the crucial problems for psychoanalysis (no different from any other field of science and culture) is that most conceptual assessment of theories are made either with a more or less explicit denigration of one or other or a cult-like adherence to another. Controversy is usually conducted on the basis of a priori assessment of these virtues and denigrations. A real engagement in the values or weaknesses of particular theories is often avoided. The academic field of psychoanalytic studies presents a resourceful ground for conceptual studies with a critical and contextual assessment of theories that to some extent tries to avoid the allegiances of particular groups and establishments, and this book is in large part a product of this academic endeavour. Wilfred Bion is undoubtedly one of the most innovative and challenging psychoanalytic thinkers of the second half of the twentieth century, and has been highly influential throughout the psychoanalytic community. His name on titles of papers indexed in the PEP database (www.pep-web.org) is still increasing exponentially, while for instance Klein and Fairbairn reached a peak in the 1990s and are now falling.

Bion was an atypical psychoanalyst and psychiatrist. He came quite late to psychoanalysis, after his mature years, in a point of the life cycle where he had been already developing his own adult thinking, and had been moulded by many thinkers and cultural languages other than Freud's semantic universe. He was more deeply moulded in his formative years by history, and was more an army officer and a want-to-be philosopher than an indoctrinated 'couch-potato'. As a physician working in the field of psychiatry, he was the opposite of a 'shrink', his aim was to widen the horizons of the patient and the psychiatrist alike.

In the course of his life Bion travelled widely, and dwelt, not only geographically (from India to the New World – Los Angeles and Brazil) but mostly intellectually between history, literature, psychiatry, psychoanalysis, art, religion, philosophy, mathematics, politics, economics ... and no doubt others. To some extent this intellectual breadth resembled Freud, but whereas Freud wrote in a linear narrative style, accumulating his points and his evidence, informing the reader with careful referencing and quotations, Bion wrote in a non-linear, labyrinthine and enigmatic style, purposely concealing and overlooking many of his sources, allegedly to achieve fresh outlooks, different vertexes of reality, unsaturated with memory and uncontaminated from intellectual prejudice. His narrative style is more Becketian than Shakespearean.

We believe there is a lot to be taken and learned from deconstructing Bion's mazes and from trying to find the hidden threads which guided him through his journey into the eye of the mind-storm. As happened with Freud, Bion offers the chance of integrating psychoanalysis with many other fields of knowledge and culture.

R.D. Hinshelwood
Norfolk
Nuno Torres
Lisbon
March 2012

Parthenope Bion Talamo last projects

Last updated: domenica, 11 febbraio, 2001[1]

Parthenope took away with her when dying a lot of projects. I want to mention here two of them that she was particularly fond and proud of:

1 The first one is a book she had been preparing since many years (to be published by Karnac Books, London) to illustrate the historical roots of her father's thoughts. As far as I can know – from what she had told me and from what I could find in her files – the title of this book should have been BION AND HIS BOOKS – PATHWAYS TO THE WORLD OF BION. I could find the outline of it, that I print here, courtesy of Luigi Talamo:

INTRODUCTION – Sub Tegmine Fagi:

i The blend of love of nature, love of art, and the awareness of man as a group animal as exemplified in the 'sub tegmine fagi' episode of the autobiography.
ii Bion's multiple cultural roots, India and England, Rome and France.
iii His experience of colonial groups, of school and war, as the humus of experience behind 'Experiences in Groups'.

PART ONE – Official and Unofficial Schooling: Learning to read books and to experience people;

i India
ii School
iii Tanks and planes
iv Oxford
v Medical School

PART TWO – Groping towards psychoanalysis:

i Psychotherapy – feel it in the past
ii Tavistock
iii Jung
iv Official psychoanalytical training

PART THREE – Psychoanalysis
i Belonging to a group: Institutional activities as a psychoanalyst
ii Los Angeles, a different relationship to psychoanalytical groups
iii The social side of psychoanalysis: homosexuality, death penalty, Dept. of Justice, San Quintino.

I could also find, together with a lot of notes and 'cogitations' about it (they cannot, though, be published, in our opinion, as they are written simply as raw material still to be deeply worked through), the following one, that I find really very touching:

TODAY, 27/02/98, AT THE AGE OF 53 YEARS, I START TO WRITE MY BOOK ON THE LIFE AND WORK OF MY FATHER, W.R. BION.
Wilfred Ruprecht Bion was gifted to a high degree with a well-tempered curiosity. He slaked, and nurtured, it through many channels, first and foremost his work with his patients, which was a continual stimulus, but also through his wide reading, his journeys, with visits to museums and galleries, his appreciation of architecture, nature and music, and, naturally, his personal relationships with other people, particularly his immediate family. I cannot think of anything of importance in which he was not interested: but he had no patience whatsoever with what might be termed mental junk-food. My aim in this book is to try to follow up some of the channels along which his curiosity flowed, with the aim of illuminating his development as a psychoanalyst, and some of the 'ingredients' which became part, in the end, of his psychoanalytical theories.

2 The second project has been planned and worked through since many years and was a shared one with Gianni Nebbiosi (one of closest friend and colleague of Parthenope and myself) and me and with the Melanie Klein Trust and Karnac Books: to prepare the Concordance of W.R. Bion's works and possibly to publish it as an hypertextual edition on a CD-ROM together with a revised edition of his complete works.

She was so lively and active!
Farewell, *Addio*, Parthenope!

Note

1 Taken from the website: www.sicap.it/merciai/parthenope/parthenope.htm, dated 1 February 2001, and accessed July 2010 (active from 2001 to 2010).

Chapter 1

Introduction

Nuno Torres and R.D. Hinshelwood

The photograph on the fly leaf of *All my Sins Remembered* (Bion 1985) shows Wilfred Bion reading a book, titled *Plato*. His widow's claim in selecting this photograph appears to be an assertion of Bion's erudition, and breadth of reading. Our volume of papers on various aspects of Bion's interests which we are introducing goes along with Francesca Bion's claim.

It therefore also goes against O'Shaughnessy's assessment:

> Earlier in his book Bléandonu discusses Bion's importing of terms from other disciplines to introduce new models through their penumbra of 'other' meaning. In this regard, I suspect Bléandonu may be a little too French in the degree of understanding he attributes to Bion of these 'other' fields, especially philosophy: such knowledge, I think, occurs more often in France than in specialist England.
>
> (O'Shaughnessy 1995, p. 857)

At the very least our book provides some research and thought about which of the claims is most valid. The question posed in this way is bound up with general cultural discussion about whether a genius draws on others' work, or whether he is graced with profound ideas that come from nowhere else. We would subscribe to the former view. But we intend to help the reader make up his/her own mind on the basis of what we have placed between these covers.

O'Shaughnessy poses the core question, a contentious issue, she calls it: 'How shall we view Bion's highly original work? As a development of what was there before? Or as a radical discontinuity?' (O'Shaughnessy 2005, p. 1926). She makes reference to Roy Schafer (1997) and agrees with him. Schafer asserted that 'Change is best approached as a matter of transformation. Consequently, we should think of ourselves as engaged in the study of transformations in theory and practice rather than radical discontinuities' (Schafer 1997, p. x). O'Shaughnessy however attributes Bion's sources to Freud and Klein, and tends not to look further.

It is very likely that philosophy was one of Bion's main foundations, since he emphasized the need for a psychoanalyst's philosophical background due to the many problems presented by psychoanalysis that involve philosophical issues (Bion, 1962, p. i; 1967a, pp. 151–152). Actually, J.O. Wisdom was one of the common references in Bion's books (1962, 1963, 1965) and also acknowledged for revisions and suggestions of earlier works (Bion, 1965). Wisdom was an important contributor to philosophy and to psychoanalysis – former president of the Society for Psychosomatic Research –who become interested in the power of psychoanalysis to explain not only mental disorder but also the yearning for what was traditionally thought of as metaphysics (Jarvie 1993). As Bion was interested in the psychoanalytic observation, notation and interpretation of non-sensuous data (empirical data that cannot be directly received by the sense organs [e.g. 1967a, pp. 165–166]), he was troubled by metaphysical issues such as the limits of reason to access *noumenon* ('things-in-themselves') addressed by Kant.

In all his work Bion contrasted *intuition* with *reason*, in order to deal with the limitations of knowledge based both on sense impressions and on previous theories about the mind. Additionally, he was also interested in the body–mind relations, which bring about the philosophical controversies on the relations between matter and the mind (e.g. Popper and Eccles 1977), and the issue of materialistic reductionism inherent to the biomedical model in which Freudian psychoanalysis was originated (Sulloway 1979). Bion strongly criticised the implicit medical model of 'symptomatic cure' and the mechanistic models in psychoanalysis (e.g. 1962, pp. 24–27; 1967a, pp. 151–157; 1970, pp. 6–26), and proposed to replace them with the notion of 'mental growth' based on a model of biological growth inherent to the flux of life (e.g. 1962, p. 70; 1963, p. 63; 1965, pp. 37–46; 1967a, p. 137; 1970, p. 71).

Like Freud, whose development was shaped by the major issues within medicine in the late nineteenth century, so Bion was also influenced by the currents in medicine and psychology in the first half of the twentieth century. Freud's Vienna was at the forefront of the development of medicine under the influence of nineteenth-century scientific achievement. Medicine moved dramatically towards an interest in causes of illnesses (aetiology), thus becoming medical science. And medical treatment aimed at the eradication of causes rather than the eradication of symptoms. In this context, Freud developed psychoanalysis. We can consider similarly those contextual developments in science, medicine and psychology which formed the background to Bion's own development from the 1930s to 1960s.

There is a growing interest in Bion Studies, around the world, with a steady growth in publications (for instance: Bion Talamo *et al.* 1998; Bion Talamo *et al.* 2000; Pines 2000; Lopez-Corvo 2005; Sandler 2006, 2010; Mawson 2011; Brown 2011). Much of this is expository, aiming to tell the reader what exactly Bion's ideas were. We want this book to reach into the penumbra of ideas and currents of opinions which form the context out of which Bion's ideas came.

Scientific thought developed in specific ways during the period between the First and Second World Wars. During this time, Bion studied history and philosophy at Oxford, and medicine at University College London. This was a time when the philosophy of science was itself debated in critical fashion with the return to Hume's suspicion of induction, and Popper's complete indictment of induction and turn to a deductive reasoning paradigm, the hypothetico-deductive method (Popper 1959).

Bion was alert to the implications of these epistemological concerns, and studied scientific thinking in comparison with schizophrenic thinking; 'The scientist whose investigations include the stuff of life itself finds himself in a situation that has a parallel in that of the patients I am describing' (Bion 1962, p. 13). But just as important to him was another development, which led him to Braithwaite (1953) rather than Popper.

Twentieth-century science evolved in the aftermath of the extraordinary mathematical predictions of relativity, and sub-atomic particles. The convergence of mathematics with physical science clearly looked like the way ahead for all science, and Bion absorbed that interest in higher and higher levels of abstract knowledge. He studied the possibilities of notation, via the logic of mathematics, but settled on the 'grid'[1], that took its schema from physical chemistry (Mendeleev's table).

The first half of the twentieth century was a period of great development in psychology as well, and for a time psychoanalysis was in the forefront. Although Bion was himself occupied for long periods with his own issues of a career, money and his own self-confidence, he was learning medicine, psychotherapy and psychoanalysis which were themselves embedded in the wider scientific culture. It is known for instance that he was interested in Kant when at Oxford, deriving from the influence of H.J. Paton,[2] later professor of philosophy, and an authority on Kant, and whilst a medical student he was very impressed with the surgeon Wilfred Trotter who knew Freud and Ernest Jones, and had written a work in social psychology (*The Herd instinct in Peace and War* – 1916), which Freud had taken seriously (Freud 1921). These represent a much broader cultural canvas which Bion had access to implicitly through his teachers and colleagues.

This book is not just about Bion's contributions to psychoanalysis. Those are now acknowledged and described by many people in an increasing number of publications of varying standards of reliability. It is easy enough to make one's own interpretation of what he is trying to say, and so we end up with a plethora of different Bions. Already two fairly clear-cut traditions are becoming apparent. At their extremes, one is a solid follower of Melanie Klein who advanced her body of ideas, especially with the theory of linking, containment and the conjunction of pre-conceptions with realisations as the basis for thinking. At the other extreme is a much more mystical man who read St John of the Cross, was committed to the 'unknown', and who radically changed our understanding of reality to suggest it is merely extended dream-work. Such categorisations are extreme and for the purpose of making the point that we see the Bion we want to make of him; and thus to put emphasis on the fundamental need to take good care of the communication processes that take place (or not) between analysts.

Our aim, however, is different, and not simply to make a new interpretation of Bion's ideas. He did work hard at understanding the problems he was faced with, the difficulties in the clinical work, the difficulties in establishing a coherent framework of concepts, and above all how to find effective ways of communicating between analysts about those problems and their possible solutions; and to these ends it is clear Bion was an active reader with a substantial library. We know, especially from his notebooks, *Cogitations* (Bion 1992), that he looked to his reading of others for inspiration. Hence, it is possible to study what Bion takes from others, what problem he is tackling at the particular time he is reading, what ideas he harvests for the problem, what he did with the ideas he found, and what use it turned out to be for him.

If we do not situate Bion within his context of problems and available ideas to be used for solutions, and we do not make an assessment of the success of his problem-solving, then we risk the empty achievement of legend-building, which is gaseous, lighter-than-air, and ultimately easily collapsible, a frequent state of psychoanalytic discussion of which Bion was the first to complain. We need more substance than legend, and Bion was very emphatic that our discussions 'must be a genuine confrontation and not an impotent beating of the air by opponents whose differences of view never meet' (Bion 1970, p. 55). By recognising where some of the ideas came from, and why and how they are used, we hope to promote a more potent form of debate within the psychoanalytic world.

Notes

1 Editors note: The 'grid' is available originally in the first page of the following publications: Bion (1962, 1963, 1965, 1967b, 1970 and 1977 [1989]).

2 Herbert James Paton, 1887–1969. White's Professor Emeritus of Moral Philosophy, Oxford.

Chapter 2

Gregariousness and the mind

Bion and Trotter, an update[1]

Nuno Torres

> Nothing can be more contrary than such a philosophy to the supine indolence of the mind, its rash arrogance, its lofty pretensions and its superstitious credulity. Every passion is mortified by it, except the love of truth; and that passion never is, nor can be carried to too high degree.
>
> Hume, in *An Enquiry Concerning Human Understanding* (1758)

If we divide Bion's work into two major periods – the 'group period' and the 'psycho-analytic period' – they are clearly linked to his psychoanalysts John Rickman and Melanie Klein. One of Rickman's aims, which Bion shared, was to apply psychoanalytic knowledge to the study of groups (Bion and Rickman, 1943 [1961]; Rickman, 1950 [1957]). Later on, Bion would follow Melanie Klein's advice and abandon the group studies to dedicate himself to individual psychoanalysis.[2]

The aim of this paper is to show that there was a third major influence on Bion's ideas and one that can be considered no less fundamental in his professional training, but mainly in his stream of thought: Wilfred Trotter. As Bion acknowledged at the end of his life in *All My Sins Remembered*: "Trotter listened with unassumed interest as if the patient's contributions flowed from the fountain of knowledge itself. It took me years of experience before I learned that this was in fact the case" (Bion, 1985, p. 38). Trotter's influence is apparent both in the group and in the psychoanalytic periods of Bion's thinking: we can find the roots of several of Bion's original propositions in Trotter's ideas, which provide a sense of coherence to the notions of group phenomena and the functioning of the individual mind.

These notions were foreign to earlier psychoanalytic theories before Bion, and represent some of his many original contributions to the enrichment of psychoanalysis. In this paper I will deal with the following notions:

- man as a gregarious and political animal,
- the mind's need for certainty, and the problem of intolerance of uncertainty,

- the focus on the "development of the mind" instead of the alleged "cure",
- the conflicts between the new ideas and the Establishment (the status quo),
- the crucial need for a suitable system of communicating ideas in psychoanalysis, and
- biological-organic concepts (opposed to mechanistic ones) to examine mental functioning.

Who was Trotter?

Wilfred Trotter (1872–1939), a general surgeon,[3] had a pioneering and central role in the history of the British psychoanalytical movement: he attended the first International Congress of Psychoanalysis in 1908 in Salzburg, and took its ideas to England (Jones, 1945). He was a great friend and loyal supporter of Ernest Jones, "apart from Freud the man who mattered most in his life" (Gillespie, 1979). In Trotter's obituary in the *International Journal of Psychoanalysis*, Jones relates he was

> one of the first two or three in England to appreciate the significance of Freud's work, which I came to know through him [...] he followed the development of Psycho-Analysis to the end of his life (he revised the translation of the Moses book, for instance) [...]. He was a member of the Council of the Royal Society that conferred their Honorary Membership on Professor Freud and he attended him medically after his removal to England
>
> (Jones, 1940, p. 114)

Trotter was also a pioneer of social psychology. In his 1916 masterpiece, *Instincts of the Herd in Peace and War*, the main idea was that besides the instincts of sex, self-preservation and nutrition there was one additional instinct that had not yet been described by psychology: the *herd instinct*. Following Pearson's ideas on the evolution of co-operation, and those of Sidis on the bio-psychological significance of gregariousness, Trotter's herd instinct represented the general tendency of some biological organisms to gregariousness: multiple-cell organisms (Metazoa), swarms, herds, societies. The assumptions underlying Trotter's concept of herd instinct were:

1. gregariousness is advantageous to the social species in facing natural selection;
2. the human mind is highly susceptible to the effects of the herd instinct;
3. the main problem of the human species is the conciliation of the rational mind with the irrational facets of gregariousness.[4]

These ideas were received enthusiastically and the book was printed six times from 1916 to 1921, and was republished in 1953. Trotter "provided the basic material for most British students of social psychology during the 1930s, including Bion and Rickman" (Harrison, 2000, p. 27), and Rickman actually mentioned that he agreed with the notion of herd instinct.[5] Trotter was also a great influence on Norman Glaister, one of the pioneers of the therapeutic community movement (Pines, 1999).

Trotter's ideas were rejected by Freud (1921) who refused the notion of a social/herd instinct per se distinct from sexual instinct or libido, and always saw social intercourse and group phenomena as manifestations of (1) libido 'diverted from its aims' (Freud, 1913), and (2) identification (1921).

Towards the end of his group period Bion was somewhat undecided between Trotter's view and Freud's (compare Bion, 1951 [1961], p. 133 with Bion 1955, pp. 153–168) but in the end of his psychoanalytic period it is clear to me that he favoured Trotter's conception, and he considered Freud's (1921) ideas as one particular version of the herd instinct; according to Bion (1970, p. 66) psychoanalysis is concerned with the mental counterpart of the characteristics of a herd animal, closely involved in a dual situation likely to stimulate the pair, or sexual, characteristics.

In the 1980s Friedman conciliated Trotter's with Freud's ideas, grounded on fresh advances in several fields of knowledge: (1) post-Freudian British and American psychoanalysis including Klein, Sullivan and Leowald; (2) developmental psychology research on the development of morality and prosocial behaviour by Piaget and followers; and (3) evolutionary biology theories and research on inclusive fitness by Hamilton and on reciprocal altruism by Trivers (Friedman, 1985).

Wilfred Trotter and Wilfred Bion

They met around 1927 when Bion did his medical internship at University College Hospital having won the Gold Medal in Surgery, and being one of Trotter's attendant dressers (Bion, 1985). Bion greatly admired Trotter who left an outstanding impression on his personality (Lyth, 1980; Bion, 1985, pp. 36–43). The following passage is particularly poignant:

> I remember the near horror with which I saw him enter a skull with powerful blows of a mallet on the chisel he held. Such was his control that he could and did penetrate the hard bone and arrest the chisel so that it in no way injured the soft tissue of the underlying brain.
>
> (Bion, 1985, p. 37)

However in his autobiography Bion does not mention that Trotter was the first to turn his mind to the psychology of group behaviour (Bléandonu, 1994, p. 39) and that Trotter's book *Instincts of the Herd in Peace and War* was to prove an important influence on his nascent theories (Boris, 1986, p. 161). According to Francesca Bion (1995) "Trotter makes observations which remind one strongly of Bion's later views". But Bion's explicit references to Trotter are actually scarce: Trotter is only included once in his bibliographic references (Bion, 1952), and as far as I was able to trace he only referred to him again in his last book, A *Memoir of the Future*, completed shortly before his death (Bion, 1975/1979 [1990], I.24, II.1).

One of the questions that arises is why did Bion not quote Trotter more often? Francesca Bion said that Trotter's book *Instincts of the Herd* was not in Bion's personal library and "It may have been among those he lost during air raids over London in the early thirties and by the fifties it was out of print" (Francesca Bion, 1995, p. 1).

Malcolm Pines (2003, personal communication) proposed that Bion may have identified with Trotter, and Harris Williams (2010a, p. 23) talks about Bion's internalization of Trotter.

When Bion wrote *Second Thoughts*, and in commenting on "The Imaginary Twin" paper, he stated:

> he [the patient] must have been the first patient to make me wonder whether the idea of cure was not introducing an irrelevant criterion in psychoanalysis.
>
> (1967a, p. 135)

This statement attests to the fact that by that time Bion had totally forgotten that Trotter had proposed this idea in 1916. Interestingly, a few pages later in the same book, Bion made some intriguing comments about the importance of forgetting the best papers (see 1967a, p. 156).

The "suspension of leadership" group approach

The "suspension of leadership" was one of the main characteristics of Bion's group technique: it is a revised notion of traditional leadership, which stressed the "participatory/democratic set of relations among members in a sophisticated group" (Robert Lipgar, 2000, personal communication). This approach was present at the very beginning of Bion's work with groups in the army: (1) the "Leaderless Group Project"; (2) the "Regimental Nomination experiment"; and (3) the "Northfield experiment", and goes on to the Tavistock experiments from 1948 until 1951.[6] The advantage of this apparent subversion of values was addressed by Trotter in analysing the factors that gave the advantage to England in the First World War:

> [T]he submission to leadership that England showed was [. . .] to a great extent spontaneous, voluntary, and undisciplined, and gave repeated

> evidence that the passage of inspiration was essentially from the common people to its leaders rather than from the leaders to the common people.
> (Trotter, 1916, pp. 248–249)

This quote clarifies Bion's "suspension of leadership" approach. The selection of officers in the WOSB (War Office Selection Boards) was achieved through a "spontaneous, voluntary, and undisciplined" experimental situation; indeed, one of the procedures in the leaderless group situations in the Edinburgh WOSB was called "spontaneous situations" (Trist, 1985, p. 7). In the "Regimental Nomination Experiment", the passage of inspiration from the common people to its leaders, addressed and prescribed by Trotter, is even more obvious, as the candidates for the Officer Boards were voted on by every soldier in a secret ballot (Trist, 1985, p. 12). Trotter and Bion's mistrust of usual leadership had very similar reasons: both considered that it was a phenomenon ruled by atavistic instincts, in essence detached from contact with reality and thinking processes (Trotter, 1916, pp. 116–117; Bion, 1961, pp. 121, 177–179).

Theoretical advances in "experiences in groups"

Trotter's ultimate assumption about "group psychology" was that it was continuous with individual psychology, an idea which precedes the similar argument of both Freud (1921) and Lewin (1935b, 1935c). As Trotter puts it: "The two fields – the social and the individual – are regarded here as absolutely continuous; [. . .] man as solitary animal is unknown to us, and every individual must present the characteristic reactions of the social animal" (Trotter, 1916, pp. 11–12). "The gregarious mental character is evident in man's behaviour, not only in crowds and other circumstances of actual association, but also in his behaviour as an individual, however isolated" (ibid., p. 42). This was also Bion's assumption in his *Experiences in Groups* (Bion, 1961, p. 169), but Bion replaced the term *herd instinct* by the physical-chemical term (probably inspired by Lewin) of *valency:* "a spontaneous, unconscious function of the gregarious quality in the personality of man" (Bion, 1961, p. 136).

According to Trotter, the interference of the herd instinct in human intellect would be the cause of mankind's inability to use its full rational potential: "[B]elief of affirmations sanctioned by the herd goes on however much such affirmations may be opposed by evidence [. . .] reason cannot enforce belief against herd suggestion" (Trotter, 1916, p. 39). Trotter had stated that this impairment of rational abilities in the group should be one of the main themes of investigation in psychology (1916, p. 39). And, in what sounds like a dialogue with his old master who had passed away a decade previously, Bion stated that the group will often wrestle with intellectual problems that the individual could solve without difficulty in another situation, and that: "One of the main objects of our study may well turn out to be precisely the phenomena that produce these perturbations of rational behaviour in the group" (Bion, 1961, p. 40). Bion's concept and definition of *group mentality* – "the unanimous expression of the will of the group, an expression of will to which individuals contribute anonymously" (1961, p. 59) – describing a primitive kind of unanimity in opinions and conduct among the group members also finds a parallel in Trotter, who refers to it as *sensitiveness to the behaviour of the herd*:

> [M]anifestations of the same tendency to homogeneity are seen in the desire for identification with the herd [...]. It is sensitiveness to the behaviour of the herd which has the most important effects upon the structure of the mind of the gregarious animal, and therefore with that of man. [...] The chances an affirmation has of being accepted could therefore be most satisfactorily expressed in terms of the bulk of the herd by which it is backed.
>
> (Trotter, 1916, pp. 32–33)

Furthermore, Bion's conception of a triad of basic assumption groups, the three types of basic group mentality – Fight–flight, Pairing and Dependence – are parallel with Trotter's triad of instincts: Self-preservation, Sex, and Nutrition.[7]

After leaving his work on groups, Bion dedicated himself to Kleinian psychoanalysis of psychoses. This transition is less abrupt than it appears at first glance, since according to the conclusions of his last paper on groups, the understanding of the emotional life of the group was only comprehensible in terms of psychotic mechanisms: "[A]dvances in the study of the group are dependent upon the development and implications of Melanie Klein's theories of internal objects, projective identification, and failure in symbol formation" (Bion, 1952, p. 247).

Epistemology and mental growth

In the following period of his work, Bion applied and developed the psychoanalytic theories of Freud and Klein in a very creative and productive manner. It is not, however, the aim of this paper to analyse this vast domain.[8] His thinking rapidly became increasingly independent of Freudian and Kleinian theories (and eventually critical of them and of his own use of them).

The problem of the scientific status of psychoanalysis and other epistemological matters became his prime concern (see also Sandler, 2006). Bion saw the epistemological consideration of psychoanalysis as a central matter in his clinical practice: as happened with his experiences in groups, his vision of psychoanalysis was that it was more important to search for new knowledge than to aim for a medical-type "cure" of the patients (1967a, pp. 149–157; 1970, pp. 6–7). It is in the "epistemological period", from 1962 onwards (according to Bléandonu, 1994), that Trotter's implicit influence can be seen to regain importance.

If epistemology is the study of the human conditions for knowledge, it can also be seen as the study of the tendency of the human mind to accept lies, or false statements (Bion's second column of his grid, e.g. 1963, pp. 48, 71).

As proposed by the empiricist Hume,[9] and followed by both Trotter (1916, p. 41) and Bion (1970, pp. 43–44), suspension of judgement, belief or understanding is required to prevent false statements.

However, Hume, Trotter and Bion all acknowledged that the human mind *needs certainty*, to have the *feel* of truth. As Trotter stated: "the desire for certitude is one of profound depth in the human mind, and possibly a necessary property of any mind" (Trotter, 1916, p. 34), and as Bion continued: "as if starvation of truth was somehow analogous to alimentary starvation" (Bion, 1967a, p. 119.). Due to this need, people easily exchange the anxiety of uncertainty for the unanimous view between the members of the group taken as an unshakable belief (e.g. Bion, 1961, p. 83). Bion later called this "the protective coat of lies" (1965) and "theory used as a barrier against the unknown" (1963, pp. 18, 99), using also the notion of "minus *K*-link", and the sign ψ in his grid (1962).

Trotter, also, "amused by the mysterious viability of the false" (Kothari and Mehta, 1998), had pointed it out:

> [B]elief of affirmations sanctioned by the herd is a normal mechanism of the human mind and [. . .] totally false opinions may appear to the older of them to possess all the character of rationally verifiable truth, and may be justified by secondary processes of rationalization[10] which it may be impossible directly to combat by argument.
>
> (Trotter, 1916, p. 39)

When an experience does not fit the shared assumptions of their herd, humans tend to evade the experience and the evidence of it (Trotter, 1916, pp. 34–35). Trotter stated that anxiety was a too expensive a price to pay for the process of learning from experience:

> Man cannot support the suspension of judgement which science so often has to enjoin. He is too anxious to feel certain to have time to know [. . .] reason intrudes as an alien and hostile power, disturbing the perfection of life and causing an unending series of conflicts.
>
> (Trotter, 1916, p. 35)

These ideas are very close to Bion's formulation of the *hatred of learning by experience* (Bion, 1961, p. 89; 1962, p. 98). For Bion, this hatred is a characteristic both of the basic assumption groups and of the psychotic part of the personality, which were considered as two sides of the same coin (Bion, 1961, pp. 187–189). In this psycho-social conceptual field we find the basis for the idea that some social systems are associated with primitive defences against psychotic anxiety:

> the assumption underlying loyalty to the K-link is that the personality ... can survive the loss of its protective coat of lies, subterfuge, evasion and hallucination and may even be fortified and enriched by the loss. It is an assumption strongly disputed by the psychotic and *a fortiori* by the group, which relies on psychotic mechanisms for its coherence and sense of well-being.
>
> (Bion, 1965, p. 129)

The idea of rational impairment, inherent to the functioning of the group, was not new. It had been mentioned earlier by Le Bon and McDougal, amongst others, and can even be traced back to Kierkegaard, in his famous assertion "the crowd is the lie".

What is new in Trotter, again developed from Hume's conceptions, is the idea that intellectual impairment is not limited to the presence of a mob. Rather it is present in the inner mentality of the individual, because he/she is under the influence of the herd even when alone (Trotter, 1916, p. 33).

This was also Bion's innovation: the moral law and moral systems seen as superior to scientific law and scientific systems that suffocate both intellectual development and learning from experience are not only a result of external group collusion but are ultimately a manifestation of an intra-psychic preponderance of the super-ego over the functions of the ego[11] (Bion, 1965, p. 38).

Empiricism, experience and psychoanalysis

The empiricist, the one who searches for truth from evidence and empirical data, proposes that *suspended judgement and belief* combined with *experience* is the only learning method. The empiricist position of Bion is indicated by his focus on observation and notation of psychoanalytic objects, instead of centring on theoretical discussions. This is very clearly expressed in the following statements, in which he contrasts the domain of a system of observation (in which he is engaged) with a system of psychoanalytical theory (in which he is not engaged).

> I do not propose to discuss the system of psychoanalytical theory. For that I refer the reader to the work of Bowlby and the Research Committee of the British Psychoanalytical Society of which he is chairman,

> Sandler and his co-workers, Segal and her introduction to Melanie Klein and Wisdom on the theories of Klein and Fairbairn. The domains of theories of observation and theories of psychoanalysis overlap, but the problem is simplified if a distinction is made and can be preserved. The workers on the theories of psychoanalysis to whom I have referred are engaged on a task which belongs uniformly to the category row F [Concepts].
>
> (Bion, 1965, p. 160)

Bion was very sensitive to the epistemological criticisms of psychoanalysis as an empirical science, especially Popper's sharp arguments, and worked hard to deal with them. In a bold epistemological movement, Bion expanded empiricism to the idealist domains when he proposed (taking up Freud's idea) that the "psychical qualities" received by consciousness – i.e. the mental counterpart of emotional experiences – are also to be considered actual experiences as much as sensorial experiences received by the senses (1962, pp. 4, 33). Here Bion was forced to bypass Kant's limitations of pure reason and the intellect, and to propose *trained intuition* as a method of contacting non-sensuous psychoanalytical objects (see Chapter 11 of this book). Through disciplined and trained metaphysical-like intuition, combined with an abstract system of notation, the non-sensuous counterparts of emotional experiences could be researched and psychoanalytic observation and knowledge could be enlarged.

The problem of communicating the psychoanalytical experience

Once some degree of mental growth and intuitive sophistication is achieved by an individual, how does he *communicate* this ineffable experience to his fellow humans? Trotter stressed that the capacity for suitable and precise intercommunication between human minds would be crucial for human evolution (Trotter, 1916, p. 62).

When Bion started to work on psychoanalytic training, the "accuracy of communication" issue emerged: "I have experience to record, but how to communicate this experience to others I am in doubt. This book *Learning by Experience* explains why" (Bion, 1962, p. v). The review of his earlier papers in 1967, presented in *Second Thoughts*, was dominated by the same concern; how to communicate accurately (to patients, colleagues, laymen and even to himself) psychoanalytic experience? "[T]he failure to communicate the non-sensuous experience on which the interpretation is based is a major misfortune of psycho-analytic practice at its present stage. I suspect it also contributes to the somewhat futile controversy about psychoanalytical theories" (1967a, p. 134). This issue became a concern of the first order: "If this communication cannot be made, the future development of analysis is imperilled and the successful discoveries made so far could be lost to the world" (Bion, 1992, p. 173).

Mind growth or reduction? Human development *versus* mental orthopaedics

Trotter pointed out a question that would cross Bion's work at least from 1962 onwards: is psychoanalysis promoting mental growth or, on the contrary, is it only a conformed adaptation to the stable-minded norm of the herd, despising the search for truth?[12]

In the words of Trotter:

> However precious such a cure psychoanalytic may be to the patient, and however interesting to the physician, its value to the species has to be judged [. . .] in relation to the question as to whether any move, however small, into the direction of an enlargement of the human mind has been made.
>
> (Trotter, 1916, p. 90)

Almost in direct response to that, Bion stated: "In psychoanalytic methodology the criterion cannot be whether a particular usage is right or wrong, meaningful or verifiable, but whether it does, or does not, promote development" (Bion, 1962, p. vii).

Trotter's remark was an extension of his concepts of normality and mental instability, and the social pressure to neutralise disturbing new ideas:

> The mental stability, then, is to be regarded as, in certain important directions, a loss [. . .] a relative intolerance of the new in thought, and a consequent narrowing of the range of facts over which satisfactory intellectual activity is possible.
>
> (Trotter, 1916, p. 55)

Trotter believed that the consensus of the stable-minded dominant group was achieved through discarding possibilities of mental progress and evolution. Bion took this question and transported it straight into the psychoanalytic institutional group:

> I leave that paper for further discussion but repeat reasons for mistrusting "cure" or "improvement" ... because the tendency to equate psychoanalysis with "treatment" and "cure" with improvement is a warning that the psychoanalysis is becoming restricted; limitation is being placed on the analysand's growth in the interest of keeping the group undisturbed.
>
> (1967a, p. 157; see also p. 137)

From this question spring many original and disquieting contributions by Bion, such as the importance of accepting mental turbulence and preventing the "poisonous" nature of certainty, desire, memory and even understanding (1970).

Biological-organic concepts (opposed to mechanistic ones) to understand mental functioning[13]

It was Trotter's attempt to make psychology and sociology consistent with evolutionary biology (Miller, 1983), and in this he used many biologically based correspondences to psychic phenomena such as for instance:

> It [gregariousness] was not at all widely looked upon as a definite fact of biology which must have consequences as precise and a significance as ascertainable as the secretion of the gastric juice or the refracting of the eye.
>
> (Trotter, 1916, p. 21)

Bion had similar assumptions, and he clarified them in a very clear way in the following passage:

> For myself, I have found it impossible to interpret the material presented to me by these patients as a manifestation of purely psychological development divorced from any concurrent physical development. I have wondered whether the psychological development was bound up with the development of ocular control in the same way that problems of development linked with oral aggression co-exist with the eruption of teeth.
>
> (1950b, p. 22)

I also suggest that Trotter's biological models, as opposed to mechanistic ones, were the seeds of Bion's contributions in the following themes:

1 The mental "digestion" of raw sensory material into food for thought, in psychic integration and growth.
2 The mental evacuation of unprocessed emotional experiences, using the mind as a muscle.
3 The conflicts between the new idea and status quo.

The mental digestion of emotional experiences – α function and "food for thought"

Trotter had proposed the digestive model of the mind in 1932: "An event experienced is an event perceived, digested, and assimilated into the substance of our being" (Trotter, 1932 [1941], p. 98). This was closely followed by Bion: "I am reminded that healthy mental growth seems to depend on truth as the living organism depends on food. If it's lacking or deficient, the personality deteriorates" (Bion, 1965, p. 38). According to Bion's biological-organic model of the mind, the products of emotional experiences can be divided in two fundamental categories: assimilated elements (α) and unassimilated elements (β).

The first assimilations must be made with the help of maternal *reverie* through the processing and transformation of raw sensory data into the mind, i.e. "mental digestion". Bion proposed the idea of a "psychosomatic alimentary canal" in the baby, which was able to receive love and understanding along with milk (Bion, 1962, p. 34). The assimilated elements have to be detoxified of anxiety by the maternal capacity to contain her emotions and to respond sensitively to the needs of the baby, and become stored ideograms that can be used for dreams and dream-thoughts.

The mental evacuation of emotional experiences – β-elements

The unassimilated elements are expelled by "the ability to believe in the possibility of ridding himself of unwanted emotions" (Bion, 1992, pp. 181–182).

The very act of expelling an idea/thought/emotion is made possible by the inability to distinguish between thoughts and things, an idea suggested by Trotter when he pointed out the analogies between intellectual processes and reflex action (Trotter, 1916, p. 15).

Following Trotter, Bion was attentive to muscular reflex actions to understand the schizoid-paranoid mechanism of elements' evacuation:

> [F]ailure to distinguish thoughts from things contributes to a sense that the actual meaning of the words [. . .] is expelled as air from his lungs is expelled. Conformably with this the patient seems to feel that his mind is an expelling organ like a lung in act of expiration ... the patient is using his eyes, and the mental counterpart of his capacity for vision, as evacuatory musculature.
>
> (Bion, 1965, p. 131)

The organic conflict between the new idea and status quo

According to Trotter in his sarcastic paper "Has the intellect a function?": "The mind likes a strange idea as little as the body likes a strange protein and resists it with similar energy [. . .] a new idea is the most quickly acting antigen known to science" (Trotter, 1939, p. 186). Bion developed a series of reflections concerning the reception of new ideas by the mind and new ideas by the establishment, and the possible outcomes of this conflict (see Bion, 1970), which seem to have sprung from this idea from Trotter.

All these biological-organic models can be framed into a vision of sociology and psychology as integrated with evolutionary biology, as intended by Trotter. In Bion's model, the development of the mind follows steps which are grounded in biologic-like processes of growth.

Final remarks: the hypothesis of human extinction in Trotter and Bion

As a scientist of the nineteenth century, Trotter was strongly impressed by the revolution caused by Darwin (1871). Like any other species, man evolved from primitive beings, and was equally subject to possible extinction. Trotter was troubled and disquieted by these thoughts:

> Without some totally revolutionary change in man's attitude towards the mind, even his very tenure of the earth may come to be threatened [...] after all man will prove but one more of nature's failures, ignominiously to be swept from her work-table to make way for another venture of her tireless curiosity and patience.
>
> (Trotter, 1916, p. 65)

Painful as it was, this idea was quickly out of fashion in the post-Second World War baby-boom zeitgeist, until thermonuclear threats and global ecological problems started to become evident later in the twentieth century. Bion, however, insisted on it throughout his entire work: "History of life on this planet shows that decay of a species is often associated with over-development of some portion of its organism [...] is there a possibility of similar over-development of mental functioning?" (Bion, 1952, p. 247). And "I do not see why he [Man] should not be another of Nature's discarded experiments" (Bion, 1979 [2000], p. 91). This emphasis gives Bion's writings an aura of oracular dread and gravity, which bring to the foreground the fragility of our existence and the responsibility for our destiny, for we are the only animal able to think about how our mind directs our thoughts and actions.

According to Bion's (1985, p. 38) posthumously published autobiography: "It was said that when Trotter did a skin graft it 'took'." I have proposed in this chapter that Trotter did a series of central "mental grafts" on Bion's vision of the world, and they "took".

Notes

1 This chapter is an abridged and updated version with permission to reprint from Jessica Kingsley Publishers, of one chapter published earlier in: Lipgar and Pines (2003) *Building on Bion: Roots: Origins and Context of Bion's Contributions to Theory and Practice*, Jessica Kingsley Publishers, London and Philadelphia.

2 The separation of these two periods is so sharply linked to Rickman and Klein that the year after Rickman's death in 1951, Bion (1952) reformulated his previous group theory in the light of the psychotic mechanisms described by Klein. And he would not publish again on groups until the year after Klein's death (Bion, 1961).

3 Trotter was a surgeon at the University College Hospital, London from 1906, a professor of surgery there from 1935 and held the office of honorary surgeon to King George V from 1928 to 1932. In the history of surgery he is especially noted for his work on the regeneration of sensory nerves in the skin.

4 The social psychology experiments of Sheriff in the 1930s about group norms and conformity, and of Lewin in the 1940s on group decision, as well as the recent models of multilevel natural selection in the 1990s by D.S. Wilson in evolutionary socio-biology supported Trotter's proposals.

5 He says:

> I see no objection to it; many animal species exhibit it; man certainly shows a tendency to shoal, or herd, or group together. [...] perhaps the herd instinct provides a matrix within which the multi-body as well as the three body forces operate
>
> (Rickman, 1950 [1957], pp. 165–167)

6 The "suspension of leadership", which deliberately refused the mythical role of "the Doctor" contrasted with Foulkes' more traditional leadership style in Northfield, in which he "took the position of an educator and discussion tended to revolve around his comments" (Hinshelwood, 1999, p. 477).

7 The connection between the *Nutrition instinct* and *Dependence basic assumption* was the following: "the first assumption is that the group exists in order to be sustained by a leader on whom it depends for nourishment, material and spiritual" (Bion, 1952, p. 235). Hence nutrition-dependence is complemented by Bion with a spiritual factor, that can be seen also as partly inspired in (1) Rickman's ideas of 'need to believe in God' (Rickman, 1938 [1957]), and (2) the correlation between dependency on the group and endowment to it of phantasised characteristics of the idealised parents (Harrison, 2000, p. 51). Hadfield also emphasised the dependence of the child upon its parents for comfort, happiness and life itself (Hadfield, 1954, p. 20). In the sense of deriving from the innate drive to look for protection from parental figures, the dependence basic assumption must be further researched in comparison with Bowlby's concepts of both the attachment and the caregiving behavioral systems (Shaver and Fraley, 2000), as well as its developments into religious beliefs (Granqvist, *et al.*, 2010).

8 See for instance Meltzer (1978 [1998], 1986), Hinshelwood (1989) and Mawson (2011).

9 See Hume (1758 [1996], pp. 110–111) and also (1779, p. 158). For a list of Bion's explicit references to Hume, see Sandler (2006).

10 According to J.T. MacCurdy, Jones borrowed from Trotter the use of the term "rationalisation", an assertion which was strongly contested by Glover (1924).

11 This idea was also proposed implicitly by Freud in *Civilization and its Discontents* (1930) when he defined the super-ego as a coercive entity simultaneously inner and external; the guardian of consensus and correlation of conduct, controlling *objective* behaviour as well as repressing and moulding *subjective* desires and thoughts.

12 Ernest Jones wrote his paper "The concept of a normal mind" (1942) in an attempt to solve Trotter's challenge. Later in 1963, Robert S. Wallerstein retakes this theme in his paper "The problem of the assessment of change in psychotherapy".

This problem was also addressed by Hinshelwood's (1997) ethically based question on psychoanalysis: *Therapy or Coercion?*

13 It is important to emphasise that biological-organic is not here synonymic of materialistic reductionism or *physicalism* in line with Descartes automata-like visions of extensive nature; quite the contrary, it is synonymous with *vitalism*, i.e. the notion that *all* life forms are animated: to a certain extent are inherently creative, non-linear and ultimately unpredictable (see Chapter 3). The process of abandoning mechanistic/inanimate models in contemporary science deeply influenced Bion; according to him:

> I hope that in time the base will be laid for a mathematical approach to biology, founded on the biological origins of mathematics, and not on an attempt to fasten on biology a mathematical structure which owes its existence to the mathematician's ability to find realisations, that approximate to his constructs, amongst the characteristics of the inanimate
>
> (Bion, 1965, p. 105)

Chapter 3

Intuition and ultimate reality in psychoanalysis

Bion's implicit use of Bergson and Whitehead's notions[1]

Nuno Torres

Introduction

The aim of this chapter is to identify the origins of Bion's concepts of psychoanalytic *intuition*, and of "*O*" (the ultimate Reality) in the building blocks of the metaphysics and process philosophy of Henri Bergson and Alfred North Whitehead.

I will present documental evidence of Bion's readings of Bergson and Whitehead, and conceptual evidence of their convergence of notions. The documental evidence was kindly provided by Francesca Bion, by means of photocopies of pages from two books from Bion's library: Bergson's (1896 [1911]) *Matter and Memory*, and Whitehead's (1911) *An Introduction to Mathematics*, in which there were sentences underlined in pencil on several pages.

Although he did not use these references explicitly, some of the central notions presented in Bergson's *Matter and Memory* and Whitehead's *An Introduction to Mathematics* are implicitly present in all of Bion's work, starting from his 1948 paper "Psychiatry at a time of crisis", followed by his papers from "Experiences in Groups" (1948–1952 [1961]), and throughout his psychoanalytic works (from 1962 to 1970).

Henri Bergson and Alfred North Whitehead

The ideas of these two philosophers brought new solutions for the old problems of metaphysics, body–mind relations and human understanding of reality, in the late nineteenth century and the first half of the twentieth century (for an in-depth study see Baldwin, 2003 and Čapek, 1971).

For Bergson, Reality is the ever-rolling stream of time in a ceaselessly changing process, for which he coined the term *durée* ("duration"). This condition can be directly grasped by introspection of the inner experience of the self, and could be described as follows:

> (1) Duration is a heterogeneous flux or becoming. (2) It is irreversible, straining always towards the future. (3) It is continually creating

> newness or novelty, and hence is intrinsically unpredictable. (4) It is the inexhaustible source of freedom. (5) Its living reality can never be communicated by images or concepts, but must be directly intuited.
>
> (Goudge, 1912 [1949], pp. 12–13)

Bergson radically altered the understanding of Reality in the philosophical mainstream at the dawn of the twentieth century: it was no longer conceived based on the model of inorganic matter as it was by modern rationalism but on the notion of biological organic development, cumulative progress, and inner growth[2] (Cohen, 1999, p. 25).

For Whitehead, also, the world was seen as organic rather than materialistic: a self-sustaining cluster of integrated *Wholes* which are involved in vital processes (Rescher, 2000, pp. 31–32). Invoking the name of Henri Bergson, Whitehead adopted "Nature is a process" as a leading principle of his philosophy. According to Whitehead's words "nature is a structure of evolving processes. The reality is the process" (1925 [1948], p. 74). In recent years, "Process Philosophy" has become a label for the ideas of Alfred North Whitehead and his supporters:

> Beneath this lay the Heracleitean doctrine that "all things flow" and the rejection of a Parmenidean/Atomistic view that nature consists of the changeable interrelations among stable, unchanging units.
>
> (Rescher, 2000, p. 3)

The ideas of Bergson (1896 [1911], 1907 [1911]) and Whitehead (1911, 1920) which were highly influential at the time, were very much in the cultural air during Bion's time as an undergraduate reading history at Oxford between 1919 and 1921; so much so that Bergson was honoured with a degree of Doctor of Letters by the University of Cambridge in 1920. Though we know that Bion was interested in Kant (see Chapter 11) through his close contact with H.J. Paton at Queens' College (Bion, 1985, pp. 7, 83) it is likely that he then or subsequently read Bergson and Whitehead.

Bergson's philosophy become widely known as an attack on Kant, and hence would not have passed unnoticed by Kantian scholars.[3] After graduating, Bion spent a year (1921–1922) at the University of Poitiers, improving his knowledge of French (Bléandonu, 1994 p. 36; Bion, 1985) so he might have read Bergson since the "Bergson controversies" were very much alive in the intellectual circles in France at the time (Mullarkey, 1999). Additionally, in 1927, Bergson won the Nobel Prize, which made him internationally (in)famous.[4]

On the other hand, A.N. Whitehead became widely known for his outstanding work *Principia Mathematica* co-authored with Bertrand Russell, a work which is quoted in Bion's (1992) *Cogitations*.

There are strong traces of Bergsonism and of Whitehead's Process Philosophy in Bion's approach to observation and investigation of groups and psychoanalysis. Some of the radical assertions in Bion's work can be clarified, to a large extent, if we recognise his debt to Bergson, to Whitehead and to the principles of Process Philosophy. The notions to be looked at in this chapter are Bion's rather original concepts of *Intuition* and the *Ultimate Reality* ("O") in psychoanalysis.[5] All these themes share the combination of analytic Reason and intuitive Revelation, which according to Cohen (1999) is the hallmark of the *Contemporary Epoch* of philosophy.

Although there are many other notions linking Bion's ideas to those of Bergson and Whitehead (such as the notions of mental growth, the notions of mathematical notation and of algebraic systems), these do not belong to the scope of this chapter. In Chapter 6, Bion's concept of the *proto-mental matrix* will also be discussed as being convergent with Bergson's views on the so-called "mind–body" problem.

Bergson's conception of the utilitarian intellect, inadequate for knowledge

In his 1896 *Matter and Memory* (pencilled in by Bion), Henri Bergson's metaphysics starts with a critique of the previous philosophical systems of Descartes, Berkeley and Kant, which according to him had raised false problems and hence false solutions. His plea is to start afresh from the common-sense perception of objects and affects, and to carefully scrutinize what the mind does with them and for what purpose. What the intellect does, in a nutshell, is to "congeal into distinct and independent things the fluidity of a continuous undivided process" (Bergson, 1896 [1911], p. 123); the intellect has a "tendency which impels us to think on all occasions of *things* rather than of movements" (ibid., p. 121).

Bergson's innovative philosophical conception of the intellect was that it has emerged in the course of biological evolution as an instrument of adaptation to the external environment and, therefore, the nervous system and brain functions are chiefly utilitarian agencies of action (Moore, 2003, pp. 67–71). For Bergson, the more complex and evolved a creature's nervous system is, the more options it has before acting, which allows an increasing time delay between perception and action (or stimulus and response); this creates an increasing area of indetermination and of "freedom of choice", reaching its peak in the biological chain of evolution in humankind's consciousness and speculative thinking about reality. This notion is very similar to Freud's (1900b, Chapter VII; 1911a; 1915c, pp. 118–122; 1915a, p. 188) description of the emergence of the secondary process and the principle of reality as an inhibition of immediate motor discharges (characteristic of the reflex arc) in order to scan the external environment and act efficiently.[6] However, in contrast to Freud's utilitarian view of the reality principle of mental functioning, Bergson proposed the existence of a contemplative–intuitive "metaphysical" kind of mental functioning, directed not at the external reality as received by the senses but to pure self-knowledge and contact with an "ultimate reality".

In the following sections I will argue that Bion followed Bergson's lead on this subject, as an alternative to the classical Freudian view of the principle of reality.

Bion and Bergson

In Bergson's view, the habit of using the intellect for utilitarian thinking about external reality, since it "is directed to action and not to pure knowledge", created a pervasive bias in philosophical thought about reality (Bergson, 1896 [1911], p. 31). Due to the mechanistic models that the intellect builds to deal with concrete spatial reality, where the body lives and must survive, all reality including mental reality is seen by the intellect as a sum of discrete events in space; but "true" reality does not begin or end, it is an endlessly indivisible temporal succession – *durée*.

Indeed, a common thread in all of Bion's work, both on groups and in psychoanalysis is a warning against the bias and inadequacy of intellectual thinking based on the utilitarian spatial sensuous perception of concrete objects. He concurrently tried to develop models that would allow the full development of thinking about mental reality as a dynamic living continuous process of change and growth; he avoided and criticised mechanistic and spatial metaphors of the mind.

Judging by the pencil markings in the margin his copy of *Matter and Memory*, Bion had paid particular attention to Bergson's statement that:

> in psychological analysis we must never forget the utilitarian character of our mental functions, which are essentially turned toward action. The second is that the habits formed in action find their way up to the sphere of speculation, where they create fictitious problems, and that metaphysics must begin by dispersing this artificial obscurity.
>
> (Bergson, 1896 [1911] p. xvii)

In congruence with this, Bion states in "Psychiatry at a time of crisis" (1948), that *Reason* aims to achieve competent action, and points out human hypertrophy of an operative intellect focused on external reality, tool building, machinery, and technology. Paralleling Bergson, Bion proposed that the rational and emotional areas of inquiry represent two different paths of human knowledge: on one hand "a kind of simian capacity for acquiring technical skills [. . .] and a capacity for full emotional and intellectual development on the other" (Bion, 1948, p. 84). Similarly, in *Experiences In Groups*, Bion stated that while people are normally concerned with where things "begin" and "end" (i.e. when the group begins and ends), his point of view is radically different, and in fact is reminiscent of Bergson's notion of ceaseless duration:

> a shift of point of view, admittedly of some magnitude, on my part, means that I am viewing group phenomena that do not "begin"; the matters with which I am concerned continue, and evolve, but they do not "begin".
>
> (Bion 1961, p. 88)[7]

In his 1962 *Learning from Experience*, Bion recurrently states that the traditional uses of the intellect in psychoanalysis are inadequate to understand living objects and dynamic situations, and are limited to the understanding of inanimate objects:

> there must be heightened risk [. . .] when, as in psychoanalysis, we are concerned with growth and we speak of "mental mechanisms" [. . .] it is likely that the implied model is more suitable to the inanimate machine than to a living organism.
>
> (1962, p. 80)

It will become clear in his later works that Bion believes *intuition*, radically different from the *intellect*, to be "something" that will allow the psychoanalyst to make contact with the dynamic psychic reality (Bion, 1962, p. 53).

In *Elements of Psychoanalysis*, Bion (1963, p. 4) restated that Reason, or "*R*" has a utilitarian objective of "dominance in the world of reality", and to "bridge the gap between an impulse and its fulfilment". By contrast the words "thought" and "idea", represented by "*I*", represent to him the realizations of "psychoanalytic objects" consisting of sense impressions transformed into elements that allow dreaming and dream-thoughts. Here there is an implicit critique of Freud's "principle of reality" as an appropriate tool to explore and understand the mind, since the capacity to contact psychic qualities should not be equated with the principle of reality as applied to the external world of objects.[8] One of the assumptions of the book *Elements of Psychoanalysis* is that pure psychoanalytic objects are always revealed in an "impure form" because the functioning of reason/intellect and the use of language are based on "sense impressions" and inspired by objects from spatial external reality.

In Bion's 1967 *Second Thoughts*, the setback of using metaphors based on the visual apprehension of physical space to understand the mind is stated very clearly in relation to Freud's diagrammatic model of the mind:

> Freud's model of the mind, based on a diagram, is based on a realization of physical space [. . .] it has facilitated understanding and discovery; but these models are inadequate.
>
> (1967a, p. 135)

Bergson, in *Matter and Memory*, had also criticised Freud's (1891) as well as other scientists' diagrams to understand sensory aphasia, diagrams which become increasingly complicated, yet unable to grasp the full complexity of reality:

> For images can never be anything but things, and thought is a movement. It is vain, therefore, to treat memory-images and ideas as ready-made things.
>
> (Bergson, 1896 [1911], pp. 124–125)

Bion seems to have partially departed from Freud and to have implicitly adopted a Bergsonian perspective. Indeed in Bion's 1970 *Attention and Interpretation*, the first sentences of the book implicitly state the basic tenets of Bergsonian metaphysics:

> Words and verbal statements [. . .] were developed from a background of sensuous experience. Reason is emotion's slave and exists to rationalize emotional experience.
>
> (p. 1)

Bergson's *Matter and Memory* stated the same assumptions:

> That which is commonly called a *fact* is not reality [. . .] but an adaptation of the real to the interests of practice and to the exigencies of social life. We break up this continuity into elements [. . .] which correspond in one case to distinct *words*, in the other to independent objects [. . .] of an intellect enslaved to certain necessities of bodily life and for the satisfaction of its wants.
>
> (1896 [1911], pp. 183–184)

After having criticized Freud's spatial diagram of the mind in 1967, in 1970, and on the same grounds, Bion turned his criticism to the three-dimensional spatial metaphor implicit in Klein's model of projective identification:

> Projective identification has hitherto been formulated in terms derived from a realization of the ordinary man's three dimensional space [. . .] Kleinian formulations depend on a visual image of a space containing all kinds of objects. [. . .] it became evident that more rigorous formulation of the theory was needed [. . .].
>
> (p. 9)

Bergson stated the problem in very similar ways in *Matter and Memory*, namely that the perception of "inner life" (i.e. mental phenomena) is distorted into artificial spatial things which are then taken erroneously as the mental reality itself.

> the utilitarian work of the mind, in what concerns the perception of our inner life, consisted in a sort of refracting of pure duration into space [...] which permits us to separate our psychical states [...] we could show that these difficulties, contradictions and problems are mainly the result of the symbolic diagrams which cover it up, diagrams which have for us become reality itself.
>
> (1896 [1911], pp. 185–187)

In order to overcome this quandary Bergson proposed a method for metaphysical philosophy which consisted in a great effort of will directed to unmaking previous habits of thinking and perceiving, to restore intuition to its original purity, and to make contact with "true knowledge" and the absolute "real" (pp. 185–186).

In the next section of this chapter, I will describe Bergson's notion of the faculty of *intuition* and its development, and argue that Bion's notion of intuition in psychoanalysis can be seen as an application to psychoanalysis of the Bergsonian notion of intuition.

The development of intuition

According to Bergson (1903 [1912]), there are two profoundly different ways of knowing: (1) the intellectual–analytic way, which moves around the object, depends on the point of view (is *relative*) and aims to profit from the object and satisfy an interest; and (2) intuition, which by an effort of imagination and in sympathy with the object, inserts itself within the state of mind of the object in order to coincide with it and what is unique in it (is *absolute*). The former reaches its peak in materialistic–positivistic science: it tends to analyse things as static and discontinuous, building words, concepts, and theories to describe observable "objects", and then using those concepts to further understanding of reality (reducing uncertainty): it is useful for getting things done, and acting, but it fails to reach to the essential reality of things precisely because it leaves out the continuous flux of life. In contrast, the intuitive form of knowing is global, immediate, reaching into the heart of reality, and reaches its peak in metaphysics; it dispenses with symbols and cannot be represented by images.

Bergson's entire work can be seen as an extended exploration of intuition and the methods for developing it (see Matthews, 1999). Bergson argued boldly that intuition can reach the *absolute* and the *infinite*, and that the barrier which prevents direct contact with the absolute is:

> the symbolic knowledge by pre-existing concepts, which proceeds from the fixed to the moving, and not the intuitive knowledge which installs itself in that which is moving and adopts the very life of things.
>
> (1903 [1912], p. 53)

The importance of a very similar notion of intuition in Bion's entire work is quite central in his approach to observation of psychoanalytic and group reality.

In *Experiences in Groups* Bion stated his intention to investigate the group phenomena through psychoanalytically developed intuition: Bion states explicitly that he is going to start afresh without any earlier psychoanalytic theories of the group in order to achieve an unprejudiced view (Bion, 1961, p. 165).

In his 1963 *Elements of Psychoanalysis* Bion proposed intuition as the main tool in the analytic work that might solve the problem of the inadequacy of the intellect for grasping dynamic mental states (p. 74). Actually Bion mentions that the book was conceived as a response to the need "to sharpen and develop intuition" (pp. 73–74). For Bion, intuition is thus a capacity and a skill that must be trained and exercised, which is what was proposed by Bergson: a laborious and painful effort to reverse the usual utilitarian work of the intellect in order to place oneself directly, by a mental expansion, within the object studied (Bergson, 1903 [1912], pp. 38–45).

Since intuition challenges the traditional Freudian dichotomy between (1) secondary process-principle of reality-sensuous perception *versus* (2) primary process/pleasure principle/Dreams and Hallucinations, the problem of how to distinguish his notion of *intuition* from *hallucination* is addressed by Bion in *Second Thoughts* (1967a, p. 164). He postulates that consciousness is able to perceive "thoughts" that exist prior to the thinker, an "ultimate reality", the existence of which is independent of the senses and cannot be "empirically verifiable" (pp. 165–166). Here, he clearly enters into the realm of Bergson's and Whitehead's Process Philosophy metaphysics, in the assumption of Reality as an infinite and indivisible continuum, as it really is before being distorted and artificially divided by the senses and the intellect (see Bergson, 1896 [1911], pp. 183–185; Whitehead, 1929 [1978], pp. 338–341)

In Bion's (1965) *Transformations*, one of the central themes of the book is the notion of intuiting the ultimate reality of the patient's mind and of what is really going on in the psychoanalytic sessions. Bion calls this the "absolute fact" or ultimate truth, the "thing-in-itself", in Kant's sense, outside the realm of possibilities for the intellect (K or Knowledge), and uses the sign O to denote this unknowable reality. Again, trained intuition is addressed as a way to come into contact with this reality: "One pole of O is trained intuitive capacity transformed to effect its juxtaposition with what is going on in the analysis" (p. 49). The other pole of O is the analyst's preconceptions of psychoanalytic theories. Bion considers that the theories usually employed by analysts to investigate the clinical material consist of attention to preconceptions, conceptions, and concepts (corresponding to rows D, E, and F, and column 4 of his "Grid" – Bion, 1977 [1989]). He considers these states of mind too limitative and not conducive to the free-floating attention and *reverie* usually regarded as desirable in the analyst. What is implied in these statements is that theories can prevent the direct contact with Reality, while trained intuition can approximate the direct contact ("juxtaposition") with O, the thing-in-itself, ultimate reality.

A concrete description of intuition in psychoanalysis can be found in Bion (1965, pp. 124–125). He links it with the mother–baby *reverie* model, based on Klein's theory of projective identification and the good-breast which detoxifies the preverbal anxiety of the baby:

> Any individual capable of making the transformations from O, when O is a psychic reality [. . .] is capable of doing for himself something analogous to the projective identification into the good breast.

The clarification of the notion of "O" takes us to the next sections of this chapter. I will argue that Bion's "O" was partially developed from his readings of Whitehead on the importance of the symbol 0 to represent the number "zero" in mathematical notation. I will also argue that Bion's notion of "O" combined Bergson's concept of intuition with Whitehead's focus on the meaning of zero (0).

Whitehead's elaboration on the number zero (0) and Bion's notion of "O"

In Whitehead's 1911 book *Introduction to Mathematics* (also found in Bion's library with lines pencilled in by him), at the start of Chapter V entitled "The symbolism of mathematics", Whitehead considered the apparatus of ideas out of which science is built, starting with the symbols of the so-called Arabic notation for arithmetic. According to him this numeral system of notation affords us the enormous importance deriving from a good notation, by relieving the mind (the brain) of unnecessary work, and setting it free to concentrate on more advanced problems.

The paragraph pencilled in by Bion in the margins of Whitehead's book was on page 44 of Chapter V (corresponding to page 64 of the second revised edition which I have) stating the following:

> [. . .] This service is performed by 0, the symbol for zero. It is extremely probable that the men who introduced 0 for this purpose had no definite conception in their minds of the number zero. They simply wanted a mark to symbolize the fact that nothing was contributed by the digit's place in which it occurs. The idea of zero probably took shape gradually from a desire to assimilate the meaning of this mark to that of the marks, 1, 2, 3 . . . 9, which do represent cardinal numbers. This would not represent the only case in which a subtle idea has been introduced into mathematics by a symbolism which in its origin was dictated by practical convenience.

It is easy to imagine Bion's fascination with these notions as he tried to develop abstract symbols for his elements of psychoanalysis and his Grid, which according to him could contribute to the full development of psychoanalytic observation and interpretation.

In the same Chapter V of the book, Whitehead focused on other features of the number zero:

> [P]robably most mathematicians of the ancient world would have been horribly puzzled by the idea of the number zero. For, after all, it is a very subtle idea, not at all obvious. [. . .] The point about zero is that we do not need to use it in the operations of daily life. No one goes out to buy zero fish. [. . .] But what is the importance of this simple symbolic procedure? It made possible the growth of the modern conception of algebraic form [. . .] it is not going too far to say that no part of modern mathematics can be properly understood without constant recurrence to it.
>
> (1911, pp. 63–66)

The symbol 0 as seen by Whitehead, essentially relates to Henri Bergson's metaphysical plea to give up the utilitarian "intellectual operations of daily life" which aim to profit from the object and satisfy a need.[9] Building on Whitehead's ideas, Bornstein (1996) further elaborated on this topic: the concept of Zero was "difficult to grasp for people who had used counting only for practical reasons such as keeping track of animals killed, number of days passed, etc." (Bornstein, 1996, pp. 32–33).

Whitehead (1911, p. 58) directed the reader to W.W. Rouse Ball's book *A Short Account of the History of Mathematics* for further clarifications on the origins of the so-called Arabic notation, which, more accurately, should be called "Arabic–Hindu" notation. According to Ball (1908, pp. 129–153) the decimal system was introduced to the Arabs in the eighth century when Indian astronomical tables were brought to Baghdad, but it was used in India before the end of the fifth century (initially the Spanish Arabs probably discarded the symbol 0 until they understood its convenience for calculus).

These historical references of the origins of the symbol 0 in ancient Hindu culture might have held special appeal for Bion and to his sense of identity as he was born in India; indeed in the book *Transformations* where the notion of "O" is introduced, he tried to apply to psychoanalysis the works of the ancient Hindu geometer Bhãskara, which Ball (1908) had also explained at length in his book.[10] However, when Bion tried to apply geometry to his conception of "mental space" (i.e. the domain of thought), an apparently insoluble paradox arose: "the domain of thoughts may be conceived of as a space occupied by no-things" (Bion, 1965, p. 106). As already seen in the previous section, this notion is a central part of both Bergson and Whitehead's Process Philosophy concept of Reality: the ultimate nature of reality is a multitude of dynamic processes of becoming and relatedness, beyond the possibilities of verbal expressions derived from the sensuous perception of objects in space (Bergson, 1896 [1911], 1903 [1912]; Whitehead, 1929).

Bergson and Whitehead: the philosophical bases for the ultimate reality in Bion

The use of the symbol "O" by Bion can be seen as congregating the notions of Bergson on the importance of metaphysical intuition and of Whitehead on the importance of the number 0.

According to Bion (1965, pp. 45–46) the "passions" Love, Hate, and Knowledge (L-, H-, and K-links), representing the utilitarian function of fulfilling a wish under the reality principle, distort the deduction of what O is (matching Whitehead's reference to practical men who distorted the importance of the symbol 0 for mathematics). Therefore, the appropriate frame of mind to enter into contact with O is akin to the contemplative attitude of a religious and mystical approach. Whitehead makes an enlightening remark on this topic:

> We hardly ever apply arithmetic in its pure metaphysical sense, without the addition of presumptions which depend for their truth on the character of the societies dominating the cosmic epoch in which we live [...]. There is no difficulty in imagining a world in which arithmetic would be an interesting fanciful topic for dreamers, but useless for practical people engrossed in the business of life.
>
> (1929, p. 199)

In *Transformations*, Bion's mystical/metaphysical approach to reality in psychoanalysis is first made explicit. Although he considered the capacity to enter into contact with O to be outside the possibility of the intellect and of Knowledge acquired through the senses, he considered it to be within the realm of the possible: "I wish to make it clear that my reason for saying O is unknowable is not that I consider human capacity unequal to the task" (1965, p. 140). Here Bion clearly favours Bergson's ideas to the detriment of Kant's.

According to Bergson (1896 [1911], pp. 184–185):

> The impotence of speculative reason, as Kant has demonstrated it, is at bottom only the impotence of an intellect enslaved to certain necessities of bodily life [...]. By unmaking that which these needs have made, we may restore to intuition its original purity and so recover contact with the real.

Bion (1965, p. 147) acknowledged that most of the prominent thinkers (philosophers and psychoanalysts alike, such as Plato, Kant, Freud, and Klein) consider that there exists a epistemic gap between phenomena and Reality – the thing-in-itself, "O", but not the mystics who are convinced of the direct accessibility of ultimate Reality. The capacity to enter into contact with O is described by Bion by means of mystical terms, such as "becoming the godhead" and an "Incarnation of a part of an independent Person, wholly outside the personality" (Bion, 1965, p. 139). He then proceeds to further elaborate what can be called a mystical vertex in psychoanalysis (pp. 148–159). Bion pinpoints the habit of the human mind which prevents "*being one* with O" by means of his notion of "column 2 statements" i.e. using "theories as a barrier against the unknown". The solution he suggests is to achieve a state of "naivety", which presupposes the acceptance of ignorance and an intuitive approach, in a typical Bergsonian way.

However, Bion acknowledged two sides of the problem: on one side the state necessary for the intuitive approach arouses fear of ignorance, and on the other the Faith that involves "becoming" O involves dread of going crazy and of megalomania (pp. 159–164). At the end of his book *Transformations* Bion summarized the typical human response to the fears and resistances of becoming "O":

> Confronted with the unknown, "the void and formless infinite", the personality of whatever age fills the void (saturates the element), provides a form (names and binds a constant conjunction) and gives boundaries to the infinite (number and position).
>
> (Bion 1965, p. 171)

He proposed a radical change in this attitude, as applied to psychoanalysis by considering every session as an evolving pattern of the concept of godhead, to which the analyst must seek to establish contact[11] (p. 171). While these ideas seem quite alien to traditional psychoanalytic thinking, the alliance of reason and revelation, science, and faith is one of the main distinctive features of both Bergson and Whitehead's works:

> [I]t must be one of the motives of a complete cosmology to construct a system of ideas which brings the aesthetic, moral, and religious interests into relation with those concepts of the world which have their origin in natural science.
>
> (Whitehead, 1929, p. xii)

> A truly intuitive philosophy would realize the much desired union of science and metaphysics.
>
> (Bergson, 1903 [1912], pp. 53–54)

And this stance was echoed by Bion in his theory of Transformations:

> Transformations may be scientific, aesthetic, religious, mystical, psychoanalytical [. . .] all these classifications have a value.
>
> (1965, p. 140)

In Bion's *Second Thoughts* (1967a), he used terms such as "fatal to good analysis" and "a major misfortune of psychoanalytic practice" to describe the lack of developed intuition, and "if premature application of a theory becomes a habit which places a screen between the psycho-analyst and the exercise of his intuition on fresh and therefore unknown material" (p. 128). He also emphasized the need to radically readjust conventional psychoanalytic mental attitudes to accommodate what could be called a mystical vertex, which implies an open mind, differentiating mystical-like transformations from previous ready-made theories such as "pathological megalomania".

In Bion's 1970 *Attention and Interpretation* there is a restatement of the self-vigilance and the active effort of discipline needed to achieve epistemological purity, naivety, and freedom from ready-made previous theories, in order to be directly in contact with the ultimate reality of what is actually taking place in each session of psychoanalysis, and thus be an effective psychoanalyst (p. 27).

Summary and conclusion

Bion's passion for philosophy gave him an unusually broad range of knowledge for a psychiatrist and a psychoanalyst. This chapter argued that Bion's readings of the works of Bergson and Whitehead deeply influenced his worldview. The importance of intuition, of discovering the new and disregarding pre-established psychoanalytic theories can be traced back to Bergson's method of intuition in metaphysics. The dissatisfaction with the reductionism of mechanistic metaphors to understand the mind and the analytic relationship, and the importance attached to dynamic processes of relatedness seems to be based on the premises of Process Philosophy, with its exuberant and contagious emphasis on Life, Growth, Novelty, and Freedom. "Life refuses to be embalmed alive", says Whitehead (1929 [1978], p. 339), and "a being which evolves freely creates something new every moment", says Bergson, 1896 [1911], p. 223). At the same time, these two thinkers accomplished what Cohen (1999) called the integration of reason and revelation, and it seems that Bion tried to do something similar in psychoanalysis with his notion of "O": combining the algebraic symbol 0 in mathematical notation with the intuitive–mystical frame of mind implicit in reverie, both needed to grasp the "ultimate reality" of the patients' mind. The process of "becoming O", through an effort of suspending previous theories and achieving a state of developed intuition, could contribute to fresh, new discoveries about what was actually taking place in the psychoanalytic session and in the group phenomena.

Notes

1 *Acknowledgements*: I want to sincerely thank Francesca Bion for kindly sending the documental material without which it would have been impossible to write

this chapter. I want also to thank Richard Morgan-Jones and R.D. Hinshelwood for their thoughtful revisions of and suggestions regarding earlier versions of this chapter.

2 In *Creative Evolution* (1907 [1911]) Bergson introduced the famous notion of *Élan Vital*, but I will not explore this concept in this chapter.

3 Indeed, in Paton's 1927 book *The Good Will: A Study in the Coherence Theory of Goodness*, he says: "among foreign writers I am much indebted to Monsieur Bergson" (p. 8).

4 According to Mullarkey (1999, p. 1) Bergson was at one point considered to be both the "greatest thinker in the world" and "the most dangerous man in the world".

5 Only very recently, in the writing of the present chapter did I become aware that Crociani-Winland (2009) had explored the parallels between these two notions of Bion and the ontology of Bergson and Deleuze from the perspective of psycho-social research, but I will not discuss these arguments here.

6 It is worth noting that Bergson quoted Freud's (1891) studies on aphasia (Bergson, 1896 [1911]), and also that Bergson agreed with Freud's (1900a, 1900b) ideas of *Interpretation of Dreams* (Bergson, 1901 [1920]). Reciprocally, Freud discussed extensively Bergson's (1900) ideas on Laughter and was in agreement with them (Freud, 1905b). It is hence possible that some of their ideas on the functioning of the mind were mutually inspired, and also influenced by common sources, including Charles Darwin on the evolutionary origins of the Mind (see Smith, 1978), which was a major influence on both Bergson (Goudge, 1912 [1949]) and on Freud (Sulloway, 1979). Both Freud and Bergson (as well as Lewin; see Chapter 7 of this book) proposed that psychic energy exists in its own right and is not reducible to physiology and physical energy; however, while Freud assumed either psychophysical parallelism (influenced by Hughlings Jackson [see Hinshelwood, 1995]) or psycho-physical interactionism (see Hinshelwood, 1997), Bergson rejected these dualistic positions and proposed that mental and physical energies were two different tendencies of the same ultimate reality (see Chapter 6 of this book on the proto-mental matrix).

7 See the Chapter 7 on Lewin and Bion, in this book, for an additional point of view on the topic of group dynamics through the concept of "social fields of forces".

8 Hinshelwood (2003) discussed Bion's notion of the contact between minds, in contrast with the contact of the mind with external reality, inanimate objects and mechanisms.

9 Says Whitehead:

> We can imagine that when it [notation 0 for number zero] had been introduced [...] practical men, of the sort who dislike fanciful ideas, deprecated the silly habit of identifying it with a number zero. But they were wrong, as such men always are when they desert their proper function of masticating food which others have prepared.
>
> (1911, p. 65)

10 It is possible that Bion followed Whitehead's note and read Ball's book. The possible relations between Bhãskara's mathematical developments of geometry and psychoanalytic notations for "mental space" opened up to Bion series of "psychoanalytic games" on the possibility of transforming emotional experiences into a "geometrically based, rigorously based, algebraic deductive system" (see Bion, 1965, pp. 93–94 and p. 122).

11 The topic of Bion's mystical vertex would require a whole study in itself, but a

mention is in order to clarify matters. The concept of "godhead" was borrowed from Meister Eckhart (Bion, 1965, p. 139), the speculative mystic condemned for heresy in the early fourteenth century. It is remarkable that many thinkers, starting with Schopenhauer (1844 [1969], pp. 613–614), have considered the equivalence between the mysticism of Eckhart and of the ancient Hindu writings of the *Vedas* and *Buddhism*. The prominent publication by D.T. Suzuki (1957) considered Eckhart's teachings concerning detachment and the "pure Nothing," as very much akin to the concept of "emptiness" in Mahayana Buddhism. He also considered to be close the mystical concept of "Zero" and "no-thing-ness", in a way which was very similar to Bion's (see Suzuki, 1957, pp. 28, 50). It is possible that Whitehead's (1911) and Ball's (1908) reference to the origin of 0 in ancient Hindu numerals encouraged Bion to further research on ancient eastern sources; indeed, references to the *Vedas* are scattered throughout Bion's posthumously published works (e.g. Bion, 1975 [2000], p. 132; 1978 [1994], p. 371; 1979 [2000], p. 330). Additionally, there are many parallels between Whitehead's and Bergson's principles of Process Philosophy, the *Vedas* and Mahayana Buddhism (e.g. Suzuki, 1957; Smith, 1972, p. 480; Odin, 1982; Long, 2007).

Chapter 4

The wider medical culture of Bion's bio-psycho-social framework

Nuno Torres and R.D. Hinshelwood

After his army career in 1917–1918, and a graduation in history in 1921, Bion decided to study medicine, and gained his medical and surgical qualifications in 1930. In medicine the "biomedical model" was the dominant one during the late nineteenth and into the twentieth centuries (Double, 2007); this model assumes disease to be fully accounted for by deviations from the norm of measurable biological-somatic variables[1] (e.g. Alexander, 1939; Engel, 1977). In a seminal paper George Engel (1977) stressed the need for a new mainstream outlook in medicine – the bio-psycho-social model – which takes seriously into account the psychological and social components unaddressed by the reductionist biomedicine. Almost thirty years earlier, Bion (1950) had proposed a model for comprehending diseases in which social, psychological and physical components are intertwined.[2] And at the end of his series of papers on groups he remarked challengingly, "The only point about collecting a group of people is that it enables us to see just how the 'political' characteristics of the human body operate" (Bion, 1951, p. 131).

The bio-psycho-social model had been introduced into medicine in the twentieth century long before Bion's (1950) and Engel's (1977). According to Double (2007), Engel's bio-psycho-social model is basically a renamed and reanimated version of Adolf Meyer's holistic psychobiological approach initiated around 1920.[3] In the 1920s, too, in the UK, Hugh Crichton-Miller, the founder of the Tavistock Clinic, aimed at a "unified psychosomatic approach to diagnosis and treatment" (Armstrong, 1980). Bion drew a great deal from Crichton-Miller's ideas, and also to the momentous research publications of Wittkower (1949) on life-stories of psychosomatic patients, and of Halliday (1948) on social epidemiology of psychosomatic diseases.

In this chapter we will address the wider context in which Bion's bio-psycho-social approach proposals emerged in 1950 apparently quite abruptly in his writing, and quickly waned as he moved from the Tavistock Clinic to his dedication to psychoanalysis.

Mind and body: the notion of psychogenic diseases and stress diseases

The idea of the social and relational being crucial in provoking abnormal forms of affective/emotional functioning that are *directly* linked to physical ill-health, has been present at least since Freud, in his concepts of psychogenic somatic symptoms, anxiety equivalents, "actual neuroses", and the social determinants of these neuroses (Freud, 1895 [1950], 1908, 1910).

Notwithstanding the dominant materialism and physicalism of Freud's physiological and medical training, certain somatic health problems associated with *functional* nervous disorders (or *neuroses*) such as neuralgias and anaesthesias, contractures and paralysis, epileptoid convulsions, tics and various forms of disturbance of vision suggested psychological and social aetiologies (Freud, 1895 [1950], p. 4). In order to explain these "mysterious" illnesses, medical and psychiatric researchers had to develop models that acknowledged both a mind in its own right and a connection between body and mind: psychophysical *interactionist* or psychophysical *parallelist* models[4] (see, e.g. Popper, 1977b). Freud's theoretical models of hysteria, as well as later models of psychosomatic diseases were among the most prominent of such *psychophysical* models (Wisdom, 1952; Sulloway, 1979). Freud's theory of "psychogenic" disease is that unsolvable conflicts of ideas can lead to bodily symptoms (Freud, 1910; Martin, 1960; pp. 71–72). This notion had its origin in Freud's work on inexplicable hysterical paralyses (Freud, 1888) in which he proposed that they were not caused by any physical lesion in the material substratum of the nervous tissue that allows electrical association between the brain and the peripheral tissue, but were solely the result of a mental alteration by which specific psychological associative paths were turned unconscious.[5] The Freudian notion of *psychogenic* allowed an understanding of psychoneurotic *functional* somatic symptoms as being an encrypted body language representing disturbing memories defensively turned unconscious.

These notions led to a prominent psychoanalytic oriented research program on the so-called *psychosomatic diseases* (e.g. see Brown, 2000, for an account of this historical development). This movement deployed unconscious conflicts and affects as the unknown aetiology and flourished in America in the 1940s and 1950s, fostered by men such as Franz Alexander and Otto Fenichel, and also to the less-known Allan Gregg and his allocation of funding to psychosomatic research from the Medical Sciences Division of the Rockefeller Foundation.[6]

According to Fenichel (1946), "unconscious affects" are of special significance in the formation of somatic symptoms which accompany states of dammed-up libido. Such affects or "affect equivalents" lose their mental content, whereas their physiological concomitants persist. Fenichel's idea was developed further by Franz Alexander and the Chicago school of psychosomatics (Alexander and

Pollock, 1968), which connected the Freudian concept of "actual neurosis" with unconscious conflicts at various levels of the psychosexual development and with specific personality structures. Closer to Fenichel's view was Florence Dunbar (1943), who saw psychosomatic disorders as devoid of symbolic significance, the result of inappropriately or inadequately expressed affect that created chronic tension and concomitantly chronic negative interactions and, finally, organic damage.

Earlier in Britain, during and after the First World War, some Freudian ideas had been included in the understanding and treatment of functional diseases in "shell-shock" war traumatised men, led by Hugh Crichton-Miller (Prideaux, 1920; Crichton-Miller, 1920b). However, Crichton-Miller was not a psychoanalyst and had a very eclectic approach, which was of considerable influence for the Tavistock Clinic identity (see Chapter 5). He proposed a psychophysical interactionist model (a "binocular model") in which emotions, mental stability and physical factors (e.g. sepsis) interacted via the endocrine and circulatory systems (Crichton-Miller 1920a).

On the other hand, since the works of the physiologist Walter Cannon and followers, it had been known that emotional deregulation affects the body directly. Cannon's (1914) research demonstrated that the *emotional reaction* to perceived threats, the so-called *fight-flight reaction*, was physiologically identical to the reaction to somatic challenges on bodily *homeostasis*, such as low oxygen or extreme temperatures.[7] The disturbances of homeostasis were called *stresses*, and if prolonged they could represent too great a strain and lead to alteration of the *internal milieu*[8] and eventually to physical collapse and death (Cannon, 1935, 1942).[9]

Hence, important developments in medicine in Germany, Britain, the US and other countries between the wars were made on the relation between physical illness and emotional/psychological stress. Growing evidence was available as to the central role of emotional factors in non-infectious diseases. This was so much the case that in 1934 the Public Health Relations Committee of the New York Academy of Medicine founded the "Committee on Emotions and Health" (Dunbar, 1935, p. xxi). According to Dunbar: "The findings of research workers in many fields have combined to modify fundamentally not only our concept of psyche and soma but also our concept of disease" (ibid., p. xiii) and "both physiology and psychoanalysis were taking the lead in providing scientific studies of the relationship at the "boundary between the ego and the outer world" (ibid., p. 58).

But at the same time as the development of much more sophisticated and effective pharmacological treatments since the Second World War, have rendered any psychological factors apparently irrelevant, the results of psychoanalytical research were eventually very disappointing. The recent comprehensive reviews of psychoanalytic research on psychosomatic diseases point out that the early mistakes of this research programme were that it followed too precisely the model of psychoneurosis and of psychogenic symptoms and looked for patterns of internal ideational conflict in the minds of the patients (Taylor, 1987; Nemiah, 1987). On the other hand, the research on *stressful life events* and psychosomatic diseases followed the physiological advances in stress research and the disillusionment with the psychoanalytic program of research and treatment[10] (Taylor, 1987, p. 39; Brown, 2000).

Hence, by the time Bion published his 1950 ideas about psychosomatics (i.e. the proto-mental system) in book format in 1961, the psychoanalytic-inspired psychosomatic research was in steady decline. Bion's proposals are actually much closer to the notion of *emotional stress* than to the notion of *psychogenic* unconscious conflicts – he named one of the group-mentality basic assumptions of *fight-flight*, borrowing Cannon's notion on the animals' reaction to perceived threats. Bion valued highly the lectures of Elliot-Smith on the physiology of the brain, while he was studying medicine at University College (Bléandonu, 1994, pp. 37–38), and his emphasis was laid on very primitive and basic emotions, pre-verbal (which from a brain anatomical perspective stem from the evolutionarily primitive limbic and sub-cortical areas), and that could manifest both physically or psychologically, or even in an indistinguishable psycho-physical blend: the proto-mental. Additionally Bion postulated that the determination of psychosomatic diseases should be sought not only in the mind but mostly in the social level and was correlated with group and social dynamics.

Bion and the bio-psycho-social integration: psychosocial medicine in England

Bion's bio-psycho-social integration was a culmination of his interest inspired by the Tavistock in the 1930s, with its integrative urge to bring biological, social and psychological studies of human beings together. This was steered by the founder of the Tavistock, Hugh Crichton-Miller as well as his very early associates, James Hadfield and Ian Suttie.

In 1946 Allan Gregg, the Medical Director of the Rockefeller Foundation, made a donation of untied funds to the Interim Planning Committee (IPC) of the Tavistock Clinic, with the objective of undertaking the social psychiatry that had developed during the Second World War.[11] Gregg "wanted to create an 'elite corps' of psychosomatic investigators *oriented* towards physiology but also *interested in* psychoanalysis yet not dominated or blindly adherent to its claims" (Brown, 2000, p. 22). The IPC was chaired by Bion, who used his findings and group techniques within the planning group itself (Trist and Murray, 1990a). Alan Gregg's passionate aim of achieving wholeness in human self-knowledge might have been contagious to Bion:

> The totality that is a human being has been divided for study into parts and systems; one cannot decry the method but one is not obliged to

> remain satisfied with its results alone [...]. The need for more knowledge here is of an excruciating obviousness. But more than mere need there is a foreshadowing of changes to come. Psychiatry is astir, neurophysiology is crescent, neurosurgery flourishes, and a star still hangs over the cradle of endocrinology.... Contributions from other fields are to seek from psychology, cultural anthropology, sociology and philosophy as well as from chemistry and physics and internal medicine to resolve the dichotomy of mind and body.
>
> (Gregg, 1936, cited in Alexander, 1939, p. 9)

By 1948, the same year of the publication of his first *Experiences in Groups* set of papers, Bion was chairman of the enormously influential medical section of the British Psychological Society (Hinshelwood, 1995). His 1948 paper "Psychiatry at a time of crisis" presents Bion's grand agenda: to integrate psychoanalysis with the study of emotions and group dynamics and contribute to mental health changes at the macro-social level.

One of the main figures of the Tavistock Group from 1935 to 1950 was Eric Wittkower, research fellow and consultant in psychosomatic medicine. In 1945, he was sponsored by the National Association of Prevention of Tuberculosis in a study of the psychological aspects of tuberculosis: Wittkower followed 785 patients and found that most of them had unresolved re-enacted conflicts over emotional dependency in their life stories. Furthermore "situations which rouse aggressiveness or endanger the delicately poised security system of the patients often precede the onset of symptoms of tuberculosis" (Wittkower, 1949, p. 137). Bion made reference to Wittkower's finding in his discussion of the non-dominant basic assumptions, though was cautious about assigning direct causality. Wittkower, like Bion, was here including the social level in the complex interplay of body and emotions.[12] Wittkower's study was published in a book prefaced by John Rickman, who was Bion's mentor, colleague and first analyst.

Indeed, John Rickman had also a very central role in the British psychosocial medicine, and his work was also an attempt to unify the medical, psychological and social approaches. In 1926 he wrote his MD thesis on a psychological factor in the aetiology of prolapse of the uterus. From 1925 to 1948 he was editor of the *British Journal of Medical Psychology* (Payne, 1957). He was a catalyst to the group of psychosocially oriented psychiatrists and medical doctors, and directly involved not only in Wittkower (1949) but also Halliday (1948) publications, that were cited by Bion in his 1950a chapter.

The notion of the sick society

In 1932, Cannon had allowed himself to consider the existence of a literal "social homeostasis", and the direct influence of social factors on bodily homeostasis. He claimed, "Steady states in society as a whole and steady states in its members are closely linked ... we are forced to recognise that the homeostasis of the individual human is largely dependent on social homeostasis" (Cannon, 1932, p. 295). These elaborations have prompted the notion that, via emotional imbalances, social influences could directly impinge on the natural balance of the body[13] (e.g. Mead, 1947). A social phenomenon characterised by rise in anxiety-equivalent somatic states, pre-neurotic defences and epidemics of psychosomatic diseases, became known as the "sick society" (Halliday, 1948).

Bion (1948, 1950c [1961]) took the notion of the sick society not only in the medical sense (of disease rates and somatically diseased individuals) but predominantly in the sociological, historical and political point of view of "social illness", meaning individual and collective alienation, political degeneracy and social self-destruction. He was probably influenced here by the consultant surgeon Wilfred Trotter (1916), for whom Bion had worked after his medical qualification, as well as by the historian Arnold Toynbee. Bion speaks admiringly of Trotter and his Darwinian-inspired apocalyptic suggestions, as Bion was ardently interested in the factors leading to social and individual development and evolution and also to social and individual decadence and catastrophe. In his 1947 address as chair of the BPS medical section (Bion, 1948), he injected a messianic grandiose tone into psychosocial medicine and social psychiatry, which in his view in combination with psychoanalysis, would have the duty of resolving the atavistic and secular paradoxes of progress and catastrophe of human societies.

In complex social systems the conflicts between individual emotional needs and social priorities, and between inspired leadership and social oppression, represent deep-seated difficulties of group co-operation. Toynbee's concept of *dominant minority*, was known to Bion. Toynbee's (1935–1961) work traced the genesis, development and decay of all of the major world civilizations in the historical record and proposed that societies had thus far failed in reconciling the powerful and primitive emotional pressures that are released in social relations with reason, intellectual development and social organisation. A substantial body of work in the sociological tradition had addressed similar questions, especially the work of authors such as Weber, Durkheim and their followers. According to Prager (1981) "both Weber and Durkheim are theoretically committed to the concern for the free individual and the belief that individuals should participate actively in social life" (p. 918).

Drawing on his study for his undergraduate degree in history, Bion presented his own version of how individuals socially co-ordinate rational organisation and the emotions, by observing much smaller "societies" than the sociologists. The work group and basic assumption group mentalities inevitably compete for ascendency And he showed how individuals could become harmfully alienated from their own social need. It was generally assumed by those interested in psychosomatic processes that it had been the rapidity of modern social change and mechanisation characteristic of the industrialised society's life-style that was at odds with people's basic emotional needs and that this led to emotional alienation and noticeably correlated levels of disease (e.g. Dunbar, 1935; Halliday, 1948). The sick society is interestingly similar to Bion's notion of group diseases, inspired by Halliday's (1948) conception of "adverse psychological-communal environment".

Bion, drawing on psychoanalysis in the 1950s, reframed this as an inherent conflict in the social human being: "The individual is a group animal at war, not simply with the group, but with himself for being a group animal and with those aspects of his personality that constitute his 'groupishness'" (Bion 1961, p. 131). This "war" manifested in the group tensions, in the mind of the individuals, and in their physical bodies, as Bion witnessed directly both in his work as individual therapist and as a group dynamics leader. In 1934, while still a trainee at the Tavistock, Bion treated Samuel Beckett who sought psychotherapy due to health problems allegedly of psychosomatic origins: while the therapy was intellectually stimulating for both, it did not progress and Beckett's body somatised with boil, tremors and abscesses (Bléandonu, 1994, pp. 44–45). As a group dynamics leader, Jock Sutherland as first-hand witness tells us that Bion in action was stressful much of the time, and some of the group members somatised through duodenal ulcer symptoms: "These effects served to bring out the depths of Bion's sensitivity and the validity of his conception of the close relation between the physical and mental at the primitive levels prominent in the group" (Sutherland, 1985, p. 52),

Conclusions

That medical phase peaked during the 1930s, with recognition that many illnesses were resistant to giving up their aetiological secrets. Prior to the age of the pharmaceutical "wonder drugs", from the 1950s, the management of illness was multifaceted, and the benefits of the placebo effect, or the "bedside manner" were more or less self-evident and even perhaps self-explanatory. The development of those views into the full-scale psychosomatic discipline of bodily diseases expressing psychological malaise was very understandable at the time. Now it may seem vague and unreliable, given the highly accurate physiological targeting of current medication, and also the current multidisciplinary biomedical research that started in the 1970s, studying the myriad of peptide molecules and receptors that chemically link the somatic regulatory processes of the body and its nervous, immune and endocrine systems (e.g. Guillemin, 1977). Only very recently evidence is becoming available of the links between social interaction systems (including early attachments, social bonding and social status) and these biochemical somatic elements and processes of the body and the nervous system (e.g.

Nelson and Panksepp, 1998). These advances in many ways support Bion's (and his forerunners') intuitions and informed speculation on the bio-psycho-social processes inherent in individual and social disease, as we have addressed elsewhere (Torres, 2010a, 2010b)

It is not surprising that Bion left his bio-psycho-social medicine and social psychiatry ambitions behind as he did the Tavistock itself. In addition to the limitations of contemporary research to uncover highly intricate bio-molecular processes and its relations to the mind and social systems, there were other determining factors: the death of Rickman, Wittkower's departure to Canada, the split of the Tavistock Clinic into the Institute (dedicated to group dynamics and institutions) and the Clinic (dedicated to psychotherapy), and his analysis with Melanie Klein who was unsympathetic to his social ideas. However, in his 1961 introduction to *Experiences in Groups* (p. 8) he still said: "I regret not having discussed sovereignty and power [...] These matters I shall discuss in a further volume, if I have time".

Notes

1 The modern biomedical model was supported by the principles of medicine defined in terms of physical abnormalities that started to grow out of the sixteenth century anatomists' discoveries that in disease the organs in the body were distorted and damaged (Sternberg, 2001). With the discovery of the role of microorganisms, the germ theory of disease was introduced (Cassel, 1964), which strengthened even more the assumption that physical disease has exclusively materialistic bio-physical causes. On philosophical grounds, this outlook belongs to the materialist doctrine and is grounded on the dogmatic assumption that the physical world is self-contained or closed and that the physical processes can and must be explained and understood entirely in terms of physical theories (see Crichton-Miller, 1920a; and Popper 1977b, p. 52, for elaborations on this topic).

2 The emphasis on a bio-psycho-social understanding of disease is getting more contemporary than ever. The World Health Organization (WHO, 2000) and the World Economic Forum (Bloom *et al.*, 2011), described the leading cause of illness and mortality in the contemporary industrialised world as a global epidemic of a cluster of chronic health problems consisting of chronic degenerative, non-communicable and non-infectious diseases, including mental disorders, heart diseases, cancers, respiratory diseases, diabetes, musculoskeletal disorders, obesity, smoking, other substances dependence (both illegal and legal), and injury as result of violence/accidents including suicide attempts. Some authors labelled this cluster of health problems as "diseases of comfort" (Choi *et al.*, 2005) and as "lifestyle related diseases" (Ackland *et al.*, 2003).

3 Adolf Meyer included in his thought some notions by Freud – he allegedly said in an unpublished lecture that Freud had formulated telling terms and formulae in the most communicable system psychiatry had seen in thirty years (Meyer, cited in Davidson, 1980, p. 140) – and also, like Freud, Meyer was influenced by the British neurologist Hughlings Jackson (Meyer, 1933).

4 The term "psychophysical parallelism" was used by Hughlings Jackson in the nineteenth century, from whom Freud took it (Hinshelwood, 1995).

5 This alteration was an abolition of the associative accessibility of the conception

of the organ or function in question: the paralysis actually followed a "cut" as it were in the train of conscious ideational association between the idea of the organ and the rest of the ideas of the conscious ego" (Freud 1888, pp. 170–172).

6 Gregg was also central in allocating money to British social psychiatry, both for the Maudsley Hospital and the Tavistock Clinic and in the fostering of Bion's bio-psycho-social interests, as we will show below.

7 The mechanism of homeostasis is the process by which the body strives to maintain a stable internal environment (such as glucose concentrations and body temperature) essential to life through the interaction of the sympathetic nervous systems and the adrenal glands (Cannon, 1932).

8 "Internal milieu" was a concept coined by the physiologist Claude Bernard, meaning the

> blood and tissue fluids, which provided a steady environment for the cells composing the body and made it independent of the vagaries of the external environment. The constancy of the internal milieu was largely maintained through the regulatory functions of the nervous system
>
> (Wiener, 1973, Vol. 2, p. 404)

9 The *flight or fight response*, which was also named "acute stress response", was later recognised by Hans Selye as the first stage of the *general adaptation syndrome*, or "stress syndrome"; Selye observed that people who had various illnesses seemed to share a quality of "sickness" that was highly similar (Sternberg, 2001). This quality has been called "disease proneness" and some have argued that psychosocial factors play a role in disease proneness to all diseases both infectious and non-infectious (Vaillant, 1979, p. 732; Ryff and Singer, 2001).

10 The general neurochemistry of the stress syndrome or general adaptation syndrome is now well understood: the body's initial reaction to emotional stress is the release of several hormones, including the glucocorticoid hormones: cortisol and cortisone (Carlson, 1994). Glucocorticoids have potent immunosuppressive properties (i.e. are immune system response-suppressing agents) and increase blood pressure and blood sugar, consequently if the state of stress is prolonged it can precipitate health problems (including physical and mental health) due to the physiological deregulation of several body systems, including the immune system and the nervous systems (Taylor, 1987).

11 This funding led to the birth of the Tavistock Institute of Human Relations, constituted at first as a division of the Tavistock Clinic, until its separate incorporation in 1947 (Trist and Murray, 1990).

12 After leaving London for Canada in 1951, he came to be the president of the American Psychosomatic Society in 1960. In the 1950s Wittkower developed "transcultural psychiatry", whose objective was to identify, verify and explain the links between mental disorder and broad psychosocial characteristics In 1955 he founded the Transcultural Psychiatric Research Review, which rapidly achieved international reputation which contributed to the relevance of the field as a legitimate and heuristic one. This journal was at essence transdisciplinary and had the collaboration of anthropologists, medical doctors, psychiatrists, psychologists and sociologists, including Margaret Mead in the advisory board of the journal.

13 In the late twentieth century these ideas were taken up again in the notion that "human relationships play a central role ... in the homeostatic regulation of physiological functions" (Nemiah, 1987, p. xxii).

Chapter 5

The Tavistock years

R.D. Hinshelwood

Bion went to the Tavistock in 1933 and left in 1948. He was there at the peak of what was the English eclectic school of psychotherapy (Brown 1964). That conceptual school was focused around James A. Hadfield and Ian Suttie, but inspired by the founder of the Tavistock Clinic, Hugh Crichton-Miller,

> The physician who has been trained to regard disease solely from the organic point of view, and the psychotherapist who has become accustomed to think exclusively in terms of mind, are both employing only monocular vision.
>
> (Crichton-Miller 1920a, p. 4)

Before he went to the Tavistock, Bion was acquainted with psychoanalysis and psychotherapy to only a moderate degree.

Wilfred Bion in the 1920s and 1930s

Bion went to Oxford in 1919, straight from the army. There he studied history, and found Oxford an intellectually stimulating and welcoming environment. Through his meeting with the philosopher H.J. Paton he developed an interest in the writings of Kant (Bléandonu 1994, p. 36). Paton was a lecturer there, and later became professor (between 1937 and 1952) – see Chapter 7. Despite this friendship, Bion failed to gain an honours degree from Oxford. Nor did he get rid of his personal and wartime ghosts. He then taught in his old school, Bishop's Stortford, until a boy made an accusation of sexual misconduct, upon which, despite Bion's vehement denial, he was sacked. He was not entirely disappointed to be rescued from a career as a schoolteacher: 'Had I been unfortunate enough to be as wise before the event as after, I might still be the extremely inept and wretched schoolteacher I was then' (Bion 1985, p. 17). He then spent some time in France, in Poitiers, where he improved his French.

He then went to the Medical School at University College, London (UCL). To study medicine, he needed to do a science entry examination, which to his dismay he only just passed. During this time he had become engaged to a very pretty girl who had subsequently broken the engagement off; and with such a dose of venom it made 'certain the wound not be, like a skilful surgical operation, aseptically carried out, but would fester and remain open' (Bion 1985, p. 27). As a medical student nursing his portfolio of failures, he needed help. Quite possibly during his clerkship as a student for Wilfred Trotter, he learned about psychoanalysis. Trotter was a well-known surgeon who had written on group behaviour – *Instincts of the Herd in Peace and War*, which had been noticed by Freud (1921). Trotter however is the person who in 1905 as a young doctor himself, pointed out Freud to Ernest Jones. In addition at University College Hospital there was Bernard Hart, a psychiatrist and one of those who early on recognised Freud (Hart 1912). He introduced psychoanalysis to the medical teaching there. And no doubt Bion would have learned from Hart during his medical training in the 1920s.

Through some route he found a therapist who offered twelve sessions, at a remarkably steep price in those days (£100 for the course). Characteristically, he failed at this psychotherapy, and subsequently, disparagingly, called this therapist Dr Feel-it-in-the-Past. Nevertheless he completed his studies and his residencies, and eventually acquired a job at the Tavistock Clinic as a trainee in 1933, and was appointed to the senior staff in 1934, presumably trained by then. He was part of the circle around James Hadfield, with whom he had some 'analysis'. It is not clear whether Dr Feel-it-in-the-Past to whom he went when a student at UCL, is Hadfield, though it seems unlikely he would not have said so.

Despite the pre-war antipathy between the Tavistock and the Psychoanalytical Society, Bion decided to train as a psychoanalyst, and at first (in 1938) sought his training analysis with John Rickman who was himself at the time in analysis with Melanie Klein. It is also probable that Bion had some dealings with Clifford Scott at this time.

The neophyte

Bion's time at the Tavistock Clinic was in two quite distinct periods divided by the years in the army in the two World Wars in which Bion served. In 1933, he was still in process of trying to 'find himself', after his war experiences in 1917–1918. He started as a trainee, and was appointed to the senior staff in 1934. Although there has been a lot written about Beckett's 'psychoanalysis' with Bion; in fact when Beckett started treatment with Bion in 1934, Bion was barely a psychotherapist in the Tavistock eclectic tradition, let alone a psychoanalyst. The Tavistock then represented a school of psychotherapy of its own, dedicated to a kind of integrative eclectic practice which included the ideas of Jung as well as Freud. As a result, the Tavistock drew opprobrium from the Psychoanalytical Society, and Ernest Jones, the founder of the Psychoanalytical Society, is said to have forbidden psychoanalysts from working at the Tavistock.

Hugh Crichton-Miller (1877–1959): The Tavistock was founded in 1920 and guided in its initial years by Hugh Crichton-Miller, who had been practising psychotherapy since before the First World War. The Tavistock grew out of his wartime experience of psychodynamic work with psychological casualties in the war. Crichton-Miller provided a strong lead with his 'philosophy of medicine, and in particular, his doctrine of psycho-physical parallelism, with the great emphasis he put on the then fashionable doctrine of focal sepsis and his slightly naïve endocrinological faith' (Dicks 1970, pp. 52–53). Crichton-Miller saw this as a binocular approach to the body and the mind and regretted 'the difficulty experienced by the average physician in achieving binocular vision' (Crichton-Miller 1935, p, 1207). We can note Bion's later use of that term, 'binocular vision' (Bion 1961, p. 8), but in his case he meant the attempt to integrate the psychological and the social sides of people. It is a strategy that later became his notion of 'vertex'. Crichton-Miller (1933) took an independent view of psychoanalysis, which put him, and the Tavistock Clinic, out of favour with Ernest Jones and the psychoanalytical society.

Thus Bion arrived at the Tavistock during a time when a certain psycho-physical integration was probably still a prevalent idea. Crichton-Miller's influence waned in the early 1930s, with new incoming staff trained elsewhere, and he resigned as director in 1933, the first year of Bion's appointment. But it is clear that something of Crichton-Miller's outlook survived as a basic outlook of Tavistock staff, and therefore rubbed off on Bion – notably the integrative approach, and the notion of achieving a binocular vision.[1]

James Hadfield (1882–1967): One of the original figures who Crichton-Millar appointed in 1920 was J.A. Hadfield. He exerted a considerable influence, on those coming to learn their psychotherapy at the Tavistock. Hadfield, with an academic background (King's College, London), took a large share of the load of teaching and training, and by 1933 was proposed as director of studies, though this brought to a head a personal rivalry between him and the director, Crichton-Miller. His own orientation leant on Jung, and William McDougal who had taught him at Oxford.

Though associated with the Clinic from its inception, Hadfield was more academic, and retained appointments at Birmingham and then London Universities. He did however practice hypnosis on shell-shock victims in the First World War, and was later responsible for the 'training analysis' of many younger psychiatrists in the 1930s. He wrote extensively though his books were regularly panned by Ernest Jones on the grounds of being divergent from Freudian psychoanalysis. He shared Crichton-Miller's interest in the relation of mind and brain, for instance,

> in the course of evolution the mind shows an ever-increasing tendency to free itself from physical control and, breaking loose from its bonds, to

> assert its independence and live a life undetermined except by the laws of its own nature.
>
> (Hadfield 1917, p. 21)

Bion was in therapy with Hadfield (1927–1935), and thus started it prior to his training at the Tavistock in 1932–1934. Possibly Hadfield was the main influence in Bion deciding to get a job there. Interestingly, Bion's autobiography mentions nothing about Hadfield or the Tavistock, and simply glosses over the time from his medical student days until his wartime service in the EMS in 1939, and in the RAMC from 1940.[2]

One suggestion made by Bléandonu about Hadfield's influence, is that Bion's conceptualisation of the three basic assumptions during his group interest in the 1940s stems from Hadfield's descriptions:

> Hadfield hypothesized the existence of a triad of drives: the sexual libido, the aggressive or self-preservative drive, and the drive towards dependence. Here we can note, in passing, the similarity between Hadfield's theory and the 'three basic assumptions groups' proposed by Bion.
>
> (Bléandonu 1994, p. 43)

Ian Suttie (1898–1935): Suttie with his wife Jane were friends of Sandor Ferenczi. They worked at the Tavistock from the early 1920s, bringing a Christian ethic, concerning love and hate. Suttie's book (1935 [1960]), *Origins of Love and Hate* (which appeared only days before he died) was prefaced by Hadfield. Money-Kyrle's critical review bitingly said, 'Dr. Suttie's book will be well received by all who wish to under-estimate the extent of infantile sexuality and aggression' (Money-Kyrle 1936, p. 138). Suttie's thesis rejected instincts, drawing all development from the loving attachment of baby to mother,

> Instead of an armament of instincts, latent or otherwise, the child is born with a simple attachment-to-mother who is the sole source of food and protection ... the need for a mother is primarily presented to the child mind as a need for company and as a discomfort in isolation
>
> (Suttie 1935 [1960], p. 37)

and 'Hatred, I consider, is just a standing reproach to the hated person, and owes all its meaning to a demand for love' (ibid.). 'Suttie, like Ferenczi, thought that it is the physician's love that cures the patient. Neurosis is a disturbance of love, of social rapport' (Heaton 1989, p. 132).

Early on in the integrative tradition of the Tavistock, Suttie (1924) used the term 'psychosocial', and is sometimes credited with a psychosocial theory (Hayward 2009). However Suttie argued, in that paper, against the view that there is a biologically directed mental recapitulation of species development. That view is found in Freud and widespread beyond at the time, especially amongst German writers. They regarded mental recapitulation as simply a part of the bodily recapitulation of the physical forms of earlier species – itself a disputed notion. He makes the case that the inheritance of psychological aspects comes at least as much through a cultural recapitulation rather than a biological one.

Suttie's notion of the psychological bonding with mother is an interesting forerunner of John Bowlby (who wrote a foreword to a later edition of Suttie's book) and contemporary attachment theory. Suttie's background was in the Scottish tradition, associated with his contemporary, the Scottish philosopher, John Macmurray. Ronald Fairbairn was another Scottish contemporary in the same tradition (Clarke 2006), and Fairbairn's notion of an object-seeking libido is reminiscent of Suttie's similar rejection of Freudian libido theory. Bowlby was of a later generation, joining the Tavistock staff after the war, and therefore long after Suttie, who died in 1935. The mother-bonding also pointed to the whole of the British object-relations development, and was contemporary with Melanie Klein's influence in the 1920s and 1930s on British psychoanalysis and psychotherapy. It may well be that his matriarchalism owes something to Klein. The Tavistock was at the heart of the British debate over the biologism, or instinctualism of Freud, and Suttie was one of its most engaging protagonists. The invitation to Jung to give his Tavistock lectures in 1935 was no doubt a part of the independent and integrative objectives. Bion is known to have gone (with his patient of the time, Samuel Beckett) to these lectures.

Kurt Lewin (1890–1947) and Eric Trist (1909–1993): Trist met Lewin in 1933 when Lewin, like the entire Frankfurt School, emigrated after Hitler came to power. Lewin stopped briefly in England (and in Israel) on his way to the United States. Trist spent time in the US after he graduated in 1935, and again contacted Lewin. Trist met people from the Tavistock during wartime, when he was involved with the War Office Selection Boards in Edinburgh. He was later involved in the resettlement schemes, designed by A.T.M. Wilson and W.R. Bion. After the war, he became a part of the Clinic when the Tavistock was reforming. His acquaintance with Lewin, the man and the ideas, informed the new approach to groups at the Tavistock. Lewin's inspiration set Trist's interest in social psychology on a profoundly theoretical path, viewing the group as a field, or as later known, a group-as-a-whole. Lewin's practice of 'sensitivity groups', was adopted by the Tavistock to give space for personal reflection in the context of others, and married with the leaderless group technique that Bion had developed with Trist during the war running the War Office Selection Boards (WOSBs). The collaboration between Trist and Lewin across the Atlantic brought the journal *Human Relations* into existence as a joint project. Lewin died at this point, and Trist left the Tavistock in 1966, though this was long after Bion left the

Tavistock in 1948. See Chapter 7 by Torres on the detailed influence of Lewin on Bion's group work.

Pearl King (2003) states that Rickman too became acquainted with Lewin's ideas in 1939, a point at which Bion was in analysis with Rickman. The relationship between Bion and Rickman progressively turned into one of collaborators over innovative projects during the Second World War, and they corresponded about the WOSBs, and Rickman acted as a kind of mentor to Bion in developing the Northfield experiment in 1943 (see Chapter 9). Lewin appears to have been important to social psychologists at around this time, just before and during the wartime.

Bion was therefore exposed to a wide variety of ideas, in his first few years as a new psychotherapist at the Tavistock Clinic. The significant ideas were those evolved there by Suttie (1935 [1960]) and Hadfield (1952), and those introduced from America on the social field by Eric Trist. The Clinic's openness to new ideas, and its avowed eclecticism and integrationism exposed Bion to current thinking in social psychology and social psychiatry, and it provided him with a freedom to think the many ideas through for himself. Though he appears to have remained without much direction in his own thinking at the time, it appears to have been a stock of knowledge and experiences from which he could draw for the rest of his life.

Wartime innovation

Before the war Bion had found his therapy with Hadfield limited, and began to think of training as a psychoanalyst, though this was discouraged. It is not clear how he found Rickman, but he intended to have an analysis that would enable him to train as a psychoanalyst (see Chapter 9). The two men clicked as persons it seems, which possibly came from a confluence of interest in Ferenczi. For Bion, Suttie's friendship with Ferenczi, and for Rickman his own analysis with Ferenczi, may have added to a common outlook. In any case, though the analysis lasted only a year, 1938–1939 (interrupted by the war), after that brief analysis Bion remained in a sort of devotion until Rickman's death in 1951. Rickman was influential in Bion's Northfield experiment and in the group work at the Tavistock after the war. Bion is known from his letters to Rickman (Vonofakos and Hinshelwood 2012) to have discussed his work in military psychiatry (and his exasperation with the military and psychiatric authorities) with Rickman by correspondence and in person. Bion was strongly interested by Rickman's theoretical and practical approaches to groups and their dynamics. Rickman, like Trist, was interested in Lewin's field theory from early on. Rickman was always behind the scenes, never working in the same institutions together. Rickman's influence drew no doubt from his own Quaker background and the willingness to allow the 'spirit to move the group' (see Kramer 2011).

By 1950, Bion was turning his back on the investigation of the social field that had so united him and Rickman, probably because he was drawn into the work with the small group of Klein's followers investigating the psychoanalytic treatment of schizophrenia. In a sense Bion had found himself during the war. There may be various reasons for this, including his rather impressive record in the First World War, which gave him a status above his peers. But there is no doubt that both of the special contributions Bion made – officer selection and rehabilitation – owe their origins either to Rickman's ideas, or to discussions with Rickman. To look at this close partnership we have to turn mostly to the existing letters he wrote to Rickman (see Chapter 9). The letters reveal Bion's dependence and his struggles to flourish, whilst rather held back by his cynical and even arrogant attitude to almost everyone else he mentions in the letters. By the time he got back to the Tavistock he seems to have found sufficient confidence in himself.

WOSBs and the leaderless group: the army had a problem as it expanded with conscription – how to select the officers, who by tradition came from the privately educated stratum of young men, but who were not sufficiently numerous to supply the expanding needs. Consequently the army needed to draw from the non-commissioned ranks. A system for officer selection at the War Office (the War Office Selection Boards or WOSBs) was set up. Bion's hatred of the way men had been let down by their inadequate officers in the First World War led him into this work with some enthusiasm. It was at this point (1940–1941) that he began to show his originality. Also, his respect for Rickman began to show and, probably behind Rickman, Lewin's field theory, which had been introduced to the WOSBs by Eric Trist, another member of the War Office team. Looking at it in field theory terms, Bion and Trist (and maybe Rickman in the background) put together groups of potential officer candidates, to discover who would emerge from the social forces in the field as a leader. This was an empirical use of the psychology of social fields. The group is the field, and the various forces play upon the individuals, with the emergence of leaders – and of course of followers (Bion 1946; see also Murray 1990).

The Northfield experiment: Bion's co-authored paper with Rickman on their Northfield experiment remains a kind of beacon in the development of group psychotherapy and the therapeutic community (Bion and Rickman 1943 [1961]). Despite its failure, the Northfield experiment endures as inspiration to British psychiatry down to the present (Harrison 2000). It was also enhanced by Bion's discovery of his terse, ironic and provocative style of writing in his section of the paper, a style which flourished from then on to entertain, stimulate and frustrate readers ever since. It was published in the medical journal *The Lancet*, and reports the rehabilitation unit that Bion ran for six weeks from January 1943. The ideas behind this came out of discussions that Bion and Rickman had over the two years before and which appear to have been initially tried out by Rickman in a unit he set up at Wharncliffe Hospital. The central idea is that the officer in charge focuses on the group of men, just as a platoon of men on active service. They are to be led towards a common enemy, which Bion defined as 'neurosis'. Each of the men was supposed to contribute to hunting down signs of the enemy and proposing methods of counter-attacking it. Much of this seems to involve the men's apathy as a sign of neurosis, and fairly simple occupational and leisure activities as the attack upon it.

The originality was not so much in terms of what actually went on, but in the thinking about how it should be proposed and actioned. The commonality of it bears the traces of Rickman's Quaker egalitarianism, and Bion's despair, learned in the First World War, over the dependency of soldiers on an inadequate leadership. The whole of the group came to be involved in identifying the problem and finding its solution. This commonality, with a minimum of divisions of labour, or of hierarchies, has the character of Rickman's Quaker influence,[3] and of the notion of the field with its supra-individual forces. The innovative approach improbably combines the appeal to grass-roots initiatives in the context of the top-down military authority. This was surely unique and a recipe for failure.[4] But short-lived though it was, the innovative originality spawned a variety of further experiments at Northfield (Harrison 2000), and in many social psychiatry projects for a couple of decades after the war. Not surprisingly Bion was soon back working in the WOSBs and as he ruefully notes in his autobiography he was the only person who finished the war with the same rank with which he entered service this time.

The old campaigner

When Bion returned to the Tavistock Clinic in 1945, he did so with many colleagues who were new to the Tavistock. Many of the old personnel were kept on as honorary staff members only. It was a new phase for the Tavistock, and a new phase in Bion's career. His experience and achievements in the war (building on his previous service in the First World War) began a reputation which took him above his most talented colleagues. In particular his experimental rehabilitation unit at Northfield Military Hospital (Bion and Rickman 1943 [1961]), and the innovatory ideas with which he backed up the new methods of officer selection helped to pioneer many post-war developments (Bion 1946). His intellectual and professional achievements indicated someone commanding a great deal of respect from others, so much so that he was elected Chair of the Medical Committee.

Bion was invited to develop his interest in groups, and in effect he conducted research groups, sometimes with patients and sometimes with staff to study group processes. He turned to a mixture of ideas. He discussed by letter and in person with Rickman, but he was influenced by the Tavistock alignment with Lewin's field theory, and published all his main papers in *Human Relations*, the joint journal. The main papers were all called 'experiences in groups' (EiG), and number I–VII.[5] The notion of group mentality is introduced as the first theoretical postulate (in EiG-II), 'I shall postulate a group mentality as a pool to which the anonymous contributions are made, and through which the impulses and desires implicit in these contributions are gratified' (Bion 1961, p. 50). One can see here an expression of the group as a supra-individual, Lewinian field of forces (desires). A great deal of actual group interaction was committed to paper in these publications which can be seen to illustrate an observer watching with the notion of a field, or group mentality in mind. In fact, Bion introduces three theoretical postulates here: (1) the group mentality; and (2) opposition to the group mentality by the individuals whose needs are thwarted; and (3) a group culture to meet that conflict. Bion writes, in EiG-II, 'The power of the group to fulfil the needs of the individual is, I suggest, challenged by the group members. The group meets this challenge by the elaboration of a characteristic culture of the group' (Bion 1961, p. 55). By culture he means a loose description of the structure, the occupation pursued, and the organisation for it.

In the next publication, EiG-III, 1949, Bion proceeds to explore the group in these terms, and concluded that they did not work very well, in a lot of instances, leaving him confused. His recall of the verbatim dialogue collapsed and he resorted, as he then said, 'to an avowedly subjective account' (1961, p. 61). He describes further the kinds of compromise cultures formed by the group. First there is a phenomenon of two people talking together, behind which, Bion says, is the assumption that they intend sex. And he remarks there must 'be considerable conflict between the desire of the pair to pursue the aim they have consciously in mind, and the emotions derived from the basic assumption that two people can be met together for only one purpose, and that a sexual one' (ibid., p. 62). Such conflict leads to the couple falling silent and another culture supervening; 'If the basic assumption about the pair is that they meet together for purposes of sex, what is the basic assumption in a group about people who meet together in a group?' (ibid., p. 63). And his answer is that they meet in order to preserve the group. He used his experience of Northfield then to elaborate the 'two techniques of the group in this endeavour of preservation – fight or flight'. And he found himself a leader of the group who did not function satisfactorily for the members to follow him in fighting or fleeing. Later in this paper (EiG-III), he introduced the dependency assumption as a way of understanding how the group attempts to form a culture that *can* include the therapist as he is functioning. Group mentality – the field of forces – had quickly given way to a focus on culture and the hidden assumptions behind them.

Bion's avowedly subjective account continued in EiG-IV, which developed his descriptions of these basic assumptive cultures, but especially the dependent assumption which compromises learning from experience. He thus headed towards an understanding of the counterpart of the basic assumptions, the sophisticated or work group. But then in EiG-V, 1950,

Bion suddenly turns to other writers on a wider front. There is a list of annotated references to this EiG, in contrast to all the others, which barely have references at all. The paper moves out from the investigation of the small group Bion is running and is a first step towards an understanding of whole societies. Volume 1 of Toynbee's 1935, 12-volume *Study of History* is there, as well as Gibbon's *Decline and Fall.* There are two treatises on money. But most interesting is Halliday's (1948 – but Bion references a 1949 edition) *Psychosocial Medicine: A Study of the Sick Society*. Halliday drew on Suttie's idea of the 'psychosocial' (Suttie 1924).

> The psychosomatic embodiment of distress and the establishment of new schemes of state welfare meant that the effectiveness of any political reformation could be assessed through reference to the new epidemiological data made available by the administration of national insurance schemes.
>
> (Hayward 2009, p. 829)

Both social and psychological aspects could be brought together, but also with political and social ones (a pillar idea of the welfare state and the National Health Service, at the time – the NHS was established in 1948). This is significant in that this EiG-V is where Bion postulates the proto-mental system for the first time. In the true Tavistock tradition of being not just eclectic but 'integral' (Dicks 1970), Bion said he would

> propose to postulate the existence of 'proto-mental' phenomena. I cannot represent my view adequately without proposing a concept that transcends experience. Clinically, I make a psychological approach, and therefore note phenomena only when they present themselves as psychological manifestations. Nevertheless, it is convenient to me to consider that the emotional state precedes the basic assumption and follows certain proto-mental phenomena of which it is an expression.
>
> (Bion 1961, p. 101)

By adding the social to the mind and body integration of Crichton-Miller, he was following Suttie to evolve the beginnings of a bio-psycho-social approach.

He arrived at this via his development of the basic assumption idea. By this date he has made all the assumptions equivalent and potential. Any one basic assumption implies that the existence of the other two is suspended (see Morgan-Jones 2010 for a recent account of the proto-mental idea). So, Bion asked, 'What is the fate of the two basic assumptions that are not operative?' (1961, p. 100). He then takes a hypothetical step by saying the hidden basic assumptions are likely to affect bodily states, and hence relates somatic conditions to psychic and group cultures. However it is also as if he had just got a copy of James Halliday's book, *Psychosocial Medicine* (1948), which connects these psychosomatic conditions to the state of wider national culture. Halliday's psychosocial notion of emotional citizenship, in fact, 'was drawn from the work of a fellow Glaswegian, none other than the heterodox analyst Ian Suttie' (Hayward 2009, p. 827), Suttie as we noted being one of Bion's colleagues in his first year at the Tavistock. Halliday's book was influential in the development of psychosomatic medicine in Britain, and his views very prevalent in the 1940s and after, and no doubt influenced those at the Tavistock. Bion bolstered his interest in the bodily side of the bio-psycho-social with the work of his colleague, Eric Wittkower, They had worked in the WOSBs together, and then Wittkower was briefly at the Tavistock in the 1940s when he wrote his report on the psychological *and* social aspects of tuberculosis, which Bion makes reference to in EiG-V (1950).

It appears therefore that around the time of this 1950 paper (EiG-V), something changed for Bion. He began to read again, and to draw widely from past reading. His thinking suddenly expanded. He had been in analysis for three to four years with Melanie Klein, from 1946, had left the Tavistock in 1948, and was beginning to commit himself to a career exclusively as a psychoanalyst. In addition, the child he was bringing up after his first wife (Betty) died following childbirth (in 1944), had now reached school age. Perhaps as a result his life began to seem much more stable when in 1951 he met Francesca, who would soon become his second wife.

Conclusions

The Tavistock represented both Bion's formative *alma mater*, before the Second World War, and also his triumphal finale in the three years after the war. We can see in the work of his colleagues in the 1930s certain ideas which may have been absorbed, as if by osmosis, by Bion. Notable there was Crichton-Miller's project for an integrative approach, especially a binocular vision of the body–mind interaction. This was the ethos of the first phase of the Tavistock itself, from 1920 and set by Crichton-Miller. It was not only a body–mind integration, but Suttie, by adding the fundamental postulate of a 'social' interaction of the baby from birth, pleaded strongly for the social to be included in there as well. And in 1950, Bion brought these three aspects together – bio-psycho-social – in the 'proto-mental system' – that which is bodily and emotional before it is psychological.

As is well-known, this apotheosis of the early Tavistock work lost impetus for Bion almost immediately afterwards, when in 1952, for Melanie Klein's seventieth birthday issue of the *International Journal of Psychoanalysis*, he reviewed his group work, deciding to convert his understanding into purely psychological terms – and in particular, Klein's psychoanalytic terms (Bion 1955).

Notes

1 Bion's first published paper 1940 'The war of nerves' is a chapter of Emanuel Miller's edited book, *The Neuroses at War* in which Crichton-Miller wrote a concluding chapter.
2 EMS was the Emergency Medical Service set up at the beginning of the war when it was anticipated that there would be large civilian casualties due to bombing. RAMC is the Royal Army Medical Corps, which provided the medical services for the Army.
3 Interestingly, another pioneer of a similar style, which gave rise to the egalitarian therapeutic community, was David Clark, also from a long-standing Quaker family.
4 Hugh Murray about the regimental nomination experiment says that 'Political and civil administrative interests found the scheme possibly subversive ("Soviets in the British Army"). Further reference to the regimental nomination was banned' (Murray 1990, p. 61).
5 'Experiences in groups' I and II were published in the first volume of the journal in 1948, III and IV were in Volume 2, 1949, V and VI were in Volume 3, 1950, and VII in Volume 4, 1951 – the last shortly after Rickman died.

Chapter 6

Bion's concept of the proto-mental and modern panpsychism

Nuno Torres

> Thinking, like the blossom, is surely nothing else but the finest evolution of the plastic forces – it is simply the general force of Nature raised to the nth degree. The organs of thought are the engendering organs of the world – the sexual organs of nature
>
> F. von Hardenberg, *Notes for a Romantic Encyclopaedia*, Note 1144

Introduction

In the context of his experiences in groups, Bion (1950c [1961]) coined an unusual term for a rather unfamiliar idea. The term was *proto-mental*, and the idea was that of a system or matrix where physical and mental were undifferentiated; he postulated that this proto-mental matrix was the source of basic pre-verbal emotions. From this proto-mental source, basic emotions could evolve and lead to primitive group-as-whole emotional field phenomena which he called *basic assumption groups*, or just *basic groups*. Additionally, if proto-mental phenomena were confined in a latent phase in the proto-mental matrix, they would manifest in certain symptoms with undifferentiated physical and mental components. Finally, he stated that the sphere of proto-mental events could not be understood by reference to the individual alone, for proto-mental phenomena are a function of the group.

Although Bion did not use the term *proto-mental* after 1961,[1] the notion of indistinct physical and mental components of sense impressions of emotional experiences was maintained throughout all his later writings, namely in his concept of α-elements.[2]

The proto-mental notion has several serious implications, among which: (1) it presupposes that body and mind have the same basic properties, so that there might a stage where physical and mental are undifferentiated; it thus implies a non-dualistic philosophical position on the so-called 'mind–body problem' that had not been hitherto explicitly discussed; and (2) it establishes a causal link connecting the dynamics of the individual in his/her social environment and the emergence of proto-mental diseases. I will only focus on the first topic in this chapter.[3]

Term proto-mental has also been used, though unrelated to Bion's writings, in contemporary philosophy. It has been thriving since the middle 1960s to describe Bergson's and/or Whitehead's allegedly panpsychist position on the body–mind problem, along with the growing interest in panpsychism in relation to philosophy of mind and quantum physics (Shimony, 1965; Čapek, 1971; Nagel, 1979; Bjelland, 1981, 1987; Atmanspacher, 2004; Skrbina, 2005; Shimony and Malin, 2006; Franck, 2008)

The aim of this chapter is to put Bion's notion of proto-mental into context in the conceptual framework of Henri Bergson's allegedly panpsychist views on matter and mind.[4] I will start with an overview on the advent of the body–mind dualism and mechanistic worldviews in Western science and in Freudian psycho-physical ideas. I will then turn to the contrasting worldview of *panpsychism*, according to which the body–matter and the psyche–mind share the same basic properties: animated sentience. The panpsychist worldview was prevalent in the natural philosophers of the Renaissance and Romanticism. It gained momentum with the developments in biology and micro-physics of the late nineteenth and first half of the twentieth century and so this was the general climate of ideas in Western culture when Bion entered adult life. The once clear-cut dividing lines between inorganic matter, simpler life forms, bodily systems of higher organisms and the human mind became blurred, in a move towards a holistic conception of reality.[5]

The soul in the machine. The body–mind split and the mechanistic worldview

In the thirteenth century, St Thomas Aquinas established the medieval Christian worldview of nature as divided into earthly and heavenly realms by harmonizing Christian theology with Aristotelian thinking (Kretzmann and Stump, 2005). According to Aristotelian physics, the heavenly movements of the celestial bodies, stars and planets, were perfect – circular and rectilinear – while the earthly or sub-lunar world was imperfect and endowed with motion of inferior types (Lewin, 1935a, p. 3). Between the sixteenth and seventeenth centuries the harmony between theology and natural science was increasingly questioned by evidence. Kepler's discovery, around 1605, that planets move in ellipses not in circles paved that way for scientists to see the gravitational laws ruling celestial bodies as mechanical rather than supernatural. Galileo's experiments in mechanics and observations in astronomy demonstrated that the same laws govern the courses of the stars and the falling of stones (Lewin, 1935a). Later, in 1687, Isaac Newton in his *Principia* explained the universe as being composed of inert material objects that move about under gravitational forces in a clockwork fashion: The whole universe behaved as a self-sustaining *machine*, without the need for divine intervention.

Based both on his studies of anatomy and of the functioning of automata, Descartes (1628/1647 [1911]), who had been educated by Jesuits, proposed that the organisms of living beings (humans, animals, and plants) were literally mechanical automata, created by God but without the need of further supernatural intervention to function.[6] The difference between humans and other inferior beings was that humans have a thinking, immortal soul which belongs to the supernatural realm (O'Leary, 2010). According to Ryle:

> When Galileo showed that his methods of scientific discovery were competent to provide a mechanical theory which should cover every occupant of space, Descartes found in himself two conflicting motives. As a man of scientific genius he could not but endorse the claims of mechanics, yet as a religious and moral man he could not accept [...] that human nature differs only in degree of complexity from clockwork. The mental could not be just a variety of the mechanical.
>
> (Ryle, 1949, pp. 18–19)

The legacy left by Descartes' works was the existence of two substances: *res extensa* (spatial extension) and *res cogitans* (thinking), and humans as composed of an extended bodily "machine" with a divine thinking soul. Descartes proposed the pineal gland as the locus of interaction between the psyche and the body[7]; but this idea was never accepted even by his contemporaries (Lokhorst, 2011). With the increasing secularisation of society and science, the divine–religious component of the thinking soul has become gradually superfluous. But the conceptual problem of the duality of substances and of the interactionism of the mind with its body–machine has remained until today.

The body–mind problem

The greatest part of the philosophical effort in the last three centuries is the attempt to resolve the Cartesian impasse on the duality of substances and the hitherto unsolvable problem of how mind and body could interact.[8] A brief summary of the problem was clearly formulated as such:

> if brain and mind are of fundamentally different kinds, and if in addition the laws of causality require causes and effects to be of a similar kind, then it is clearly impossible to brain to generate mind or mind to affect brain.
>
> (Wozniak, 1992, p. 3)

Ryle lucidly described what he called the absurdity of the dominant body–mind Cartesian dualistic doctrine through the expression "ghost in the machine" (Ryle, 1949). Some thinkers have avoided the problem by advocating *materialistic reductionism*, denying the existence of mental events in-them-selves, i.e. the *ghost*.[9] This proposal is that mind is in reality reducible to states of the material world, which could in principle be fully described in terms of its microphysical components (Humphrey, 2000, p. 5; Robinson, 2005). Materialistic reductionism, also known as *physicalism*, flourished in the nineteenth century, and was the position of the *Berliner Physicalische Gesellschaft* founded in 1845 by Brücke and Du-Bois Reymond (and of their so-called "Helmholtz School of Medicine"), clearly stated in the following passage:

> Brücke and I pledged a solemn oath to put in power this truth: No other forces than the common physical chemical ones are active within the organism. [...] the chemical physical forces inherent in matter, reducible to the force of attraction and repulsion.
>
> (Du-Bois Reymond, 1842, p. 19; cited in Bernfeld, 1944, p. 348)

Others, who did not rule out the existence of the mind as a real substance – the "ghost" in Ryle's terms – avoided the problem by advocating *psycho-physical parallelism*. This position was originally put forward in the 1690s in Leibniz's doctrine of pre-established harmony between mind and body, which run in parallel although there is no connection/interaction between them.[10]

The parallelist position was tacitly accepted during the greater part of the nineteenth century, and was explicitly formulated in 1884 by the British neurologist Hughlings Jackson in his *Doctrine of Concomitance*: this allowed the investigation of either the material brain or the psychological mind as separate spheres (Hinshelwood, 1997, p. 36). Although Jackson was aware of the philosophical problems regarding body–mind, this doctrine was adopted for practical reasons, and was intended to separate the disciplines of neurology and psychiatry both conceptually and institutionally (Hinshelwood, 1995; York and Steinberg, 2011).

A brief note on Freud and the body–mind problem

The problem of body–mind connection has been present in psychoanalysis from its inception. Freud started his career as a physiologist at the so-called "Helmholtz School of Medicine" and its materialistic programme of explaining all living phenomena exclusively by the physical–chemical forces inherent in matter (Sulloway, 1979, p. 62). However, Freud's clinical work as a psychiatrist, the influence of Charcot and Breuer and of the ideas of Hughlings Jackson, among others, led him to focus on the mind – the "ghost" as it were – as an entity in its own right:

> "Psychical treatment" denotes, rather, treatment taking its start in the mind, [...] by measures which operate in the first instance and immediately upon the human mind. Foremost among such measures is the use

> of words; and words are the essential tool of mental treatment. A layman [. . .] will feel that he is being asked to believe in magic. And he will not be so very wrong, for the words which we use in our everyday speech are nothing other than watered-down magic.
>
> (Freud, 1890, p. 283)

As a neurologist turned psychiatrist, Freud's implicit (but conflicting) position on the body–mind tended to move between psycho-physical parallelism and interactionism (Hinshelwood, 1997; Smith, 1999). The concept of *functional* neurotic symptoms (e.g. hysterical paralyses and conversions) can be understood in the following way: the proper functioning, so to speak, of the body–machine was temporarily disrupted by psychic conflicts turned unconscious. Once these mental conflicts were made conscious by the talking cure, the body returned to its normal functioning. From 1900 onwards, with the *Interpretation of Dreams*, and after having discarded his "project for a scientific psychology" Freud definitely left behind his psycho-physiological concerns. In *The Unconscious* he explicitly emphasized that he was not interested in the insolvable problems of psycho-physical parallelism, and wanted to focus on unconscious mental processes as objects of pure psychological research (Freud, 1915a, pp. 167–168).

Psychosomatics, emotions, and the body–mind connection

Between the 1930s and the 1950s the psychoanalytically inspired psychosomatic authors revived the dualistic body–mind problem with concepts such as "organ neurosis" (Schultz, 1932; Alexander, 1936) and the expression of neurotic conflicts in terms of organic disorders (Deutsch, 1939), and with it the classical unsolvable questions of interactionism, reductionism and parallelism. According to Hoch:

> [M]any of the publications in psychosomatic medicine follow a disquietingly dualistic approach and some even implied a new form of dualism in which the soul completely masters the body. Many less philosophical but practical-minded are now speaking about emotional and physiological inter-relationships.
>
> (Hoch, 1952)

Hoch reiterated the importance of what he called the "holistic concept of man", a form of non-dualism, in which mental and physical share the same basic properties:

> Most likely we are not dealing here with two different functions [*mental and physiological*] but with the hierarchy of the same function which is

perceived subjectively psychologically, and objectively physiologically. The second is not a concomitant or a shadow of the first, or vice versa, but the same.

(Hoch, 1952)

By the start of the 1950s a "holistic conception of man" was supported by the consistent findings that emotions and emotional changes were inevitably tied to both the mental functioning and physiological manifestations of the same organism (Cannon, 1932, 1935, 1942; Dunbar, 1935; Gillespie, 1942; Halliday, 1948; Wisdom, 1952; Hoch, 1952).

Bion's idea of emotions as arising from enmeshed physiological and mental components in the proto-mental matrix did not use traditional psychoanalytic models but was updated with the contemporary state of emotion research and with this "holistic approach" in psychosomatic medicine.[11] For instance, Halliday, who was quoted in Bion's 1950 paper, says:

[T]he autonomic nervous system is related to the central nervous system which, by virtue of its integrating functions, organizes, mediates and distributes the vital energy that moves us (i.e. *emotion*) into its various patterns of liberation and bodily expression called "emotions".

(Halliday, 1948, p. 233, emphasis in the original)

Bion and the body–mind

Although Bion never systematically and explicitly spelled out his philosophical position on the body–mind question, it is obvious in his definitions of the proto-mental matrix that he neither implies dualism of substances (psycho-physical parallelism or interactionism) nor materialistic reductionism. I propose that this was an implicit framework not only in the concept of proto-mental matrix but also in Bion's thinking as a whole, namely about the α-elements.[12] This may have happened for several reasons. Due to his initial higher education in history, before training in medicine, Bion was not tied up in the logical-mathematical determinism and the attached mechanistic worldview ruling in natural sciences; in his 1950 paper on the proto-mental, out of the nine bibliographic references, six are from history, one from economics and two from psychosomatic medicine from a holistic perspective (Halliday, 1948; Wittkower, 1949). By 1950 he had been working for almost two decades at the Tavistock, absorbing its holistic, integrative, and eclectic approach to disease (see Chapter 4 on "The wider medical culture").

Overall, Bion approached the body–mind problem from a totally different angle than Cartesian dualism. To Bion, there was a primary indistinctiveness between the bodily and the mental, but without ever reducing one to the other, a vision which is in principle philosophically compatible with panpsychism.[13] I will now turn to the description of the monistic view of panpsychism.

Body–mind union in panpsychism

Panpsychism is defined as the philosophical view that all matter has the ingredients of mind embedded within it, i.e. "the view that the basic physical constituents of the universe have mental properties" (Nagel, 1979, p. 181). According to Skrbina (2005) the term derives from "Pampsychia" ("The All-Souls") coined by the Italian philosopher Patrizi in his 1591 work *Nova de universis philosophia*. Patrizi – who like other Italian naturalists of the renaissance had a deep dislike of Aristotelian philosophy – supported Plato's concept of *anima mundi* (world-soul) and its particular manifestations in the natural world.

Panpsychist views have been the alternative for the split worldview derived from official medieval doctrines, in particular those of Aquinas. Aquinas adopted the theses that (1) the soul and God are supernatural entities; (2) only humans possess a soul; and (3) only humans, animals and plants possess *life* – defined as self-generated motion or being animated, while the rest of the natural world is lifeless.[14] This has been the prevailing Christian position, fundamentally unchanged for nearly 800 years (Skrbina, 2005). With the advance of natural sciences and with the secularization of western society, these notions have evolved into mechanicism, psycho-physical parallelism and materialistic reductionism.

In the eighteenth and nineteenth centuries, several German Idealist and Romantic philosophers such as Fichte, Schelling Goethe, Haeckel and von Hardenberg,[15] who opposed dualistic, mechanistic and materialistic views (Heidelberger, 2005), articulated aspects of a holistic philosophy of nature which were implicitly panpsychist (Skrbina, 2005). This view reached its peak in the *Naturphilosophie* inspired by Schelling, which according to Sulloway (1979, p. 146) subsisted in nineteenth-century German medicine and may have surfaced implicitly in Freud's interest in dreams, the notions of Life and Death instincts and the *Id*.[16]

Darwin's theory of evolution, published in 1859, initiated a string of new arguments for panpsychism. In 1874, the English physicist W.K. Clifford proposed a form of panpsychism in his theory of *Mind-Stuff*, building on the works on protoplasm by the biologist T. Huxley (1870), both of them influenced by Darwin's ideas that that "all life shared a common ancestry, and that conscious humans had no claim to ontological uniqueness" (Skrbina, 2005, p. 188). According to Clifford: "A moving molecule of inorganic matter does not possess mind, or consciousness; but it possesses a small piece of mind-stuff" (Clifford, 1874, p. 85).

The transition from the nineteenth to the twentieth century was of particular importance, with panpsychist views appearing in the writings of Peirce, James, Bradàley, Royce, Bergson, and Whitehead (Skrbina, 2005).

The postulate of panpsychism is that what we call *matter* is not totally inert or dead-like and has embedded in it some *mental*-like properties. The critical assessment of this postulate depends in great measure on what one means by the terms *matter* and *mind*, as well the by evidence or knowledge available about the disciplines studying them. The modern panpsychist tendencies of Bergson, as well as those of Whitehead, arose vis-à-vis the advances in biology, neuroscience and physics of their time.

Bergson's panpsychism, and Bion

Bergson (1896 [1911]) initially focused on demonstrating the continuum between the evidence of intentionality and memory, present in the lowest levels of living matter (protoplasm) and the simplest organisms (protozoa), and the mindful behaviour of more complex organisms and humans:

> [W]e find that living matter, even as a simple mass of protoplasm, is already irritable and contractile, that it is open to the influence of external stimulation, and answers to it by mechanical, physical, and chemical reactions. As we rise in the organic series, we find a division of physiological labour. Nerve cells appear, are diversified, tend to group themselves into a system; at the same time, the animal reacts by more varied movements to external stimulation [. . .] and the same impression, which makes the organism aware of changes in the environment, determines it or prepares it to adapt itself to them.
>
> (Bergson, 1896 [1911), pp. 17–18)

Bergson proposed later in *Mind-Energy* that there was virtual intentionality and memory in the simplest constituents of matter itself (Bergson, 1911). What we ordinarily call *mind* and *consciousness* was nothing else than differentiated, complex, and specialized forms of movement and memory that were universally present in reality as a whole.

A copy of Bergson's *Matter and Memory* was in Bion's library (see Chapter 3), and we may assume he read it fairly attentively since he made marks in pencil in the margins of several paragraphs. He may also have read *Mind-Energy*, as it had been available in English since 1920. From Bergson's proposal of the existence of mentality and adaptability to the environment in a mass of protoplasm, it was just a small step to Bion's idea of proto-mental phenomena linked to the social environment. These proto-mental phenomena could thus manifest themselves both by movements and intentions to move (*e-motions*) and by physical–chemical reactions and organic alterations in the body of the individuals, as a function of group dynamics (Bion, 1950c [1961]).

Bergson considered matter as the lowest degree of mind: hence matter and mind were not different substances, they had the same basic properties, and the difference between them was reducible to the "difference in the *rhythm*, vibration or 'tension' of duration" (Čapek, 1971, p. 199). According to Čapek, Bergson's "vibratory conception of matter" anticipated by more than thirty years the perplexities of quantum physics, namely Heisenberg's uncertainty principle in 1927 and DeBroglie's discovery of the wave-like nature of matter in 1924.

The first decades of Bion's adult life were precisely the times of the quantum revolution and the discovery of the "dematerialisation" of the physical world;[17] Popper (1977a, p. 8) claimed that with quantum physics materialism had transcended itself and that the physical theory of matter might be said to be no longer materialistic. In 1950, Bertrand Russell observed that matter in modern physics becomes "as allusive as fleeting thoughts" and in 1951 David Bohm pointed out some striking resemblances between the mental processes and quantum phenomena (Čapek, 1971, p. 308). Hence, with the revolutions in physics in the first half of the twentieth century (which literally exploded in the form of the atom and hydrogen bombs) the notion of matter that had formerly been so concrete and palpable became as "ghostly" and elusive as the mind itself. Bion was undoubtedly not alone in his awareness of these issues and they must have been obvious to all who might have influenced him.

The term proto-mental as related to Bergson

The term "proto-mental" has been used to describe Bergson's (and also Whitehead's) concept of matter: Shimony made specific reference to the term "proto-mental" to describe Whitehead's concept of "actual occasions" (Shimony 1965, p. 254); Čapek (1971) reviewed these notions some years after Shimony and proposed also that Bergson regarded physical events as "proto-mental entities". Also according to Popper, these two philosophers proposed that all matter has a quality that might be described as "proto-psychical" (Popper, 1977b, p. 53). However, the attribution of proto-mental and proto-psychical notions to Whitehead and Bergson, appears to have been made by Shimony in 1965 and restated by Čapek in 1971 and Popper in 1977b, long after Bion's first use of the term in his 1950 paper. Bjelland (1981) critically reviewed Capek's notion of proto-mentalism in Whitehead and Bergson, noting that it "provides the sole detailed and systematic exposition of Bergsonian proto-mentalism available in English" (p. 180).

Did Bion read subsequent authors in French, and did the term proto-mental appear in the French philosophical literature before 1950, when Bion first used the term? According to another paper by Bjelland (1987), in a French collection of essays and personal communications from Bergson to friends and colleagues, it is recorded that Bergson told Jean de la Harpe that his "metaphysical research program is best viewed as a version of panpsychist or proto-mentalist pluralism" (Béguin and Thévenaz, 1943, p. 358, cited in

Bjelland, 1987, p. 19). Did Bion read this book, and borrow the term proto-mental from it? It is a possibility, since he was fluent in French. However, it is also possible that Bion could have independently coined the term. Whatever the case, there is a clear convergence of notions between Bergson and Bion's concepts of proto-mental.

Final remarks

The proto-mental idea which Bion adopted in 1950 is inherent in Bergsonian ideas, although he linked it to the psychosomatic trend in medicine at the time and the integrative policies of the Tavistock Clinic in the 1920s, 1930s and 1940s; the concept can be seen as an attempt to ground in a philosophically sound way the holistic connection between psychosomatics and social field phenomena (a bio-psycho-social approach – see also Chapter 6), avoiding the unsolvable conundrums of body–mind dualism. It does not necessarily imply full engagement of either Bion, or Bergson to panpsychist beliefs, but it comes close to it. A matter for further research is the suggestion that Bion's proto-mental matrix notion is compatible with emergentism and downward causation inherent in General Systems Theory: von Bertalanffy was visiting professor at the University of London in 1948–1949 and was a fellow of the Rockefeller Foundation, hence his influence could also have easily reached Bion at the time.

Bion's concept of the proto-mental matrix has been difficult to integrate with the psychoanalytic study of groups. With recent advances in multidisciplinary research on emotions, affective neuroscience and neuro-psychoanalysis, and concepts such as the *proto-self* (Damasio, 2000) and of *Simple Ego-like Life Form* (Panksepp, 2004), it might become more fully appreciated as a valid heuristic to understand primitive group phenomena and related emotional dynamics in a holistic manner. The notion of proto-mental matrix can also become integrated with psychoanalytic notions of emotional containment in groups and institutions (Hinshelwood, 1987, 2001) and their links to psychosomatic health (Morgan-Jones, 2010; Morgan-Jones and Torres, 2010).

Notes

1 In his 1961 rewriting of his 1952 paper "Group-Dynamics: A Review" for the publication of the book *Experiences in Groups*, Bion maintained the concept of the proto-mental.

2 For writings on this topic see Meltzer (1986), Imbasciati (1998 [2006], 2002), and Torres (2008, 2010a). Mancia and Longhin (2000) and Ferro (2006) have implicitly connected β-elements to proto-mental phenomena (using the term *proto-emotional*).

3 I have written previously on the second topic and its implications elsewhere (Torres, 1999, 2000, 2008, 2010a, 2010b; Morgan-Jones and Torres, 2010).

4 Some authors argue that Bergson was not completely a panpsychist, but that he "flirted with panpsychism" (Skrbina, 2005).

5 The notions of "emergentism" and "downward causation" are also holistic conceptions, which link several layers of reality (matter, biology, mind and social structures) and different levels of organization within each of the previously mentioned layers (e.g. in biology: cells, organisms, ecosystems), without presupposing panpsychism (see Popper, 1977b). However, these concepts were fully developed later, mainly in the 1960s by von Bertalanffy in his general systems theory and by Roger Sperry in psychobiology (Corning, 2002). Most philosophers of mind today favour emergentism over panpsychism, but the debate is far from finished.

6 According to Descartes:

> the body of a living man differs from that of a dead man just as does a watch or other automaton (i.e. a machine that moves of itself), [. . .] from the same watch or other machine when it is broken and when the principle of its movement ceases to act [. . .] it is not less natural for a clock, made of the requisite number of wheels, to indicate the hours, than for a tree which has sprung from this or that seed, to produce a particular fruit.
>
> (Descartes, 1628/1647 [1911], pp. 300–333)

7 In the article on "How the soul and the body act on one another" he says:

> the soul has its principal seat in the little gland which exists in the middle of the brain [. . .] Reciprocally, likewise, the machine of the body is so formed that from the simple fact that this gland is diversely moved by the soul, [. . .] it thrusts the spirits which surround it towards the pores of the brain, which conduct them by the nerves into the muscles, by which means it causes them to move the limbs.
>
> (Descartes, 1628/1647 [1911], p. 347)

8 For detailed discussions on the body–mind problem, namely the notions of monism, dualism, interactionism, emergentism, reductionism, epiphenomenalism, parallelism, idealism, materialism, and the several possible logical combinations between them, see e.g. Wisdom, 1952; Popper, 1977b; Edelman, 1992; Humphrey, 2000.

9 Thomas Hobbes, in his 1641 *Objections to Descartes' Meditations'* was perhaps the first to propose that Descartes' *cogito* (thinking) was not necessarily incorporeal ("ghostly") and thus opened the way for materialistic reductionism. La Mettrie in his 1748 *L'Homme machine* (*Machine Man* or *Man a Machine* according to the two different translations to English) described human beings as self-moving mechanisms and sought a neurological basis for mental activity.

10 Says Leibniz:

> Souls follow their laws which consist in a certain development of perceptions, according to the goods and the evils; and bodies also follow their laws, which consist in the laws of motion; and nevertheless these two beings of entirely different kind are in perfect accord, and correspond like two clocks perfectly regulated on the same basis. This is what I call Pre-established Harmony [. . .] souls harmonize with bodies and among themselves, in virtue of the pre-established harmony, and not at all by a mutual physical influence
>
> (Leibniz, 1679/1704 [1890], pp. 165–166, 235)

11 According to Gregg (1953) psychoanalysis had enriched the holistic approach to the study of man in medicine, but there were many unsolved problems, such as

finding a common terminology and semantics. Concomitantly Rapaport (1953), tried to organize a systematic psycho-analytic theory of emotions. However, the integration of psychoanalytic theory with neurophysiological emotion research was never really accomplished in full and is still a work in progress (Panksepp, 1999).

12 For instance:

> It may be useful to suppose that there exists in reality a psycho-somatic breast and an infantile psycho-somatic alimentary canal corresponding to the breast. This breast is an object the infant needs to supply it with milk and good internal objects.
>
> (Bion, 1962, p. 34)

Also Bion's definition of β-elements is very clear on this point: "This term represents the earliest matrix from which thoughts can be supposed to arise. It partakes of the quality of inanimate object and psychic object without any form of distinction between the two" (Bion, 1963, p. 22). See also Chapter 2 on "Bion and Trotter" and Torres (2010a).

13 It is debatable if Bion's position is also compatible with emergentism, which states that sentience is not a fundamental property of matter, but that it has emerged as something new in complex organisms. The notions of emergence and downward causation (see for instance Popper, 1977b) are surely compatible with Bion's proto-mental matrix dynamics. I will not discuss these matters in detail here.

14 The etymologies of the synonym words "soul", "mind", "psyche", as well as "animate" (from Latin *anima*) are extremely complex since they have origins in Germanic, Latin and Greek words, and have accumulated a wealth of meanings amalgamated from different contexts. To avoid the confusion of meanings, Clifford (1874) adopted the name *sentience*, which has entered common usage in contemporary philosophy of mind. For a review of the concept of mind, psyche and soul see, e.g. MacDonald (2003).

15 Von Herdenberg adopted the pseudonym Novalis for his published writings and until recently he was regarded primarily as a poet.

16 I have addressed the parallels and differences between Freud's *Id* and Bion's *proto-mental matrix* elsewhere (Torres, 2008, 2010a).

17 Godwin (1991) compared Bion's theories about mental development, with the post-modern theoretical physicist David Bohm's theory of the implicate order in physics.

Chapter 7

The psycho-social field dynamics

Kurt Lewin and Bion[1]

Nuno Torres

> Our mind is frail as our senses are; it would lose itself in the complexity of the world if that complexity were not harmonious.
>
> Poincaré (1907 [1914], *Science and Method*, p. 30)

Introduction

Most theoretical approaches to explain human behaviour tend to follow one of two implicit reductionist models: either the causes of behaviour are reduced to inborn and acquired *individual traits* or reduced to permanent or momentary *social* influences and categories (Lewis, 2000). Occasionally some minds are able to challenge the reductionist paradigms and achieve "binocular visions", developing models embracing both the individual and their social environment, as well as their complex interactional dynamics.[2] Among these are pioneers such as Sigmund Freud and Adolf Meyer (see Bowlby, 1988), and undoubtedly also Wilfred Bion and Kurt Lewin.

The most distinctive assumption shared by Lewin and Bion is that individual and group behaviour are truly indissociable, and should be understood as a dynamic whole in a way similar to the figure/ground reversal phenomenon of optical perception (Bion, 1949b [1961], pp. 86–87; 1951 [1961], p. 134; 1970, p. 66; Lewin, 1935a, p. 3). Based on this assumption, they achieved and inspired groundbreaking integration of the psyche and the social to improve human relations and development in a broad range of social units and institutions (Allport, 1948 [1951]; de Board, 1978; Trist, 1985; Trist and Murray, 1990a, 1993, 1997; Thelen, 1985; Schermer, 1985; Khaleelee and Miller, 1985; Hinshelwood, 1999).

The aim of this chapter is to illustrate that Kurt Lewin's pioneering work on group dynamics influenced some of Bion's psycho-social concepts and was a solid bridge which assisted Bion in combining his innovative ideas on psychiatry and psychoanalysis with group phenomena and social science. Hence, some of Bion's concepts on the psycho-social can be seen in the light of Lewin's models, enriching the contributions of both authors to the comprehension of the complexity of human psycho-social dynamic systems.[3]

Lewin and Bion

Both Lewin and Bion went through the two world wars: in the First World War as enemy soldiers (and both were awarded medals for bravery), while in the Second World War they were on the same side; they developed some of their early psycho-social methods to increase the chances of the Allies and democracy against the Axis powers and totalitarianism. Their experiences at war very likely influenced their ideas, not least because group psychology, morale and *esprit de corps* (themes which they both researched) are central issues for an army in combat[4] (Harrison, 2000).

Despite having witnessed first-hand mass destruction and human mayhem at its worst, both of them believed a fresh psychological science, to which they largely contributed, could help change mankind for the better (Lewin, 1939 [1951], 1943b [1951], 1947a, 1947b; Bion, 1946, 1948a [1961]).

As part of what Cartwright and Zander (1953, p. 5) called "an empiricist rebellion in social science" starting in the 1920s, Lewin and Bion were pioneers in experiments with entire groups and institutions.[5] The "Tavistock" approach to group dynamics was clearly influenced by both Bion and Lewin (Trist and Murray, 1990a, 1993, 1997; Khaleelee and Miller, 1985). The journal *Human Relations* was co-created in 1947 by the Tavistock Institute in which Bion had a prominent role and Lewin's Research Centre for Group Dynamics at the Massachusetts Institute of Technology with the purpose of integrating Lewin's field theory and object relations psychoanalysis (Trist and Murray, 1990a, p. 8). In the first two years of its publication, the journal printed two papers by Lewin (1947a, 1947b) and two by Bion (1948a [1961], 1948b [1961]). Lewin focused on the development of social sciences in order to make them useful for preventing the destructive capacities unleashed by man's use of natural sciences. This plea was quite similar to Bion's address to the medical section of the British Psychological Society in 1947, which was published in his paper "Psychiatry at a time of crisis" (Bion, 1948).

There were, on the other hand, vast differences between the two: Lewin was an experimental social psychologist inspired by gestaltism, who mostly did laboratorial controlled observation;[6] Bion was an army officer and psychoanalytically oriented psychiatrist, who always worked directly in real-life institutional settings on the brink of crisis.

Additionally, whereas Lewin relied on positivistic quantitative and statistical data as evidence, Bion used subjectivist qualitative and narrative accounts not unlike clinical case studies. But this division of methodologies is less substantially clear-cut than it would seem at first sight: Lewin wanted to understand individual cases and severely criticized the simplistic misuse of statistics (Lewin, 1935a) and Bion's group theories led to several experimental and quantitative approaches: among these were the research programme established in 1950 at the Human Dynamics Laboratory in Chicago by Stock and Thelen (1958) and the Q-sort research methods of Stephenson (1953, cited in Brown, 2003, p. 286), Armelius and Armelius (1985), Lipgar (1998) and Brown (2003); they also led to clinical-based research in psychiatry and psychopathology, including Karterud and his colleagues (Karterud and Foss, 1989; Karterud, 2000) and myself (Torres, 2008, 2010a).

Lewin's influence on Bion

There is so far scarce evidence that Bion had first-hand knowledge of Lewin's ideas, apart from few oral sources, people who worked with Bion and John Rickman in the 1940s (De Maré, 1985, pp. 111–112; see also Harrison, 2000, pp. 64–65). The most explicit link between Lewin's ideas and Bion's seems to be Eric Trist, a psychologist who was manifestly enthusiastic about Lewin, who become also a close colleague and a great admirer of Bion (Trist, 1985, 1993; Hinshelwood, 1999).

In his autobiography, Eric Trist (1993) states that as a student he was mainly interested in psychoanalysis and gestalt psychology. After graduating in psychology (in 1933) he visited Kurt Lewin in the USA and became "utterly hooked". When the Second World War broke out Trist worked at the Maudsley Psychiatric Hospital in London, where he wanted to implement Lewin's ideas by considering the environment as a therapeutically active social field (Trist, 1985, p. 5). At that time Trist had several contacts with the army group of the Tavistock Clinic, including Rickman and Bion, who asked him to join them, and in early 1942 he become the psychologist for the experimental team of the War Office Selection Boards (WOSBs), together with Bion and Sutherland. During the last two years of the war Trist became chief psychologist to the Civil Resettlement Units (CRUs) implementing the methods of the therapeutic community initiated by Bion and Rickman at Northfield (Trist, 1985, pp. 22–24; Trist and Murray, 1990b, p. 42). Trist developed follow-up studies showing statistical evidence that repatriated soldiers in CRUs had significantly higher adjustment in fifteen major life roles: according to him this meant there was hard evidence for Bion's idea that integration of psycho-social therapy and participation in a therapeutic community could be life-enhancing and promote personal growth (Curle and Trist, 1947, cit. in Trist, 1985, p. 24). After the war, Trist continued to work with Bion at the Tavistock and was his assistant in his original therapy groups (Trist, 1993).

It is very likely that during the whole of this period Eric Trist exposed Bion to Lewin's concepts and experiments. The hypothesis that Bion became aware of Lewin's ideas from 1942 onwards when Trist joined the WOSB to work with him can be supported by the fact that some of Lewin's central notions and terms were absent in Bion's (1940) "The war of nerves", his first paper on psycho-social dynamics, and started to appear in Bion's papers from 1943 onwards.

In "The war of nerves" Bion (1940) relied on an amalgamation of military strategy and psychoanalytic object-relations notions and shared Glover's view in *War, Sadism and Pacifism* that "knowledge obtained from individuals is applicable to a society with sufficient exactness to make that application valuable" (Glover, 1933 cited in Bion, 1940, p. 184). Bion also wrote that it was a grave shortcoming to base his proposals about group phenomena only on speculation, due to the lack of scientific evidence on groups; this sentence implies that he did not have any contact with Lewin's experimental group dynamics papers.

In contrast, in 1943 after Bion had worked closely with Eric Trist for two years, his second paper (Bion and Rickman, 1943 [1961]), starts with an implicit Lewinian gestaltic assumption: "in the treatment of the individual, neurosis is displayed as a problem of the individual, in the treatment of a group it must be displayed as a problem of the group" (p. 11). This statement shows a change of framework, in which the group is not seen as a linear sum of individuals, but is a qualitatively different entity in its own right, which can be addressed literally "as-a-whole" (a *Gestalt*). In the conclusions of their experiments, Bion and Rickman (1943 [1961], pp. 25–26) relied on concepts addressing the dynamic and structural properties of the group and the "social field". These theoretical and methodological assumptions are totally congruent with Lewin's (1939 [1951]) "Experiments in social space" and are clearly an application of Lewin *et al.*'s (1939) principles explaining aggressive behaviour based on the properties of the group structure.

How is it possible that the social psychologist Lewin's ideas, based on positivistic empirical data collection methods, could ever appeal to Bion and be compatible with his psychoanalytic and object-relations' ideas? This question takes us to the next section, showing how Lewin's model of the mind is in reality harmonious with Bion's psychoanalytic-oriented approach.

Lewin's model of the mind

Although Lewin relied on positivistic laboratory data, his theoretical model is clearly anti-behaviourist, and proposes the mind as a result of the complex dynamical interaction of psychical energies, psychic structures and the experienced environment (Lewin, 1935b, 1935c). In point of fact, it is similar in many ways to Freud's model of the mind in its meta-psychological five dimensions (Rapaport and Gill, 1959; Sandler, 1997): dynamic, economic, structural–topographical, genetic–developmental, and adaptive. How much Lewin was influenced by Freud is a matter for further research, since Lewin reveals that partially endorsed Freud's ideas (Lewin 1935a, p. 22; 1935c, p. 102; 1935d, pp. 180–181; 1935e, p. 242). For instance: "we often find facts which Freud first brought to our attention, thereby rendering a great service" (Lewin 1935d, pp. 180–181). He also stated that despite disagreements with the Freudian method of research, co-operation between the two approaches should prove fruitful, and on some points psychoanalysis was superior to any kind of theory based on an experimental procedure (Lewin, 1937 [1999]).

Indeed Lewin's model included the following features:

- Psychic energies derived from the pressure of needs, which tend to discharge to the lowest state of tension, creating psychic tensions while undischarged.
- A tendency for immediate discharge (akin to Freud's primary process and pleasure principle) and a tendency to delay discharge when a wish must be attained through long continued effort (akin to Freud's secondary process and reality principle).
- Unfulfilled wishes that remain in a tense system, and may not appear in consciousness for a long time but can assert themselves most strongly on some occasions (akin to Freud's notion of "dammed-up" psychic energy).
- Discharge may result by means of a substitute completion or compensation (akin to the idea of discharge through neurotic activities by Freud).
- Several strata or layers of the mind, the content of some of which is only accessible in dreams or hypnotic states (akin to the unconscious).
- A structure within the psychic totality of the mind that must be defined as the self in a narrower sense (akin to Freud's idea of the ego).
- The formation of these psychical systems is based on the ontogenic development and shows a specific historical component in each individual.

In Lewinian infantile psychology (1935b, 1935c) there was also place for something like "internal objects" analogous to Kleinian ideas: they would correspond to objects existing in what Lewin called the unrealistic strata (fantasy and dreams) of the individual's mind: "The description of the child's environment would be incomplete without including the whole world of phantasy which is so important for the child's behavior and so closely connected with its ideals and with its ideal goals" (Lewin, 1935c, p. 76). But Lewin developed his research of the mind much further in the realm of social–environmental influences and much less in the internal world than Freud and Klein did. In the following sections I will compare Lewin's approach to Bion's.

Psycho-social field dynamics: the group atmosphere and the group-as-a-whole

Lewin proposed with conceptual rigour the existence of the dynamic properties of the *psychological* environment (1935c, p. 79). His concept of *social field of forces* denotes a constellation of individual and environmental factors ("social facts") interacting dynamically: for instance individual wishes of children that came across environmental barriers or attractors, including parental prohibitions, praise, punishments and rewards (1935c, p. 75). The *pressure* of the social world affecting the individual is described by the notions of *social atmosphere* or *social climate* (Lewin, 1936 [1951], p. 5). By 1933, Lewin and colleagues (e.g. Lewin, *et al.*, 1939) experimented the effects of different "group social climates and atmospheres" induced in clubs for schoolboys by experimentally manipulating the style of adult leadership: authoritarian, democratic, and laissez-faire. The concept of "group-as-a-whole" was introduced and was operationalized through assessments *both* of the group *and* of the individuals (which included Moreno's sociometry, independent observers, in-depth interviews, Rorschach tests, and teachers' ratings of students). These multi-method data allowed the integration of sociological or "group-centred" data with psychological or "individual-centred" data. According to Lewin:

> Groups are sociological wholes; the unity of these sociological wholes can be defined operationally in the same way as a unity of any other dynamic whole [. . .]. Such a definition takes mysticism out of the group conception and brings the problem down to a thoroughly empirical and testable basis. At the same time it means a full recognition of the fact that properties of a social group, such as its organization, its stability, its goals, are something different from the organization, the stability, and the goals of the individuals in it.
>
> (Lewin, 1939 [1951], p. 60)

In papers written between 1946 to 1952 Bion also used not only the notions of *group field*, but also of *group atmosphere* and *group-as-a-whole* (e.g. Bion, 1946, p. 78, 1961, pp. 21, 32, 34, 47, 51).

At the WOSBs the traditional individual-based assessments of the candidates were complemented with the whole group as the test situation (Bion, 1946; Trist, 1985; Trist and Murray, 1990b). However, Bion and his team moulded the notion of group-as-a-whole in a perspective reversal to the aims of officer selection: they did not pre-establish leadership as Lewin and his colleagues; instead the leaders – the men showing more aptitude to be army officers – were left to emerge from the group field dynamics, with as little interference as possible from the assessment team. Another innovative method making use of group-as-a-whole assessments at the WOSB was the "Regimental Nomination Procedure" (Trist, 1985; Murray, 1990). Eric Trist adapted this idea as a form of Moreno's Sociometry (Murray, 1990, p. 59), which was one of the methods used by Lewin *et al.* (1939). This procedure proved extremely useful in identifying suitable candidates, and additionally in predicting the pass rates of candidates in the WOSBs (Murray, 1990, pp. 60–61).

Group discussions: a method for social and therapeutic change

From 1941 to 1946, by means of controlled experiments, Lewin and his colleagues meticulously tested the effects of small group discussions on behaviour change, and used them as the first step in a chain of procedures to persuade people to modify behaviour more effectively than mass propaganda, lecturing and individual advice (Lewin, 1943a, 1943b [1951], 1944 [1951]). In his experiments to change food habits, Lewin developed methods for small group decision of "goals set up by the group as a whole to the group as a whole", which proved to be much more effective than lecturing and individual advice (Lewin, 1943a, pp. 55–56).

Small group discussions were also reported by Bion and Rickman (1943 [1961]) and Bion (1946) – in contrast with the individual patient treatment which was traditional in psychiatry – as an essential tool for therapeutic change both of the individual and of the "social field" of the institution-as-a-whole. Bion's (1946) use of small group discussions at Northfield Hospital, initially also aimed to persuade the patients "to face their enemy instead of running away from it" (p. 79). Like Lewin's objective of changing inappropriate food habits, Bion's objective was to change neurotic behaviour. But Bion was looking for more than an effective social manipulation technique; he wanted to "produce self-respecting men socially adjusted to the community and therefore willing to accept its responsibilities whether in peace or war" (Bion and Rickman, 1943, p. 13).

To accomplish this task the individuals had to become conscious of the phenomena guiding their behaviour as group members: it became clear to him that knowledge of deeper unconscious intra-group and intra-psychic tensions had to be made available by the group experiences of individuals, and this became his main aim (Bion, 1946, 1948a [1961], 1961).

The programme of group experiments Bion started in 1946 at the Interim Planning Committee of the Tavistock Clinic – the so-called "Operation Phoenix" (Trist and Murray, 1990a) – was the clarification *in situ* by the whole-group, including himself, of these unknown tensions, forces, and emotions through methods of exploratory psychoanalytic-oriented groups (Bion, 1961).

The group within the individual

According to Lewin (e.g. 1936 [1951]), and stating the obvious for a social psychologist, for most of the time people act not purely as individuals but simultaneously as a member of social group(s) in terms of aspirations, goals, and behaviours. But a radical and puzzling discovery arising from the experiments by Lewin and his colleagues was that the effect of the group on individual behaviour was not limited to classical sociological categories such as family, gender, political parties, clubs, and so forth; it was also operative even if a group had only existed for few minutes, the participants did not know each other before nor had regular contacts afterwards. There was a significant effect which was stable, or even increased through time at later follow-ups, of these fleeting group decisions: "In case of group decision, the eagerness seems to be relatively independent of personal preference; the individual seems to act mainly as a 'group member'" (Lewin, 1948 [1999], p. 283). Bion reported a similar phenomenon in his therapeutic groups at the Tavistock Clinic:

> it is possible to show that some of their [members of the group] daily conflicts are arising from their attempt to reconcile the demands of everyday thinking and the demands of their membership of the group [...] patients produce material in a steady stream to support the view that their membership [...] exerts a widespread influence on their mental lives when the group disperses as well as in the short period when they meet as a group.
>
> (Bion, 1949b, p. 86)

The theoretical problem is what kind of 'binding force' would be strong enough so that the individual mind becomes largely a function of their membership of these group(s) and not of their putative individuality? The response from both Lewin and Bion was to propose the existence of a psychological/emotional influence, which was metaphorically similar and as powerful in binding individual minds as electromagnetic field forces bind atoms and molecules: valence/valency.[7]

Primary psycho-social forces: valence/valency

The theoretical term of *valence* was coined by Lewin in concord with Edward Tollman (Lewin, 1935b), to designate imperative social–environmental facts that *attract* the individual's mind, as they are perceived as means for satisfying needs or wishes. He first used the term to signify the many things that attract the child (to eating, to climbing, to grasping, to sucking, etc.).

In the adult, valence was related also to powerful attractions to groups and group standards, as these are perceived as having a vital value (Lewin, 1945 [1951]). In fact, the divergence between an individual's behaviour and the standard behaviour of the group(s) they belong to brings about ridicule, severe treatment, and possibly ejection from the group, so most individuals tend to stay pretty close to their group(s') standards: "In other words, the group level itself acquires value. It becomes a positive valence corresponding to a central force field [...] keeping the individual in line with the standards of the group" (1948 [1999], p. 281). Bion, on the other hand, coined the concept *valency* to designate an emotional force that describes the "capacity for spontaneous instinctive co-operation", an "unconscious function of the gregarious quality in the personality of man" and part of the "equipment of a herd animal",[8] to act according to common basic emotional standards, i.e. the "basic assumption groups" (Bion, 1950a, pp. 116–117; 1951 [1961], p. 133, 136; 1952, p. 170).

> I wish also to use it '*valency*' to indicate a readiness to combine on levels that can hardly be called mental at all but are characterised by behaviour in human beings that is more analogous to tropism in plants than to purposive behaviour.
>
> (Bion, 1950a, pp. 116–117)

Lewin had also used the concept of *tropism* as a biological metaphor of the social–environmental influence on human behaviour (Lewin, 1935c, p. 69), so it is possible that Bion borrowed the idea from Lewin. But while Lewin explained the individual's valence to group standards in fairly straightforward terms (avoidance of ridicule, and so forth), Bion tried to dig deeper into the unconscious dynamics of valency using the Kleinian notions of internal objects and persecutory anxiety (Bion, 1949b, p. 90).

At this point Bion entered into totally new territory, and tried to conciliate different theoretical models – a psychoanalytic model of Kleinian object-relations, and a group dynamics model comprised of an amalgamation of his own ideas, Trotter's and Rickman's ideas, and also "Lewinian" concepts. The unresolved intricacies of this effort have been discussed at length by several authors elsewhere (e.g. Miller, 1998a, 1998b; Sanfuentes, 2003; Torres, 2003, 2010b). In brief it could be said that Bion considers group behaviour in a binocular way: as both a manifestation of a "group animal" driven instinctively to inter-dependence, warfare, and sexual reproduction, as well as of the individuals' mental defences against primitive (psychotic) anxieties. For Bion this would help to explain phenomena such as the construction of psychotic-like and absurd common-sense social consensus, the rigid maintenance of *establishments* and *status quo* at the expense of social development and mental growth, and the alienation of individual distinctiveness and responsibility associated with basic assumption (primitive and archaic) forms of leadership (Bion, 1961).

The problem of leadership

Both Lewin and Bion, not least for personal reasons,[9] were motivated to develop sophisticated forms of leadership that could embody equilibrium between emotions/intellect, individual/social interests, and hence allow the healthy social development of human societies and organizations and its members.

Kurt Lewin was a firm believer in the virtues of democracy, but was also aware of its paradoxes. To him: "The democratic leader does not impose his goals on the group as does the autocratic leader: the policy determination in democracy is done by the group as a whole. Still the democratic leader should 'lead'" (Lewin, 1943, p. 39). Here we can find another major agreement between Lewin and Bion, in the sense that Bion's type of leadership fits perfectly into the former paradoxical definition: "I take advantage of this position [leader] to establish no rules of procedure and to put forward no agenda" (Bion, 1961, p. 77) and "The group always make it clear that they expect me to act with authority as the leader of the group, and this responsibility I accept, though not in the way the group expect" (Bion, 1961, p. 82). Bion (1948a, pp. 38–39) verified that when he, as the work-group leader, apparently "suspended leadership" the group searched impulsively for other leaders. Lewin called them "indigenous leaders": "The goal of the democratic leader will have to ... make himself superfluous, to be replaced by indigenous leaders from the group" (1943b, p. 39). The "indigenous leaders", however, were seen by Bion in his groups as no more than "puppets" of the primitive basic assumption levels, and were chosen from amongst the most disturbed elements of the group: "without exception, a thoroughgoing psychiatric case" (1961, p. 119).

Lewin (1943b), however, believed democracy was a goal reachable through mass training. Here we can find a major disagreement between Lewin and Bion. According to Bion, things were far more complex: the appropriate "leader would be the one who could approach unconscious group forces while maintaining connection to reality, augmenting the insight of the members of the group as to their functioning" (1961, pp. 177–178).

Final remarks and conclusion

It would be unfair and extreme to say that Lewin was the single most important influence on Bion's group ideas. In fact, all of the social and scientific movements of the first half of the twentieth century and numerous conceptual cross-fertilizations led to a fairly coherent group psychology on both sides of the Atlantic (Cartwright and Zander, 1953; Hinshelwood, 1999; 2004; Harrison, 2000). But Bion's (1940) intuitions on psycho-social phenomena may have found a firm basis in Kurt Lewin's rigorous conceptual system and hard evidence on "social fields". It is also likely that Lewin's notions appealed to Bion since they were compatible with a psychoanalytic and object-relations oriented approach, as I have argued above.

Moreover, Lewin's use of analogies and concepts from dynamical physics inspired by Henri Poincaré's pioneering works on the topology of dynamic systems, were updated to the complexities which also appealed to Bion. In his later works (1962, 1963, 1970), Bion also quoted Poincaré, namely the notion of *selected fact* which makes it possible to grasp the "whole-ness" and order in the apparent disorder and overwhelming complexity of the world. The conceptual promises in Lewin's notions were hence compatible with

Bion's inherent bold aspirations to overcome the limitations of psychiatry and psychoanalysis and to combine them with other disciplines namely social sciences, philosophy and history (Bion, 1948b).

Notes

1 *Acknowledgements*: I want to sincerely thank Robert Lipgar for his thoughtful comments and important suggestions of earlier versions of this chapter, and also R.D. Hinshelwood for his assistance and inspiration.

2 According to Bion and Rickman (1943 [1961], p. 26) "There is a useful future in the study of the interplay of individual and social psychology, viewed as equally important interacting elements". This type of model only emerged in the mainstream of psychology in the late twentieth century, through what Lewis (2000) called "transformational models", rejecting the idea that the individual and the social environment are ever independent or exist as "pure" forms. Instead these features interact and transform themselves at each point in time (e.g. Sameroff, 1975; Bronfenbrenner, 1979). Bronfenbrenner (2005) described these types of models as *Process-Person-Context* models. In the area of psychoanalytic studies, Hinshelwood (1987), Schermer and Pines (1995) and Hinshelwood and Chiesa (2001) have fostered this type of model, as Hollway (2008) did more recently in the area psycho-social research methods.

3 I use here the term *complexity* in its technical sense, in the context of complexity theory and dynamical systems theory, applied to psychology and social sciences (see e.g. Eidelson, 1997; Lewis and Granic, 2000). See also Hinshelwood (1987, Chapter 17) for an example of application of complexity theory to a psychoanalytic view of organizations.

4 Sandler (2003) has addressed Bion's First World War memoirs and their relations with his later concepts. See also Chapter 5 of this book on Bion's "Tavistock Years".

5 Earlier pioneers of group experiments at the beginning of the twentieth century, namely Jacob Moreno and Trigant Burrow are described in Pines (1999) and Hinshelwood (2004).

6 Lewin expanded the gestalt concepts of Max Wertheimer and Wolfgang Kohler into the field of personality and motivation (see Lewin, 1935b, 1935e, p. 240), by adding notions from the physics of dynamical systems inspired by Poincaré's works on topology (1907, cited in Lewin, 1935a, p. 66).

7 Valence (also spelled valency) in chemistry is the property of an element that determines the number of other atoms with which an atom of the element can combine.

8 For a study of the origins and implications of the concept of *gregariousness* and *herd instinct* in Bion see Chapter 2 on Bion and Trotter.

9 Lewin was obliged to leave his beloved Germany in 1933 due to the most infamous autocratic leadership mankind has ever produced; Bion was bitterly resentful of bad leadership at least since his First World War experiences: "the sooner people realize the criminal folly of their leaders the better" (Bion, 1918 [1997], p. 127).

Chapter 8

Bion's analysts

Malcolm Pines and R.D. Hinshelwood

Bion came to psychoanalysis slowly and had four attempts at therapy – the last two, with John Rickman and Melanie Klein, being full analyses. In the second part of his autobiography, *All My Sins Remembered* (1985), he writes about an 'analyst' to whom he had been for 'cure' to dispel the anxiety from which he was suffering after scholastic and athletic failures at Oxford in the early 1920s. He was told that he would require about 12 sessions, but as he was not cured in this time and ran into debt with his analyst, he stopped treatment. He is contemptuous of this analyst, calling him 'Dr Feel-It-In-The-Past'! His analyst even sent him a patient, an adolescent boy, with whom he again failed.

James Hadfield (1882–1967): We know that for several years he was in some form of psychotherapy with Dr Hadfield, a well-known eclectic psychotherapist of the times, and author of *Mental Health and the Psychoneuroses* (1952), whom Bion described as 'charming and intelligent'. Hadfield was one of seven doctors employed by Hugh Crichton-Miller when founding the Tavistock Clinic, in 1920 (Dicks 1970). When Bion went to work there, in 1933, as an assistant doctor (in effect, a trainee), Hadfield was in a commanding position and served as Bion's trainer in psychotherapy. Hadfield rejected the significance of the transference, and using free associations and dream interpretation, he emphasised the importance of linking the symptom with the nuclear incidents from the past. He also modified Freud's dual instinct theory to become a three-pronged motivation – a sexual libido, an aggressive/self-preservative drive, and a drive towards dependence. Interestingly, as Bléandonu points out 'Here we can note, in passing, the similarity between Hadfield's theory and the three "basic assumption" groups proposed by Bion' (1994, p. 43). Like others in Hadfield's circle, Bion became disillusioned by the limitations of Hadfield's theories – and maybe by the therapy. Clearly, he had a contempt for this man; but he also described himself as an imposter in his first attempts to set up as a Harley Street consultant psychotherapist.

John Rickman

Just before the Second World War started, Bion broke off with Hadfield and went to see John Rickman. He writes

> In those days he was blunt-spoken and frighteningly impatient of cant. I liked him; I agreed with great misgivings, to start analysis. To my surprise, his interpretations appeared to me to be reminiscent of common sense; they reminded me of real life. I was astonished because common sense did not seem to be grand enough ... I thought Rickman liked me. But there was some kind of emotional turbulence, with its high and low pressure areas, which extinguished the analysis as far as Rickman and I were concerned. It stopped; though not before it had also extinguished any spark of respect that might have been entertained for me by my pre-psychoanalytic colleagues before I had penetrated far enough to be independent.
>
> (Bion 1985, p. 46)

Despite the reservations about the turbulence between them, he seems from the evidence of the letters he subsequently wrote, until Rickman's death, that Bion retained a very high opinion of him, almost idolising him (see Chapter 9, on the letters to Rickman).

Bion was in analysis with Rickman for little more than one year between 1937 to 1939. The original intention was a training analysis to enable Bion to become a psychoanalyst with the British Psychoanalytical Society. However the war intervened in 1939, the analysis was broken off, and their relationship change radically to become eventually collaborators on significant developments in military psychiatry during the war. Rickman was then a leading member of the British Psychoanalytical Society and clearly from the few clinical examples that he gives in his papers, he was a man of very considerable analytic understanding and technical skill. He had been in analysis with Freud, Ferenczi and Klein, a large, warm, friendly man whose writing is that of a highly cultivated and cultured individual with a broad grasp of scientific method, comparative religion and anthropology. He wished to place psychoanalysis in perspective against sociology and anthropology, and to show the relevance of a general theory of psychoanalysis to the study of group tensions both on the local level, as well as national and international levels. His thought is not speculative, mystical or loosely philosophical. He does not take deep plunges into the unconscious; he draws his models from structural theory, object relations theory and from Melanie Klein and Freud. He emphasises the ahistorical data in psychoanalysis, the essential data, which is present and discernible at the time of observation as it is in science generally. He was in demand for essays on general topics by popular magazines such as *New Era*, and wrote editorials for such as *The Lancet* often anonymously.

He refers only rarely in his papers to Bion, mostly in discussing what he calls operational research into group tensions, that is, the study of group-cohesive and group-disruptive forces.[1] Clearly he writes then of Bion as a colleague and partner in research. Though Bion frequently writes of himself as inept or lazy, Rickman regarded Bion as a pioneer in this field which nobody should undertake who wants a peaceful life (Rickman 1938 [2003]). Bion described Rickman as a man who never attached enough importance to not overworking and therefore wasted himself very badly. 'He had a very good brain, but I think for the last 10 years there was a falling off. He did not himself realise it, luckily. The surprising thing is that so few others noticed it either, though it was very marked' (Bion 1985, p. 107).

It is clear that Rickman helped Bion out of his then long-lasting and chronic state of cynicism and depression. The analysis came to an end abruptly in 1939, shortly after Bion's mother had died, and when Rickman joined the Emergency Medical Service at Haymeads. This service (EMS) was set up to cope with the large scale of civilian casualties expected from bombing. There Rickman began experimenting with new ideas, that he developed at Wharncliffe Hospital, and which were developed later by Bion at Northfield in 1943 (Bion and Rickman 1943 [1961]). In the obituary to Rickman by Sylvia Payne, she quotes Bion as saying,

> John Rickman had a great capacity for grasping the value of a new idea. I appreciated this when I found, during the war, that he had heard of some views I had expressed about the occupational therapy of soldiers in Psychiatric hospitals and had then and there set about translating them, nebulous though they were, into action at Wharncliffe. I visited him there and he told me about it. It was a fascinating account, illuminated by flashes of humour, punctuated with generous tributes to the merits of what were assumed to be my ideas, but never once betraying the least awareness of how much the scheme he was describing was the child of his own creative imagination.
>
> I remember thinking then at Wharncliffe and later at Northfield what a good combatant officer he might have made. He used his abilities and his knowledge to persuade the men in hospital to have a look at themselves and so seemed on the verge of achieving a new kind of leadership in which men were brought to face the unknown territories from which arise the diseases of a sick society.
>
> (quoted in Payne 1952, pp. 55–56)

Payne also noted that an issue that Rickman gave prime importance to was 'the need to study the technique of communication between a speaker or teacher and his audience' (Payne 1952, p. 56); an issue which may well have stuck with Bion who ten years later introduced his book, *Learning from Experience*,

> I have experience to record, but how to communicate this experience to others I am in doubt; this book explains why. For a time I thought of concentrating on analysis of trainees. I am confident that psycho-analysts are right in thinking that this is the only really effective method of passing on analytic experience that we have at present; but to limit one's energies to this activity smacks of the esoteric cult. On the other hand, publication of a book, such as this, may seem premature. Nevertheless I believe it may be possible to give some idea of the world that is revealed by the attempt to understand our understanding.
>
> (Bion 1962, p. v)

Rickman was a Quaker, and it may be that his approach to groups which so influenced Bion, resulted in the quietist, non-managerial style of leaderless group with which they were both identified. There is a question of primacy here, which does not necessarily go in Bion's favour. As Harrison (2000) who researched in detail the Northfield work of Bion as well as various others, including T.F. Main and Michael Foulkes, decided that Rickman was the inspiration behind the scenes there. Tom Main said in an untranscribed interview in 1984 with Harrison,

> Rickman is much undervalued. Lot of what Bion says is borrowed direct from Rickman, at that period [i.e. the Second World War]. I don't mean that Bion isn't an original man. He's a most remarkable and original man. Really he is.... But Rickman showed him.... Deserves credit.

Nevertheless Bion and Rickman worked on the ideas for the Northfield 'experiment' in 1943, though Bion with an increasing confidence took the lead as administrative psychiatrist in charge of the rehabilitation wing. His debt to Rickman is immense since prior to Northfield, Bion was instrumental with Trist, Wittkower and others in setting up the novel WOSBs (War Office Selection Boards – Bion 1946). Their success owes not a little to Bion's originality in developing the apparently leaderless groups, from which potential officers could show their emerging leadership. And in turn, Bion owed something to Rickman as a kind of mentor in enabling Bion to make his contribution there. That experience seemed to energise him to take on the development of the Northfield work.

The writing of their joint article on Northfield bears the hallmark of Rickman's group dynamic sophistication and Bion's striking originality of language. When enquiring of British wartime psychiatry in September 1945, Jacques Lacan gave a flowery portrait of Bion at the time,

> these two men, of whom it could be said that the flame of creation burns within – in one as if frozen in an immobile and moonlike mask, accentuated by the fine commas of a black moustache, which, no less than the

> large physique and the swimmer's chest that hold it up, contradict Kretschmer's formulae, when everything tells us we are in the presence of one of those beings who are solitary in even their highest achievements, and as we find confirmed in this man's adventures in Flanders, where he followed his tank, switch in hand, into the breach, and paradoxically thus forced the iron gates of fate.
>
> (Lacan 1947, English translation in Bléandonu 1994, p. 278)

This says as much about Lacan's literary gifts as about his observations, but nevertheless we do get a graphic picture of Bion and the sense of his large presence, with the equally large Rickman.

Bion had come to life under Rickman, and one could almost wonder if the effect of their collaborations was just as important to Bion at that time in his life, as the effect of the analysis. Shortly after the analysis Bion met and married a very charming, intelligent and successful actress. His achievement in courting a woman was a significant step forward for him. He was in his early forties. Their marriage inevitably disrupted by the wartime nevertheless produced a pregnancy and Betty's death in childbirth a few years later (1944) was one of the greatest blows of his troubled life.

Melanie Klein

After the war, Rickman suggested that they should not continue analysis because of their joint wartime experience. Bion agreed, for he had already considered the possibility of approaching Melanie Klein. He writes,

> Melanie Klein, of whom I had heard and had some chance of observing from a distance on one or two occasions, was a handsome, dignified and somewhat intimidating woman. My experience of association with women had not been encouraging or conducive to growth of any belief in a successful outcome.
>
> (Bion 1985, pp. 66–67)

Bion's flourishing as a result of Rickman as a kind of mentor seemed unusual in his life so far, and it appears he believed that his general experience of women needed perhaps a comparable therapeutic spur. She agreed to accept him and he writes that at that time he had looked at the theories of Melanie Klein and could not make head or tail of what he read.

Of his analysis with Melanie Klein, he writes that

> it pursued what I am inclined to think was a normal course; I retailed the variety of preoccupations; worries about the child, the household, financial anxieties. Mrs Klein remained unmoved and unmoving. I was very glad that she did, but that did not lead to the abandonment of my

> grievance. I suppose I expected to be supported in what I considered to be very moderate affluence. Melanie Klein, however, was not easily led away from her awareness of a universe that is not subject to the needs and wishes of human beings, even when they came to her for analysis.
>
> (Bion 1985, p. 67)

He says in his autobiography (Bion 1985) when he was given an interpretation, he used very occasionally to feel it was correct; more usually, he thought it was nonsense, but hardly worth arguing about, since he did not regard the interpretation as much more than the expression of one of Mrs Klein's opinions, unsupported by any evidence. As his analysis continued, he realised more and more that what he had to learn about in analysis was to listen to what his own sense told him.

> I did not become more amenable to her views but more aware of my disagreement. Nonetheless, there was something about that series of experiences with her that made me feel gratitude to her and a wish to be independent of the burden of time and expense of money and effort involved. At last, after some years, we parted. She, I think, felt I still had a lot to learn from her, but she agreed to the termination – partly no doubt through the realisation that enough of WRB was enough.
>
> (Bion 1985, p. 68)

Around 1950, a new flourishing occurred. We can see in his series of papers arising from his group researches at the Tavistock Clinic a sudden change in style that occurred with the fifth of these, 'Experiences in Groups V', published in *Human Relations* in 1950. Here he begins to take off theoretically. It is as if the form of his thinking about his observations changed, and he looked for more inspiration from elsewhere than Rickman. This paper suddenly cites nine works; the rest of the papers cite a total of three (one cited in EiG VI – Toynbee also cited in EiG-V; and Freud twice in EiG-VII) from a variety of disciplines from Gibbon to Halliday, from economics to Anglo-Saxon history. There is a sudden explosion, almost, of new interestingly innovative sources.

Though there is no evidence whatever that this creativity is directly to do with his analysis with Klein, his creativity did begin to stir itself again, during the analysis. Not long after, in 1951 he met and fell in love with Francesca, a social scientist at the Tavistock Clinic. Looking at the love letters to her (see Sayers 2002) he developed a new tone to his writing. He became light-hearted, passionate, romantic, idealised the woman whom he loved and began once again to become excited by life and by the exploration of his mind and his soul. Should this be connected with his analysis, his later self-conscious autobiographical writings appears to claim that Melanie Klein had relatively little effect upon him.

However, his scientific writing, too, conveys a contrary view. In 1952, he attempted to introduce her theories into his review of group dynamics, in a way that some considered restricting of his originality; we know that she considered his interest in groups to be a resistance to proper psychoanalysis. This was written specifically for the symposium of the *International Journal of Psychoanalysis*, to celebrate Klein's seventieth birthday, and appears as a reconsideration of his own groups theories out of a respect for hers.

In 1953, just as his analysis with Klein was finishing, he gave the first of his papers on schizophrenia (titled 'Notes on the theory of schizophrenia' and published 1954) to the International Psychoanalytic Congress in London. She attended this session of the Congress and made a response from the floor, describing the impact that people with schizophrenia have on the analyst. It is so demolishing they either drop the patient and drop working with schizophrenia altogether, or they become extremely positive attempting to deny the negative countertransference. Notes in the archives of the Wellcome Library in London, show that Bion must have shown her a version of the paper, and she prepared her notes before the Congress. She was very involved in her analysand's work. Bion was in turn very much his teacher's pupil, slogging it out with these difficult patients, interpreting their negativity, and collaborating in this with Klein's other loyal followers, Hanna Segal and Herbert Rosenfeld.

At the Geneva Congress, in 1955, he was with Eliot Jacques and Melanie Klein. He writes:

> Melanie is extremely demanding. I suppose it is because she has had so many attacks and so little genuine happiness in her life, that she always feels sucked dry; I don't know quite how it is. I think she fishes for a compliment, gets it, rejects it, and then says 'But all the same, I think he (or she or it or them) is really quite friendly to me'. I am supposed to be in a state of nerves about my paper. In fact, I don't give a damn about it. But she likes to reassure me. Later she will want to stop me being conceited about it.
>
> (Bion 1955a [1985], p. 116)

He was humorously critical of the way in which Melanie Klein was always surrounded by her supporters. 'If Melanie had her way, and she has a lot of it, she would make the whole Klein group quite ridiculous in everyone's eyes' (Bion 1955b [1985], p. 117). His observations of Klein are as ironically humorous as those on people's behaviour in groups. At the same time, a graphic description comes through of a charmingly vulnerable human being, like many of the rest of us.

Nevertheless, between 1954 and 1959, he published no less than six papers, on schizophrenia, using Melanie Klein's theories (Klein 1946), a formidable output of one paper per year, demonstrating perhaps the powerful adherence to her advice to relinquish his interest in groups (and perhaps in

Rickman). It indicates the beginning of a powerful surge of Bion's hitherto quiescent creativity, one which lasted to the end of his life.

The occasional references that he makes to Melanie Klein are always ambivalent and have a grudging note of admiration; he always looks to see what faults he can find in her. It is clear that he was not an easy member of the Kleinian group nor of any group. His discussions in *Attention and Interpretation* (1970) regarding the fraught relations between the mystic (or genius) and the 'Establishment' of a group or organisation, may have been drawn from his own fractious relations with organisations, from his boarding school to the army and onwards. Behind the text there was perhaps his own heartfelt experience of being always against the authorities perhaps, in consequence, one of the reasons he fled London for California in 1967. Such speculation is unverifiable. But the suggestion here is that Bion was still in search of something; as he put it in the quote (1985, p. 67, above) a need to abandon his grievance.

Far away in California, he may have felt more able to become himself rather than the representative of a group, and it was during those years (1967–1979) that his speculative writings changed in the deepest way. His two autobiographical books reveal, however, the deep pain, distress, cynicism and self-distrust that remained intrinsic to his personality. His dialogues with himself are lacerating in quality and it is with a great sense of relief that we can turn to his joyful letters to his wife and to his children. His grievances towards authority, and ultimately towards himself were aspects of his personality that were not cured by his analyses, but which he reconciled himself to live with. Given the cruel contempt he felt for authorities at the beginning of his life, and its translation into the lacerating self-criticism of his later life, may also have been expressed more abstractly in his writing when he said, stoically,

> We find it necessary to differentiate between the pain of a broken leg and the pain, say, of bereavement; sometimes we prefer not to, but exchange mental for physical pain and vice versa. Physician and psycho-analyst are alike in considering that the disease should be recognized by the physician; in psycho-analysis recognition must be by the sufferer too. The physician considers recognition of the pain subordinate to its cure; the psycho-analyst's view is expressed by Doctor Johnson's letter to Bennet Langton: 'Whether to see life as it is, will give us much consolation, I know not; but the consolation which is drawn from truth, if any there be, is solid and durable; that which may be derived from errour must be, like its original, fallacious and fugitive.'
>
> (Bion 1970, pp. 6–7)

And satisfyingly, 'The patient who will not suffer pain fails to "suffer" pleasure'. So, speculatively is he musing on the limited outcome of his analysis – truth but not cure?

Conclusions

What then can we say of the influence of Rickman and Klein on Wilfred Bion? Clearly Rickman introduced him to his own sophisticated study of religion, anthropology and of group dynamics. Rickman's genius was to be able to turn abstract, and inward-looking psychoanalytic ideas into practical plans of action. And complimenting Bion thus, he could help in the wartime experiments – the War Office Selection Boards and Northfield – and the post-war group research they corresponded about. Giving support and strength to Bion's slowly increasing confidence, Rickman remained a truly good friend – may be the only one Bion had.

In his longer analysis with Melanie Klein (1946–1953), did she help him? She gave him the opportunity for an identity with a professional and intellectual group at the very peak of the group's creativity during the 1950s. Such a group identity was, of course, a mixed blessing for Bion with his uncertain self-identity. Did she help with his own personal problems? The suggestion indicated in this paper, was that with the help of both his analysts – John Rickman as a mentor and friend, and Melanie Klein as psychoanalyst – Bion did find a way to flourish creatively in his work, in his intellectual development, and in his family life. Probably not a bad balance sheet.

But Bion gives little acknowledgement. His pervading distrust of all women, apart from his beloved first and second wives, coloured his attitude towards Klein. Clearly, he saw through her, but we can infer that he respected her as an analyst in that she saw through him, and was not deceived and manipulated by him into offering him support for his underlying sense of grievance. With Rickman, he seemed to gain the ability to value others, fell in love with his first wife, and in a sense he fell in love with Rickman. Their enduring relationship at Northfield and throughout wartime Britain saw him begin to turn his acidic cynicism into enquiry, and to debunk conventional ways of thinking.

Bion was something of a success at his analyses, having been such a failure after Oxford, if we measure it in terms of the release of his originality and the capacity to express it in a compelling way. He became one of the most successful people in his chosen career. His analysts – and perhaps his wives – should be most proud of that achievement, together with Bion himself.

Note

1 Rickman observed the group processes in a Russian village when he worked in a Quaker medical unit during the First World War he saw how the village elders (Staritsi) made decisions which accorded with the restoration of good communal relations after a member had committed a crime. If the crime had been committed by an outsider the result was very different.

Chapter 9

Letters to John Rickman

Transition 1939–1951

Dimitris Vonofakos and R.D. Hinshelwood

This chapter examines the transition of Wilfred Bion from troubled First World War veteran to innovative psychoanalytic thinker during the Second World War and its aftermath. It draws upon the recently published letters by Bion to John Rickman.[1] The material is a collection of 29 letters, 27 from Wilfred Bion to John Rickman, one addressed to Mrs Rickman and one from Rickman to Bion (Vonofakos and Hinshelwood 2012).

Introduction

Bion's First World War experience was probably little short of a war neurosis, or as it would now be called a post-traumatic stress disorder, which cast a long shadow down through his life. He was not reserved about writing about it (Bion 1997, 1982, 1985), and his ability to find the right words to convey his feelings was almost certainly one of the most fundamental ways in which he struggled to 'contain' the experience. This cloud over his life began to clear 20 years later from about 1937 when he embarked on his training as a psychoanalyst, until 1951 when he married his second wife. There are probably many contributing factors in this, including his work as a respected (though querulous) veteran in the Second World War, his first marriage in 1940, his two analyses, and his second marriage. Between these two dates, the period of the letters, Bion had an intense attachment to John Rickman, first as an analysand for a period just short of two years, interrupted by the war, and then as a colleague working on the development of psychoanalysis as a tool for thinking practically about groups.

The letters give a window into this evolving collaboration between the two. There is little doubt that the senior partner in this dance of geniuses was Rickman, who had the extraordinary ability to find not just theoretical explanations, but actually useful functions for psychoanalytic ideas in social groups and problems. The point of noting these letters is that they help a little in understanding how that thinking developed, but more than that they plot Bion's slow emergence from his brooding unhappiness, sense of failure and even non-existence, towards a springboard for his enormous creativity.

Covering the period of Bion's mid-life transition, the letters are addressed to Rickman in increasing degrees of familiarity, while one is also addressed to Mrs Rickman thanking her for an evening's hospitality as well as reaffirming the blossoming relationship between the two men. Occasional reference to parts of this correspondence have appeared elsewhere (see Harrison 2000; King 2003). But until recently, this material had not been fully transcribed and published as a complete historical artefact.

The two Wilfred Bions

Study of the letters illustrates a kind of 180 degree turnaround for a man who was all but broken from his terrifying experiences in the First World War and was stumbling along in unsatisfying and unproductive personal and professional relationships. He became the fearless, passionate and innovative 'wunderkind' of the British psychoanalytic establishment leaving a lasting legacy in every psychoanalytic study he was involved in.

In 1940 Bion wrote a lacklustre paper; as Bléandonu starkly writes:

> Bion contributed an essay on the 'War of nerves' written in a rather dogmatic style. This essay bears interesting comparison with the first article he wrote for The Lancet in 1943. The two pieces are very different, and it is difficult to see evidence of the genius of the later works in the laboured lucubrations of the early essay.
>
> (Bléandonu 1994, p. 52)

The letters give a different sense of Bion, and of his experience of himself and others, than the autobiography (Bion 1985). The hindsight gained from having achieved a position of eminence allowed him to create a memory of a very different kind of experience he recorded in the letters.

The autobiography, is now familiar. It was, he said, 'trying to tell the story of *my* business – part of which was the problem of existing' (1985, p. 33), and he does so with a crucifying self-mockery and the most abject descriptions of his worthlessness, 'DSO, Mention in Dispatches, Legion of Honour – all very fast-fading reassurances, which at best had failed dismally to convince me' (ibid., p. 12). He described his interview at University College Hospital, where the dean of the Medical School, he says, 'was again wondering if the unprepossessing mass of ineptitude before him, concealed some possibility that had not so far emerged. So did I, though even less hopefully' (ibid., p. 19). The self-description makes the reader wince, either because of the truth of the pain, or because of embarrassment at the literary exaggeration. But the self-deprecating humour emerges elsewhere. For instance, after the war, 'I cannot remember being awarded a Victory Medal, but I am sure that a grateful establishment would have inflicted one on my completion of so many years of undetected nothingness', (ibid., p. 62). And his attitude to others is no longer as irascible as appeared in the letters, but an affectionate jocularity that went for their whimsical oddities,

> The two Colonels to whom I was subordinate were as civil as their station in life called on them to be. But in war there is no particular reason for joyful anticipation of the prospect of prolonged co-operation. They suggested a billet in Whip-ma Whap-ma Gate. No they didn't know why it was called that. I was made aware that that was the kind of idiotic remark, a display of irrelevant curiosity typical of a psychoanalyst – or more exactly of me.
>
> (ibid., p. 51)

Bion is extremely amusing in that dry English way where the whimsy of others is simply a foil to the amusing worthlessness of himself.

This contrasts with the bitterness of the cynicism in the letters where the humour is acidic, and often more acidic than humorous. For instance, in reporting the papers read at a meeting, he mentions Baynes, the translator of Jung,

> Baynes I find hard to criticize because I have always found, and found again last time, that when they talk of either history or myth the Jungians seem to me to do so with a very inadequate historical or mythological equipment whatever, according to their own lights, their psychological credentials may be. And when I detect quite serious inaccuracies in the first two I begin to suspect the last as well.
>
> (15 March 1940)

And about psychiatric colleagues,

> Unfortunately the fate of genuine psychiatry and psychotherapy seems to me to be wrapped up very closely with the fate of practically every free mental or cultural activity. If 'we' win this war then the position of the Maudsley-minded will not I think be very important. But if the fascist-Nazi-outfit wins then the Maudsley wins and it will be goodbye to any real hope of human advance for many a long years.
>
> (14 December 1941)

The contempt for others in the letters written in the 1940s, contrasts with the self-contempt in the autobiography. What happened, it is not easy to know, and indeed not the job of this chapter to investigate. But it might be worth noting that, in between the two, in 1958, Bion wrote a paper 'On arrogance', where he says about a certain class of patient that they exhibit

> references to curiosity, arrogance, and stupidity which are so dispersed and separated from each other that their relatedness may escape detection. I

> shall suggest that their appearance should be taken by the analyst as evidence that he is dealing with a psychological disaster. The meaning with which I wish to invest the term 'arrogance' may be indicated by supposing that in the personality where life instincts predominate pride becomes self-respect, where death instincts predominate, pride becomes arrogance.
>
> (Bion 1958a, p. 144)

To what extent has Bion taken to heart the full significance of the disasters that he suffered (boarding school, First World War, and the death of his wife straight after childbirth)? It is tempting to think that his subsequent analysis, and his subsequent marriage, helped him to address his scorn and contempt – though his substitution of self-denigration is hardly a full working-through. Whatever the truth of these speculations, the importance of the letters is the slightly different story from the later published autobiography.

Wilfred Bion in the 1920s and 1930s

After the war, Bion had much cause for brooding on his accumulated failures. He did not gain an honours degree at Oxford, and then subsequently while teaching for a while at his old school, Bishop's Stortford College, a boy made an accusation of sexual misconduct (probably quite unfounded), upon which Bion was promptly sacked. Later, while at medical school (University College, London) he felt considerable failure including his fiancée breaking off their engagement, and turned then to therapy. Perhaps on Wilfred Trotter's advice he found a somewhat expensive therapist who offered 12 sessions, but subsequently called this inadequate therapist, 'Dr-Feel-it-in-Past'. However when he was appointed to a job at the Tavistock Clinic, he met James Hadfield, and again embarked on some therapy with Hadfield, again without great benefit. Finally, and obviously with some perseverance, Bion found his way to Rickman for a psychoanalysis in 1937, with the intention of training as a psychoanalyst.

Meeting John Rickman: Rickman was at the time a prominent psychoanalyst in the British Psychoanalytical Society (King 2003). And the two men, although from very different backgrounds, develop an enduring relationship. At the time of their meeting, Rickman was just a few years older than Bion but at a very different stage in his professional career. He had finished his medical studies before the war and due to his Quaker faith, which adhered to pacifistic principles, he opted for travel to Russia to carry out relief work there providing medical cover to rural, isolated parts of the country. On his return, already married to Lydia, he specialised in psychiatry and soon after left for Vienna to be analysed by Freud.[2] He came back from Vienna two years later and took up a post at St Thomas' Hospital in London and was elected a member of the Psychoanalytical Society. From that point onwards until his death, Rickman was integral in the workings of the Society in various roles and capacities: in areas of training, education, publishing and eventually as its third president from 1947–1950. But Rickman did not stop there; he had numerous other associations and posts throughout the three decades of his working life. Some of these were: assistant-editor and editor of the *British Journal of Medical Psychology* for 24 years (1925–1949), editor of the *International Journal of Psychoanalysis*, a member of the editorial team of the Tavistock Institute's *Human Relations* and author of several anonymous editorials in *The Lancet* where he applied his psychoanalytic thinking to everyday social phenomena. All in all, Rickman's capacity for work was truly remarkable.

As a person, Rickman was a large, friendly man, due partly to his Quaker background, a very attentive listener (Kramer 2011). He was fascinated with the study of social phenomena and was very well-read in psychoanalytic literature but also had the ability to write in very simple language and appeal to a wide audience. In fact by the time of their first meeting, and in contrast to Bion, Rickman was already an established psychoanalyst and well-respected social scientist.

Bion's psychoanalytic treatment with Rickman lasted for under two years as it was interrupted when Rickman joined the Emergency Medical Service (EMS) as a Civilian Psychiatrist at Haymeads EMS Hospital,[3] prior to the outbreak of war. However his short period was enough to make a considerable impression on Bion and for a strong positive transference to develop. In fact, his description of his time in analytic work with Rickman is strikingly different from his previous, 'Feel-it-in-the-past' experience:

> To my surprise [Rickman's] interpretations appeared to me to be reminiscent of common sense; they reminded me of real lie. I was astonished because common sense did not seem to be grand enough. Rickman's interpretations and his behaviour stirred up the dead embers of the pile of rubbish which was all that I could see ... ashes ... ashes ... I thought Rickman liked me.
>
> (Bion 1985, p. 46)

Analysis with Rickman seemed to stir up something deep inside Bion's personality for the first time. From that moment a 'new' Bion started steadily emerging over the course of their relationship evolving to become colleagues and friends. By 1951, Rickman attended Bion's wedding, although he died only a few weeks later.

The Bion–Rickman correspondence (1939–1951)

The letters divide into four periods:

1 The analytic phase (9 September 1939–15 March 1940) – five letters (one by Rickman)

2 The student phase (18 December 1940–14 December 1941) – six letters
3 The collegial phase (12 July 1942–7 December 1944) – ten letters (one to Mrs Rickman)
4 The path to independence (13 January 1945–17 June 1951) – eight letters

The analytic phase (9 September 1939–15 March 1940)

The Letters start after the interruption of the analysis, when Rickman went to Haymeads. Bion wrote shortly after, 'I hope it will before very long be possible to do something about the analysis but obviously it has to wait at present' (9 September 1939), and a couple of months later,

> I would like to press on by hook or crook with the whole of my training as, although I have felt very pleased, I have also been able to feel I know enough now to know how much I am still missing.
>
> (7 November 1939)

Rickman replied however with

> nothing definite to say about my return to London for the continuation of our work. All I can say about that is that at the moment I am here and may be moved at any time and anywhere. If I get shifted to London I will certainly let you know.
>
> (4 December 1939)

So Bion wondered rather desperately if

> there could be any objection to my trying to get a little further with my analysis by transferring to someone else for the time being? I hate the idea of it and I do not even know if it is practicable financially; but I should feel happier if I had a talk, say with Dr Glover, about the business if you think something might be gained and nothing lost by doing so.
>
> (30 January 1940)

He is at this point beginning to court Betty Jardine, and will marry her later in 1940, so he may have felt the need to discuss such issues with his analyst. However, there is no mention in any of the letters of his romance, despite it being, probably, an enormously important achievement of the brief analysis. At this stage, the letters are characterised by their formal analyst–analysand relationship, and they address each other with their formal titles (Dr Rickman/Dr Bion).

Up to this point, Bion had been giving his time to the Emergency Medical Service (EMS), set up at the beginning of the war to deal with civilian casualties,

> I've now landed as group psychiatrist and am trying to find out just what that means. It *ought* to mean something really important but it feels at present as if 'passive defence' has eaten its way into the mentality of the service and become a complete lack of initiative.
>
> (9 September 1939)

He seems to find the army work mundane and his characteristic scorn is turned on his colleagues in the EMS. Being in London, Bion gave news of various meetings of the Psychoanalytical Society and various discussions with analytic colleagues. He was vainly trying to continue to make a living as a doctor in Harley Street. However, he appeared resigned to an imminent change and a return to army life.

> I look like being swept into the army. I have been offered a consultant job and as my practice will not come back – I have only seen one new patient since the war and have never had more than two – I can see no other course. I can't pretend to feel pleased about this but it may after all present a very useful opportunity to get work done of which I ought to know more than I know at present.
>
> (15 March 1940)

Whatever disasters underlay his cynicism, Bion felt confident enough to write a chapter for an edited volume by Emmanuel Miller. This was Bion's first published piece, the rather pedestrian 'The war of nerves' (1940). In addition he demonstrated confidence in his own analytic work, which he attributed to his own analysis,

> I have been getting on very happily with my work and the analysis I have been doing has, I think, been fairly good although I knew this can be very deceptive. I've been particularly glad to find that I seemed to be able to draw on quite early bits of my own analysis which I thought I had forgotten.
>
> (7 November 1939)

In 1940, Bion was posted as a 'command psychiatrist' in Northern Command, in Chester and subsequently an 'area psychiatrist' in York. The latter post was viewed by Bion as a demotion; he had expected to remain at general headquarters and help organise the work of area psychiatrists at regional level around the country. The experience did little to change his mind on the value of his intellectual abilities as well as to improve his embittered relationship with the army (Bléandonu, 1994, p. 55).

The student phase (18 December 1940–14 December 1941)

His contact with Rickman intensified. The overt hankering to continue analysis has died away. The letters were now more regular and he took an active interest in Rickman's work,

> I shall be very glad to come over to Wharncliffe and think I can manage it all right. It will be a relief to hear talk which is backed by some psychological knowledge for once.
>
> (18 December 1940)

Rickman was posted to Wharncliffe a few months earlier (August 1940) to build on the experimental work he started at Haymeads, and which eventually led up to the 'Northfield experiment' with Bion in early 1943. Rickman's innovative work at Wharncliffe contrasted with Bion's post at York, where he seemed to have felt both alienated and unappreciated by his superiors often alluding to his own superiority,

> I wrote a memorandum on a scheme for a special hospital training which I sent to my D.M.S. [Defence Medical Service] and Rees. It has not had one single comment made upon it except that Rees said the style was 'too diffuse'. So we take our psychotherapy fairly lightly here.
>
> (18 December 1940)

Rickman, however, gave generous attention, which strengthened Bion's sense of confidence in his own ideas,

> Just a line to thank you for making me so very comfortable at Wharncliffe last weekend. I enjoyed seeing you again very much indeed and it was most refreshing to get somewhere where at least a sane attempt was being made to get work done.
>
> I dug out my memorandum when I got back here and was pleased to find that it did seem to suggest something like the scheme you are in fact carrying out. Not the least value of a parallel military training course seems to me to be that a patient is given a world to adjust to that is nothing like so severe as the isolated unsupported world which is presented to him by the bed-ridden existence, aimless and disoriented, which he has to face in the special hospitals.
>
> (9 January 1941)

Here Bion pleads with Rickman to 'get him invited' to the hospital and he starts forwarding his ideas to Rickman in the form of memoranda. Bion was now writing as to his mentor, a man of experience, generous with his time, and encouraging Bion's to take an interest in therapeutic environments.

Furthermore, he has now become 'My dear Rickman' and the letters discuss more personal matters including his new wife, Betty Jardine's, acting career as well as instances when Rickman had visited them both at home. In stark contrast is his personal frustration at the lack of professional recognition for himself,

> They look pretty indifferent and out of date on going over them but I send them unchanged. It is a comment on our outlook that although Rees has had them in his pocket for 7 months there has never even been a {breath} of discussion.
>
> (4 February 1941)

Seemingly, he can only hang on to Rickman's coat-tails at this time, 'I hope I shall be at the next meeting you have at the Wharncliffe. Please get me invited!' (4 February 1941). And Rickman is courteous apparently in offering a full critique of Bion's ideas (27 July 1941).

Reflecting on his experience of his post in York, Bion is amused and somewhat supercilious about the army's attitude to psychiatrists; and typically, the psychiatrists also come off badly,

> the position of the Maudsley people, and of others in the same line of business in the army, extraordinarily weak ... one of my strongest impressions during this second dose of the army has been the feeling of amazement at the lack of elementary knowledge of hygiene (mental) in the layman and a corresponding misgiving, to use no strange word, that the psychiatrists had failed very seriously in their education of the public.
>
> (14 December 1941)

There is no doubt for Bion who is to blame, which 'can only belong to those who never make any attempt to tackle those latent anxieties. The Maudsley-minded look askance at the psychiatrists who *do* tackle those fears – but do nothing themselves' (14 December 1941). There is no detailed description of what work he was doing, or what the many reports and memoranda are about – perhaps that was secret material a censor would cut. But we can see from subsequent research on the War Office Selection Boards (WOSBs) that he was in fact developing these ideas, and forms of practice (well summarised in Harrison 2000). These memoranda no longer exist, but clearly Rickman had a significant contribution from a distance, and appears to have inspired Bion with his own ideas on rehabilitation and therapeutic environments at Haymeads and Wharncliffe.

The collegial phase (12 July 1942–7 December 1944)

In this period Bion and Rickman's most famous work took place. Their short-lived 'experiment' at Northfield Military Hospital was very influential. They work now as colleagues, sharing ideas,

> I do not know why you say you owe anything to my performances; it is quite clear to me that the indebtedness is all the other way and I, in common with all others who have had the good fortune to have your criticism and help, have felt that anything I have done springs time and again from a stimulating and productive line of though suggested by yourself. If you tried to dispute this I could easily muster an overwhelming number of votes against you!
>
> (7 December 1944)

From early 1941, Bion had been in Edinburgh developing new forms of officer selection, WOSBs. Bion has been credited with the core idea of the leaderless group, though this has been disputed (Vinden, 1977). Nevertheless, Bion and his colleagues, Trist and Sutherland, spotted the potential of this novel exercise for officer selection (Bion 1946).

At last, Bion does write in more detail, balancing, as it were Rickman's ideas. The first of these letters (12 July 1942), much longer than its predecessors, makes three significant and important points.

- *The place of psychiatrists*: Bion now recognises much more respect within the army for the contribution of psychiatrists, reporting 'the emergence of the psychiatrists as the leg on which the whole organisation hangs' (12 July 1942). Not that it remains constant, for his derogatory attitudes emerged a year later, 'Army psychiatry is I think now settling down – down is the operative word – to the banal and fool proof level of all R.A.M.C. [Royal Army Medical Corps] Activity' (7 July 1944). However, Bion was growing in stature, both in the army, and also in the growing equality with his mentor.
- *Tackling pessimism*: Bion sees his role as curing the mental state he calls pessimism, and he congratulated himself on his success; he is satisfied with

> the influence we have had in checking quite dangerous pessimism and doing something to change it into suitable activity. In this respect I felt myself to have played a big part; because when I first met the A.G. [Adjutant General] he was saying that officer material was bound to deteriorate and indeed this had been published in an official document circulated to all boards and elsewhere. I tackled

> this point at once and pointed out that it was quite fallacious. I said that by all [permanent?] officers should not deteriorate in an army at war and that on the contrary the army, if all were well, should sprout officers. I said that if it has not doing so it was because the climate was wrong and that as soon as a new atmosphere was abroad one could expect the new shoots to come in instead of being frozen off.... I flatter myself that I was the first person to put this view and that I almost instantaneously reversed the direction of thought about officer production.
>
> (12 July 1942)

- *Colleague selection*: Although posterity has assigned to Bion the provenance of the leaderless group idea, he did not mention this at all in his description to Rickman in this, or subsequent letters. Instead the idea he was proud of is different, though related: 'But the thing about which I am keenest is to come to the touch tomorrow. I have been saying that no candidate should be allowed to come forward unless he has been voted for by his platoon or company' (12 July 1942). And his enthusiasm is so strong that he sees a future for his ideas radically converting selection processes across a wide sweep,

> In other words in this country the filter of examinations, selections etc. is so defective that there is nothing to choose between the filtrate and the original liquor.... And it seems to me that the work that the army does in this matter of selection is something which will *have* to be applied, when peace comes, by all examining and selecting boards in this country, whether for Universities or Scholarships, or Civic Service, or, most formidable strong-hold of all, for Parliament itself.
>
> (12 July 1942)

Bion then solicited Rickman's co-operation, 'the point I am really anxious about is to engage you interest in the matter and beg you seriously to consider applying to come into it' (12 July 1942). He is no longer the supplicant, and his confidence has shot to the other end of the scale.

There was a long gap in the correspondence of nine months or so because, finally, they worked together. Rickman on being made major had been transferred to Northfield in July 1942, and took responsibility for a psychiatric ward. Probably with Rickman's influence, Bion arrived at the beginning of January 1943 to take responsibility for the training wing which took soldiers for rehabilitation back to active service. Though they had different responsibilities, they clearly collaborated over the ideas behind the practical development of Bion's wing. And both were moved on when the experiment provoked opposition from the military authorities.

They met socially now, and after one evening Bion wrote to thank Mrs Rickman for her hospitality, and commented on the disappointment after Northfield, though Bion still personalised it, 'that for the time being I shall have to be working without Major Rickman' (1 March 1943). No doubt part of that meeting was to plan the influential paper on Northfield published in *The Lancet* later that year (Bion and Rickman, 1943 [1961]).

The existing letters for some time report little except progress on drafts of the paper. Bion returned to work at WOSBs now at Winchester. And he expresses the opinion that

> The more I look at it the more it seems to me that some very serious look needs to be done along analytical and field theory lines to elucidate the problems underlying the promotion of leaders and governors and the present system by which those people are recruited from the 'self-selected minorities'.
>
> (7 March 1943)

The reference to Lewin's 'field theory' came from Bion's association with Eric Trist[4] on the WOSBs (in Edinburgh), but Rickman too was aware of Lewin. Disappointed at no longer working together, they could write a paper together, and feel the collegiality in their common ideas. Though there was hesitation, 'I felt very dis-satisfied with my part and the alterations seem to have made it worse' (12 November 1943), Bion was now being consulted, 'Maine [*sic*] said he was going to suggest a meeting with yourself and myself on Saturday night' (12 November 1943). And, 'Wilson, Hargreaves and Rodger had a sort of confab with me about the P. of W. and I gave my views' (13 January 1944). There were clearly War Office projects that both Rickman and Bion were now being asked their opinion on – a project on 'officer reception', and rehabilitating prisoners of war. At difficult times however, Bion's mocking cynicism still comes through, 'I begin to see the supreme merits of not seeing too much' (13 January 1944).

The letters become infrequent during 1944. Betty became pregnant in May–June, and in July, Bion went for a while to France shortly after D-day. After the disappointment of the project they worked on so closely, they were going their own ways. In December 1944, Rickman suffered his first heart attack, and was discharged from the army. Again Bion is disappointed to lose his colleague, and gives him another tribute, 'I do not know why you say you owe anything to my performances; it is quite clear to me that the indebtedness is all the other way' (7 July 1944).

By this time, there was a collegial relationship between the two men. Though he still lapsed at times into his humorous mocking of the inadequacies of his colleagues, his work returning to the WOSBs, was enormously respected.[5] His paper on the core idea of the WOSBs in 1946, unfortunately but typically does not acknowledge others. One of the great things that Bion seems to have learned from Rickman, and perhaps helped to maximise, was Rickman's talent for making psychoanalytic ideas practically useful, and not just theoretically explanatory.

The path to independence (13 January 1945–17 June 1951)

During this period, Rickman had recovered from his first heart attack, but was now out of the experimental world of military technology. He was discharged from the army on medical grounds and returned to civilian life. He continued to be organisationally active at the British Psychoanalytical Society and at the Tavistock Clinic establishing good relations between these two institutions, and also advising on the regeneration of the Cassel Hospital when Tom Main arrived there. From now on the letters are sparse. Nevertheless, all the thinking they did together formed the backbone to Bion's groundbreaking, post-war work in group dynamics.

In response to a long letter from Rickman which seems to have continued his thinking, Bion writes reflectively,

> As I see it there are two main threads in society which are tolerably clearly defined: it seems to me that it is the nature of the human animal to combine two contradictory characteristics. He is, for want of a better word, extremely ambitious and he is also physically very poorly endowed. The latter characteristic forces him into close associations which the former make him unable to tolerate.... The second thread seems to me to be the way in which society lends itself to the progress of the very ambitious solitary. He cannot admit his dependence and cannot tolerate equality; as a result he goes into politics where he hopes to achieve predominance for himself.... As a result communities are always controlled by those sections of the populace which are the most cantankerous and quarrelsome.
>
> (13 January 1945)

On 27 February Bion's first child, Parthenope, was born while he was in France and three days later Betty died of a pulmonary embolism. He had both an emotional and a practical turmoil to sort out. So after a long ten-month gap Bion wrote soberly, 'Many thanks for your note. I am sure you are right about a paper on the Intra-groups tension idea but I feel singularly unable to produce anything worthwhile' (27 November 1945). He did not mention his family tragedy, though of course they may have had personal or telephone contact. Nevertheless he extemporises in the letter with a number of conditions for group therapy, including the happy injunction, 'The individual must be allowed to go hang in the sense that interpretations are primarily directed to that aspect of his associations which are significantly shared by the group' (27 November 1945). He was back at the Tavistock now, and starting a group 'next Friday' (30 November).

On 1 January 1946, Bion took the first staff group at the Tavistock with some 30 people. His letter of the next day gives a good picture of the way he worked as he began his 'Tavistock groups'. One particularly vivid segment is the following,

> The group hunted round a bit and then Dr. Stein took the floor to explain, since I wouldn't, what he thought Dr. Bion wanted. The group fell on this with gratitude and Dr. Stein took over the group. Then they petered out again. Then the topic of Dr. Bion cropped up, but without much assistance from Dr. Bion. A certain amount of heat began to be generated at this point and I then intervened to point out that they were angry with me because it was becoming clear that when I had said 'group therapy' I meant 'group' therapy and not therapy by Dr. Bion. I said that when I hadn't taken the lead they had first fallen back on themselves and had then squeezed Dr. Stein into the job since I wouldn't.
>
> (2 January 1946)

He did not give details of his patient group, but promised to talk of it when they met. But continued with his speculations in the next letter, after apparently a productive reply from Rickman,

> I find that one important thing with patients – dreadfully important and I kick myself for not having seen it before – is the need to let them make their own experiments and approaches however hard and sterile they may appear to be.
>
> (28 January 1946)

Soon after, he was demobbed (May 1945), and finally restarted his analytic training. He began an analysis with a new psychoanalyst, Melanie Klein, perhaps at the recommendation of Rickman who had also been to Klein before the war.

The letters then lapsed for some years. When he is courting Francesca, and they are house hunting, Rickman wrote, perhaps to congratulate the couple. In his reply, Bion is affectionate, and the grating cynicism and mockery has abated,

> Your second letter also was very welcome. Not only for the news it brings, but because it comes from you with whom I started my first steps on the path to this goal. There must be a great many who have you to thank for that and I hope it makes you as pleased to know it as I think it should.
>
> (19 April 1951)

The final letter (17 June 1951) was soon after the wedding with Francesca (9 June 1951) thanking Rickman for his wedding present, a bowl. Both Francesca and Wilfred sign the letter. Two weeks later Rickman died of another heart attack.

The tone of his writing in this last phase looks increasingly familiar as he discusses 'the nature of the human animal', the contradictory characteristics human beings are endowed with, the friction between society and the individual as well as the new, tentative concepts he is coming up with in an effort to conceptualise human relationships. We are also afforded a close look at how he conceptualised the 'essentials' of group therapy and how all this was run through and discussed with Rickman in concise but detailed letters. Their close relationship seemed to have continued undiminished after the end of the war, despite the less frequent letters. He still drew inspiration from Rickman.

Conclusion

The study of this collection of personal letters complements Bion's later autobiographical work accounts. We witness an evolving relationship between the two men which gradually transforms their association from one being characterised by analytic transference to an energising and inspiring mentorship. Rickman's influence appeared to have been solidly therapeutic at first (Bion's first marriage) but then to have planted the seeds for Bion's later work in group dynamics and psychoanalysis. This is most evident in Bion's excitement with Rickman's work in therapeutic institutions, at a time when little seemed to interest Bion. During that 'student' period, Bion was introduced into a new area of work, the social field.

In their joint work on therapeutic institutions for the rehabilitation of soldiers, there was little Bion could draw on other than his intensely personal experience at boarding school, and in the army in the First World War. That period might be called Bion's crash-course in social and institutional processes. Its lasting effect on him endured through his group work at the Tavistock in the 1940s, and on to the speculative work in *Attention and Interpretation* (Bion 1970) in Los Angeles. He never really left his interest in the 'nature of the human animal' (13 January 1945). Perhaps it served an emotional purpose, too.

The change of tone in Bion's writing is most evident following his involvement in the work of the WOSBs and his subsequent letter to Rickman outlining his involvement and inviting him to join the work undertaken there (12 July 1942). This represented the first documented instance where Bion was able to channel his military experience and insight into the production of original, groundbreaking work. This transformative process is now clearly seen to owe a great deal to Rickman's supportive presence.

In her study of another collection of Bion's letters (1951–72), those to his fiancé and second wife, Francesca, Sayers (2002) argues that it was their love affair which altered his perceptions of himself and the world. The evidence of these letters to Rickman is that the metamorphosis from 'Bion the troubled' to 'Bion the creative' was a slower process that took place during the evolving relationship with Rickman and that 'love' affair which was formed in the idealisation of the transference.

Notes

1 These letters are housed in the Archives of the British Psychoanalytical Society, in London. We are grateful to the Honorary Archivist, Ken Robinson, for permission to have them published and to the staff of the Institute of Psychoanalysis library for help with finding these letters. We also thank Tom Harrison for originally mentioning their existence. We have asked Francesca Bion, Bion's widow, and Lucy Baruch, Rickman's daughter, about the other side of the correspondence but it appears to be no longer in existence. The archival and research work for this project was supported by a grant from the Institute for the History and Work of Therapeutic Environments (IHWTE) and Planned Environment Therapy Trust (PETT).

2 Later in his life, and prior to his initial meeting with Bion, Rickman would have further analytic sessions with both Ferenczi and Klein.

3 Rickman saw fundamental differences between the First and Second World War thinking that in the latter case the (Quaker) stance of non-participation would not suffice and was not morally correct (Harrison, 2009, personal communication).

4 'Field theory' had been developed by Kurt Lewin by applying gestalt psychology to social groups. In 1933 Lewin, like the entire staff of the Frankfurt School, emigrated to the US. He stopped briefly in England where Trist met him. Later Trist spent time in the US after he graduated in 1935, and again contacted Lewin then at the Centre for Group Dynamics at MIT.

5 See Hinshelwood (1999) for archival material demonstrating the respect Ronald Hargreaves, at the War Office, had for Bion over others who had worked at Northfield.

Chapter 10

Freud's influence on Bion's thought

Links and transformations

Christina Wieland

I this chapter I shall restrict myself only to one aspect of Bion's work – Freud's influence.

Bion, especially early Bion, is regarded generally a Kleinian and there is no doubt that Klein (who was his second analyst) exercised a pervasive influence on him and his work. At the same time we can say that Bion's work is to a great degree an extensive dialogue with Freud. David Bell goes further when he writes that Bion's work can be thought of as an 'English return to Freud' (Bell 2011). In this he particularly stresses that Bion like Freud 'makes a distinction between the world as it is and the world as I would like it to be' (Bell 2011: 84). This stress on the distinction between the reality principle and the pleasure principle remains central throughout Bion's work and gives a fundamentally classical quality to his work.

I shall argue that this classical approach to psychoanalysis, due to Freud's pervasive influence, permeates Bion's work while at the same time new radical developments take place. Sometimes defined and referred to by name, at other times Freud's influence is simply implied. Yet at other times Freudian concepts such as 'repression' or 'the unconscious' remain but their meaning has changed and is defined by the new theory of the mind that he introduced. Sometimes he is explicit about these changes and sometimes he is not. I shall attempt to examine chronologically Bion's work from the point of view of Freud's influence, both stated and unstated, on his work.

The Appendix shows all the explicit references to Freud in Bion's theoretical works. I have not included his lectures, his autobiographical works, or *The Memoir of the Future* because, valuable and imaginative as they are, do not constitute new theoretical contributions to psychoanalysis.

However there are much more references to Freud than those explicitly stated in the text and in the Appendix. It would be an impossible task to examine all of Freud's references, stated or unstated, and their impact on Bion's theories. In what follows I try to examine Freud's influence at the major junctions in the development of Bion's thought and the transformation of Freudian concepts in the process.

I have structured this paper chronologically around the three periods of Bion's work, which form the three major areas of his thought:

1 groups,
2 psychosis, and
3 theory of thinking.

Experiences in groups

Early papers 1948–1952

Bion's first innovative work was in the theory of groups. His theory of group dynamics came directly out of his work with therapeutic groups at the Tavistock Clinic and was therefore based exclusively on group experience. *Experiences in Groups* was first published in 1961 and comprised of several papers on groups published between 1948 and 1952 as well as of an extensive chapter entitled 'Re-View'.

Freud is not mentioned very much in the original papers but Freud's strong presence is felt through Bion's new important concept of the 'work group'. One cannot avoid the conclusion that the work group (*W*), which is task oriented and based on the co-operation of the members of the group, is based on Freud's reality principle. And Bion himself recognised the similarity of his *W* with some of the characteristics that Freud attributed to the ego (1961, p. 127). However Bion's dichotomy between 'work group' and 'basic assumption group' does not follow Freud's dichotomy between reality principle and pleasure principle. Rather the basic assumption groups are based on Melanie Klein's psychotic mechanisms. So already the bringing together of Klein and Freud to create a new perspective, that Bion has achieved in his later works, begins here.

The Re-View itself is a protracted debate with Freud but only as a way of clarifying his differences from him. He concludes that Freud's theory of groups as governed by family dynamics is not so much wrong as incomplete. Bion makes a bold statement:

> I think that the central position in group dynamics is occupied by the more primitive mechanisms that Melanie Klein has described as peculiar to the paranoid-schizoid and depressive positions. In other words I feel ... that it is not simply a matter of the incompleteness of the illumination provided by Freud's discovery of the family group as the prototype of all groups, but the fact that this incompleteness leaves out the source of the main emotional drives of the group.
>
> (1961, p. 188)

Nowhere did Bion confront Freud so directly and in such detail as in the Re-View, which is basically a long, protracted debate with Freud. However, as this debate with Freud's ideas was written after the theory had already been formed, it cannot count as influence although we can say that it is not possible that Bion did not have Freud's ideas in mind as he made his observations in group dynamics, however much he tried to divest himself of all 'memory and desire'.

Second Thoughts

Theory of psychosis – attacks on thinking and bizarre objects

A look at the Appendix shows us that, throughout his work, Bion used the same Freud papers again and again. Amongst these papers Freud's 'Formulation of the two principles of mental functioning' published in 1911, occupies a central position. One cannot overstate the influence that this paper had on Bion as it permeates his work and appears again and again either in an explicit or implicit way. It forms a kind of leitmotiv that constantly reminds us of Bion's dedication to the reality principle and to scientific work.

The discussion of Freud's paper in some detail introduces a new element into Bion's work which had been up to that point based on Klein's theories. The development of a 'mental apparatus' whose function is to apprehend, and work with, reality (both external and internal) makes its appearance first in Bion's 1956 paper 'Development of schizophrenic thought' and in more detail in his 1957 paper 'The differentiation of the psychotic from the non-psychotic personalities'. In this sense Freud's influence begins here. The 'reality principle', and an 'apparatus' that has as its purpose the awareness of reality, enters a hitherto Kleinian framework and takes central stage. With this a new framework begins to develop, in which Freud and Klein come together in a new, characteristically Bionian way.

Freud's paper delineates the two principles of mental life – the pleasure principle and the reality principle. Freud makes a clear distinction here between 'the older, primary processes' which aims at pursuing pleasure and avoiding unpleasure', and the development of a new principle that aim at establishing what is real rather than what is pleasurable. With characteristic eloquence he writes:

> A new principle of mental functioning was thus introduced; what was presented in the mind was no longer what was agreeable but what was real, even if it happened to be disagreeable. This setting-up of the *reality principle* proved to be a momentous step.
>
> (1911a, p. 219. Italics in the original)

Instead of motor discharge that expresses frustration, meaningful action to change the environment can now be undertaken. But to do this a map of the environment needs to be created in the mind. In other words the establishment of the reality principle presupposes a change in the mental apparatus. Freud explains this by stressing the significance of the sense-organs that are directed towards the external world and the 'consciousness' attached to them.[1] This rudimentary consciousness, in scanning the external world for sense data, develops '*attention*' as a way of meeting the sense data halfway and '*notation*' as a rudimentary memory. *Judgement* comes also into existence as a way of deciding whether something was true or false, i.e. existed in reality or was just a hallucination. Finally Freud lists *action* to be taken to alter the environment.[2] This kind of action is rational action based on the data collected by the scanning of the environment and is fundamentally different from motor discharge calculated to get rid of unpleasant stimuli.[3]

Bion defines psychosis as an attack on the mental apparatus, especially that part of it that is concerned with awareness of external reality (as described by Freud). This attack is so destructive that the mental apparatus is split into minute fragments that are projected out into objects which they engulf. He coined the term 'bizarre objects' to describe the result of the fragments of the mental apparatus being expelled so that they enter into objects in external reality. The bizarre reality that follows this fragmentation, projection and re-introjection of the fragments was Bion's description of an active psychosis.

When the psychotic attempts to re-introject what he has projected he re-introjects only bizarre objects which have now become persecutors. In this way the balance between projection and introjection that leads to a realistic image of the external and internal worlds and to the development of thought, is replaced by projective identification. The link between the external and the internal world is attacked as well as the link between objects. In this process, *thought* itself, including primitive or pre-verbal thought which he sees as the link between ideographs (1957),[4] is also attacked and destroyed. The result is a disaster from which the psychotic cannot recover because, due to the severe splitting and destruction of his mental apparatus, he lacks the very equipment which will help him recover. Bion calls this a primitive disaster which continues to be active.

This conceptualisation of psychosis is different from Freud's idea of psychosis as a withdrawal from reality. It is rather an integration of Klein's theories of splitting, fragmentation and projective identification with Freud's theory of a mental apparatus which has as its aim the perception or reality. The fragmentation and projection of the mental apparatus might appear as a withdrawal from reality as Freud suggested. Bion, however, maintains that the psychotic's ego never completely withdraws from reality but its contact with reality is masked by an omnipotent phantasy whose function is to create a state that is neither life not death. In this way the contact with reality is never completely lost and the phenomena associated with neurosis are never completely absent from the analysis of psychotics. The parallel existence of a psychotic and a non-psychotic personality implies a different type of splitting from Klein's splitting and fragmentation which are part of the paranoid–schizoid position. It implies more Freud's splitting of the ego as described in his paper 'Splitting of the ego in the process of defence' (1938 [1940]).

The second modification he makes of Freud is that the withdrawal from reality is an illusion which depends on the attack and mutilation of the apparatus for awareness of reality.

The conclusion is that the psychotic contains in his personality a part that is neurotic and a part that is psychotic. These parts co-exist in 'negative juxtaposition' to each other.

So Bion implies two types of splitting in this paper. First, the excessive splitting and attack on the mental apparatus which can be better described as fragmentation. This relates to Klein's differentiation between splitting and fragmentation in her paper 'A note on depression in the schizophrenic' (1960). In demonstrating fragmentation Klein evokes Schreber's splitting of himself into 60 souls (Freud 1911b). For Bion the two types of splitting would be (1) the attack on the mental apparatus and its fragmentation; (2) the splitting between the psychotic and the neurotic part of the personality which is more in line with Freud's notion of the splitting of the ego as described in his papers on 'fetishism' (1927a) and his posthumous paper 'Splitting of the ego in the process of defence' (1938 [1940]).

Due to this parallel existence of a neurotic and a psychotic personality, the psychotic has an awareness of the external world in the non-psychotic part of his personality which also makes psychoanalytic treatment possible.

However this is not without its precedents in Freud who also remarked that psychotic patients very rarely withdraw from reality completely. He writes:

> The problem of psychoses would be simple and perspicuous if the ego's detachment from reality could be carried through completely; but this seems to happen only rarely or perhaps never. Even in a state so far removed from reality of the external world as one of hallucinatory confusion, one learns from patients after their recovery that at the time in some corner of their mind (as they put it) there was a normal person hidden, who, like a detached spectator, watched the hubbub of illness go past him
>
> (1938, pp. 201–202)

Also it has been brought to my attention that Mauritz Katan also postulated a psychotic and a non-psychotic part of the personality, before Bion's present formulation, at an IPA Congress where Bion also presented a paper (Bob Hinshelwood: personal communication).

However what Bion added was that every personality, not only the psychotic, contains these two parts, a neurotic part and a psychotic part, and that it is the prevalence of the one over the other that determines whether a person is neurotic or psychotic.

This last statement changes not only our perception of psychosis and neurosis but also what normality, or what human nature, is. This leads to a different view of disturbances in the personality and therefore how psychoanalytic treatment is conducted. For we cannot avoid the conclusion here that even in a neurotic personality what needs to be treated is the psychotic part. This is in line with Kleinian thinking about the deepest levels of the mind and with Kleinian analysis. However Bion's model of a *mental apparatus* comes directly from Freud. The very notion of a mental apparatus has no equivalent in Klein.

I have gone into some detail discussing this paper as the marriage of Freud and Klein achieved here is to continue throughout Bion's work. Freud's apparatus for the perception of reality and Klein's concepts of splitting, fragmentation and projective identification come together to form this new theory of psychosis.

Hallucination and attacks on linking

Bion continued to explore psychosis in his subsequent papers. In his paper 'On hallucination' (1958b) he discusses in some detail Freud's paper 'Constructions in analysis' (1937) where Freud discusses psychotic symptoms as an attempt by the patient to cure himself. Expanding on this Bion discusses hallucination as a 'way of unburdening the psychic apparatus of unwanted stimuli' (1958b, p. 79) in this way bringing the discussion back to Freud's two principles.

But Bion's final formulation of psychosis is in terms of an attack on links elaborated in his paper 'Attacks on linking' (1959). Freud's influence is weak here and the paper is overwhelmingly Kleinian.

Theory of thinking – alpha function and reverie

Bion's theory of thinking came directly out of his work on psychosis where the attacks on thinking and linking were central in understanding the psychotic's state of mind. The inability of the psychotic to bear reality – external or internal – led Bion eventually to the idea that reality, whether external or internal, was only bearable if it was filtered through the mind and was transformed into symbolic units. This can only happen originally through another mind. This other mind is usually the mother's.

The mother's capacity to 'digest' the baby's emotional experience, i.e. the baby's own reality, and return it to him in a form he can take back into himself is what Bion called 'alpha-function'.[5] Bion imagines an exchange between mother and baby whereby the baby projects into the mother his fear of death. The mother after she has been able to digest this experience in her own mind she gives it back to the baby in a form that he can take back into himself. In this exchange between mother and baby the baby does not just take back his own experience, but also the mother's capacity to deal with it, i.e. *her* alpha function. In this way the baby's capacity to tolerate his own experience increases as his alpha function develops slowly out of the mother's alpha function. This presupposes a *present* mother tuned into the baby's experience.

The transformation of Freud's mental apparatus into 'alpha function' is arguably Bion's most lasting contribution to psychoanalysis. In this new view of the mind the mental apparatus is not formed through the demands of reality alone, but through another mind capable of taking in another person's reality. The demands of reality are made bearable only through another mind capable of bearing reality. The *present* object is important here.

However, a more complex process emerges as Bion, like Freud, saw *thought* emerging as a result of an *absent* object. Only the absent object can become a thought, and in this sense thought comes in to bridge the gap that the object leaves. However, his consideration of the conditions under which thought arises combines once again Freud and Klein. For thought can emerge only if the baby can tolerate absence. And the baby can tolerate absence only if he *can tolerate frustration*.

So, although thought arises out of an *absent* object, the toleration of frustration depends partly on a previous *present* object (and partly on the innate personality of the baby). Bion attributed to the baby's innate personality and innate capacity to tolerate frustration an important part in this process. In optimal circumstances these two factors work together and the adaptation of mother and baby to each other is very important.

This combination of a present *and* an absent object to create 'thought', and an 'apparatus for thinking', is important in the theory. Here we see once again the meeting of Freud's idea that thought and absence are related (1925) and Klein's idea that meaningful absence is really loss – the loss of something the baby felt he once possessed and possesses no more (1935) – and therefore thought depends on the baby's capacity to mourn the object. But what Bion adds is the intermediary step, the most important step in the creation of thought – the creation of alpha function. In this sense no mourning can proceed if alpha function has not developed.

The development of alpha function and of thinking depends on the mother's capacity for *reverie*. Reverie is another term coined by Bion to describe the mother's (and the analyst's) state of mind. In *Learning from Experience* he defines it as 'being open to the reception of any "objects" from the loved object and is therefore capable of reception of the infant's projective identifications whether they are felt by the infant to be good or bad' (Bion 1962: 36).

The concept of reverie has a great deal in common with Freud's 'free floating attention'. Yet the framework is very different and therefore changes the concept itself. The framework is one of object relations and of the baby's *intentional action* (projective identification) to reach the object. This makes reverie such a different concept – one that takes into consideration that very interaction between mother and baby and analyst and patient – yet one that owes a great deal to Freud's free floating attention.

The similarities with, and differences from, Freud's framework are now clearer. Freud's 'mental apparatus' emerged as a result of 'searching the environment' as described in 'The two principles' (1911a). Alpha function, on the other hand, emerges as a result of the projection of the baby's impulses into a mother who is capable of receiving them and transforming them into something that the baby can take back into himself. The transformation of Freud's mental apparatus, a formation that is the result of an *isolated individual* 'searching the environment', into 'alpha function', a function that is the result of an *emotional relation to an object* capable of receiving the projections and of transforming them, is a transformation of both Klein and Freud.

We can say that 'searching the environment' has a different meaning for Bion from that of Freud. The mother searches for any need that comes from the baby, and the baby searches for a suitable 'container' (another one of Bion's original contributions to psychoanalysis).[6] Mother's mind as a realistic container of the baby's anxieties includes mother's need to understand the baby's needs. In this K – the emotional wish to know another human being – is very important. It could be argued that Freud's free floating attention has the same emotional meaning of needing to understand another human being and in this case Bion's new concept of reverie is only an elaboration of Freud's original (clinical) formulation within an object relations framework.

Learning from Experience

Alpha function and its vicissitudes

Learning from Experience is a treatise on alpha function, its development, its failure and its reversal/distortion/perversion. Freud's mental apparatus and Bion's 'apparatus for thinking' have now been transformed into 'alpha function' which has more in common, not with Freud's 'thought', but with Freud's 'dreamwork'. Not surprisingly then that in *Learning from Experience* the most frequent references to Freud come from *The Interpretation of Dreams* (1900a, 1900b).

Dream, dreamwork and contact-barrier

Bion's understanding of the dream and its function within the psyche differs from Freud's but he shares with Freud the importance and centrality of the dream within the psyche. Bion's concept of dreamwork is synonymous with alpha function that transforms experience into alpha elements. The dream is the mental representation and transformation of experience into 'mind'. What is common with Freud's dream is exactly this function of transformation of experience. However for Bion it is the 'waking dream' (Ferro 2011) that is important.

What does it mean that our experience of the world is a 'dream'? I understand it to mean that it is transformed into symbolic units which are meaningful and coherent and can therefore be built on. The experience can be communicated to others and can be controlled within the personality through the creation of conscious and unconscious and through the regulation of affect. But, and it is a big but, it is not to be trusted as necessarily corresponding to external reality. Meaning and reality are not necessarily the same. The dream does not tell us whether something is true or not. It tells us that it is meaningful, it has a structure, and that it exists in relation to other things internal or external. Maybe that is why Bion had to create the grid – a system that has two axes: the vertical axis representing human meaning in the dream, the myth, preconception, conception etc. and the horizontal axis representing the reality principle i.e. the rigorous testing of whether something is true or not (always within a relationship) which he represented by the horizontal axis.

In Bion's new formulation the dream works through the 'contact barrier' which consists of a fluid accumulation of alpha elements and which both unites and separates conscious from unconscious. He borrowed the term from Freud who used it to refer to the neurological entity that connects the neurons in the brain and which later came to be known as the 'synapse' (Freud 1895). Like the synapse, Bion's contact barrier both separates and unites. He defines the contact barrier as identical to a 'dream' which transforms an emotional experience into alpha elements. In this sense, contact-barrier, the dream, and alpha function are identical.

He gives an example of the operation of the contact-barrier, or of the 'dream' in operation, by referring to a man talking to a friend. The dream, he writes, acts as a barrier to prevent the man being overwhelmed by the emotions that come from talking to a friend while at the same time he remains aware that he is talking to a friend. By contrast, the psychotic, whose alpha function is faulty, cannot achieve this kind of separation of conscious and unconscious. He is aware of everything but cannot make use of his experience as he is overwhelmed by impressions and emotions. Everything is equally present but nothing has any resonance. In this way the dream, or contact-barrier, protects the personality from what would virtually be a psychotic state.

Dreamwork is concerned with the transformation of experience into units of mind but not with their accuracy. This problem Bion addressed with the creation of the grid where the development of thoughts was constantly checked by the reality principle. Scientific work depends very much on this constant check. A well-balanced mind will have both axes operating together.

When the 'dream' and 'alpha function' in Bion's system operate successfully, the stored alpha elements can be either separated from consciousness or retrieved at will and used by the personality as needed. The 'contact-barrier' both separates *and* connects conscious and unconscious.

This is a different type of unconscious from that of Freud's system Ucs, and Bion's contact-barrier is very different from Freud's 'repression barrier'. Bion's unconscious is not repressed because it is not acceptable to consciousness. It is rather separated from consciousness in order to allow the personality to focus on what went on at a particular moment. The communication between conscious and unconscious is a two-way traffic that is regulated by alpha function. In this sense Bion's unconscious is more akin to Freud's preconscious. Bion does not comment on this and it is not certain whether he realised how different his unconscious was from Freud's.

The statement can be made that Freud's 'dream' *gives access* to the unconscious whereas Bion's dream and dreamwork *constitutes* the unconscious which is constantly formed and re-formed and is available for use by consciousness.

Bion's dichotomy is not between conscious and unconscious but between alpha elements and beta elements[7] or between alpha elements and bizarre objects. There is also the dichotomy between 'contact-barrier' and 'beta screen'.[8] The beta screen however has more in common with the notion of a pathological organisation than with the concept of Freud's unconscious. This is in line with Bion's Kleinian framework, his interest in psychotic mechanisms and his dedication to the mechanisms of splitting, fragmentation and projective identification rather than to Freud's theory of the repression barrier and the unconscious.[9]

K, −K and the container/contained model

The theory of K and its relation to the container/contained (represented by the ♀ and ♂ symbols) is the final formulation of Bion's model of 'learning from experience' and is an important formalisation of his theory of the mind and its development – positive or negative. Although K can be at least compared or contrasted to Freud's 'Wissentrieb'[10] Bion does not make any reference to Freud (or to Klein's epistemophilic instinct). K as an emotional experience that defines the interaction between two minds is of course different from both Freud's and Klein's concepts but one cannot help but wonder whether there has been another one of these silent and implicit transformations of classical concepts that Bion has so often achieved. The result of a meaningful interaction between container and contained to create K makes the internalisation of the container/contained possible and leads to the benign cycle known as 'learning from experience'.

However, when frustration or envy predominate, minus K (−K) coupled with a negative container/contained predominates leading to psychotic processes. Minus K (−K) is defined as an internalised object that malignantly and wilfully misunderstands. Bion gives a chilling description of this internalised object:

> its predominant characteristic I can only describe as 'without-ness'. It is an internal object without an exterior. It is an alimentary canal without a body. It is a super-ego that has hardly any characteristics of the super-ego as understood in psycho-analysis: it is a 'super'-ego. It is an envious assertion of moral superirority without morals. In short it is the resultant of an envious stripping and denudation of all good and is itself destined to continue the process of stripping.... The process of denudation will continue till − (♂) and − (♀) represent hardly more than an empty superiority-inferiority that in turn degenerates to nullity.
>
> (1962: 97)

This description of −K and −(♀♂) and of the 'ego-destructive superego' that is installed within the personality has strong similarities with Freud's severe superego that destroys the ego defined by Freud as a 'pure culture of the death instinct' (Freud 1923). Yet once again Bion does not mention Freud.

Other points of debate

Bion's engagement with Freud in *Learning from Experience* is extensive and I have only focused on central points of influence.

There are various minor modifications of Freud's theories that take place in *Learning from Experience*. On p. 29 the co-existence of the pleasure and the reality principle is postulated by Bion. However, this had already been postulated by Klein when she asserted that an elementary ego is there from the beginning of life. Bion however makes no reference to Klein.

Another difference from Freud is to distinguish between different functions of thought: for instance through projective identification thoughts can take the function of evacuation (p. 83). This has already been observed by Bion himself in his papers on psychosis.

On pp. 53–54 he engages with Freud's understanding of consciousness as 'the sense-organ of psychic reality' and finds Freud's theory unsatisfactory. This is an instance where Bion argues clearly and coherently about the advantage of his own theory of alpha function as compared to Freud's theory of consciousness.

Elements of Psychoanalysis (1963)

Freud's influence is felt throughout this book in two different ways – the use of the myth, especially the Oedipus myth; and the creation of the 'grid'.

Myth/dreams

Bion set out to restore the myth 'to its place in our methods so that it can play the vitalising part it has in history (and in Freud's discovery of psycho-analysis' (1963: 66).

The myth has a great deal in common with the dream and we can say that personal myths are a type of dreams that can be used as preconceptions looking for a realisation in the development of thoughts represented by the vertical axis. The scientific work that is needed to be applied on preconceptions, conceptions etc. in the search for K is provided by the horizontal axis of the grid. The horizontal axis is based almost exclusively on Freud's reality principle.

The grid

The grid is a matrix that shows the development of thoughts (vertical axis) as well as the statements that could be made about these thoughts (horizontal axis). Freud's attributes of the reality principle as laid out in 'The two principles' (1911a) enter once again here on the horizontal axis. With the exception of Column 2 the rest of the horizontal axis, *definitory hypothesis, attention, notation, inquiry, action*, are taken from, or related to, Freud's 'Two principles' which Bion uses as the basic blocks of scientific work whether it is carried out in the laboratory, in the consulting room, or in life.

Column 2 represents the basic danger to the discovery of truth and to the scientific endeavour as it belongs to the transference–countertransference feelings that, if not examined and understood, they obscure, or disguise, or deny the true state of affairs. Column 2 is also a place of no curiosity and no doubt.

However as Gerard Bléandonu comments, Freud may be present even in Column 2. He wonders about the Greek letter psi which Bion uses for this column and speculates that this might have been taken from the Greek 'proton psevdos' (the first lie) which Freud used in 1895 to explain hysteria (Bléandonu 1994: 166). However Bléandonu seems to have taken this from Francisco Corrao who first commented on this.[11]

The vertical axis that describes the development of thoughts is based to a great degree on Klein's theory of projective identification; Bion's modification of Freud's theory of dreams and myths; and Bion's own theory of the development of thoughts.

The two axes combine to create a mental space where analytic work, whether in the consulting room or in ordinary life, can be understood. Bion insisted however that the grid should not be used during the session but only afterwards as a space for reflection on what went on.

The grid can be seen as a marriage of Freud and Klein to create a new concept/baby, a new space, or a new way of understanding and working with clinical material. It is a way of encapsulating and formalising his theory of the development of thoughts and of the scientific work that has to be applied on such thoughts. The grid is a continuous reminder of Bion's commitment to scientific work and we know that whatever changes and innovations Bion made to his thinking he never abandoned the grid which figures in all publications of his theoretical works.

Later works – the theory of O; faith; no memory or desire

After the *Elements of Psychoanalysis* Freud's influence on Bion's theoretical work seems to be declining. References to Freud occur frequently in *Transformations* but they are more incidental for the main thrust of the book which is more influenced by philosophers and mystics. However one could argue that the theory of O – 'the thing-in-itself' (a term he took from Kant) – which is unknowable and can be known only if translated into K, is not unlike Freud's (and Klein's) theory of the instincts which can only be known through their mental representations. Again Bion makes no reference to Freud (or Klein).

In *Attention and Interpretation* (1970) and his late book *Two Papers: 'The Grid' and 'Caesura'* (1977), Bion is preoccupied with the state of mind that is proper to the psychoanalyst. He quotes a letter that Freud sent to Lou Andrea Salome in which he talks about 'blinding himself artificially' so that he could 'focus all light on one spot'. From now on Freud's letter becomes central to Bion's development of his clinical thinking in which the state of 'no memory or desire' is seen as the appropriate state of mind of the analyst.

One could argue here that this is a restatement of a state of 'reverie' formulated many years before. Or alternatively that the state of 'no memory or desire' is not unlike the state of neutrality recommended by Freud as the proper state of mind of the analyst or the state of mind for any scientific work. Yet Bion mentions neither of these possibilities and one is left with the feeling that Bion meant something more than neutrality. This something more is encapsulated in the concept of F (standing for faith) and the state of intuition that Bion thought a necessary state for practising psychoanalysis.

The paradox of Bion's later works is that as Freud's letter to Lou Andrea Salome becomes central to Bion's development of his thinking (in fact as central as the 'two principles') the influence of Freud is declining and Bion seems to be using Freud's idea of 'blinding himself artificially' to develop his own ideas of 'F', 'intuitive link', symmetry and polyvalence.[12]

Conclusion

I have argued that Freud's influence on Bion's work has been extensive and pervasive although confined to a few key papers and declined sharply in

Bion's later work. It is not clear whether he read Freud extensively or whether he chose a few key texts and key ideas to engage with, and to integrate into the Kleinian framework. However the use he makes of these key papers and ideas is extensive and transformative.

We can say that Bion used Freud to transform Klein, or used Klein to transform Freud. I think that both statements are true. The result is a new framework where the classical psychoanalytic idea that truth can be discovered by a detached individual observer is integrated into the object-related fluidity of the Kleinian model without giving up the scientific basis of the psychoanalytic endeavour. This resulted in the transformation of the 'mental apparatus' – a concept that evokes a world of technology and mechanics – into the model of 'container/contained' (♂/♀) – an organic, dynamic concept that evokes sex, pregnancy and birth – *but without losing the idea of the reality principle.*

Bion's dedication to the reality principle, and to a scientific approach to psychoanalysis, remained unchanged all throughout his varied work. We can say that Bion's creation of the grid as a system for checking reality away from the passions, desires and frustrations evoked during a session, is a tribute to the reality principle. For him, as for Freud, the aim of psychoanalysis remains the pursuit of (emotional) truth – even if it means the pursuit of the lie or the liar, as it came to mean for Bion in his later work. But even this is not that different from the classical model of psychoanalysis. The examination of symptoms and defensive systems as elaborate lies covering up the truth is Freud's earliest discovery in *Studies in Hysteria* (Freud and Breuer 1895). Work in psychoanalysis has always consisted of understanding, pursuing and exposing the lie but maybe never completely stated as clearly as in Bion's statements.

As I have shown earlier Bion's concept of 'reverie' may illustrate his use of classical concepts in a new way and within a different framework.

Reverie as a state of mother's mind (and of course of the analyst's) exists within an object relations framework. Freud's 'free floating attention', on the other hand, exists within the framework of the isolated individual and of an observer who does not influence his object (in other words within a Newtonian world). This 'isolated individual' 'searches the environment' for sense data and uses judgment to decide what is true and what is not (Freud 1911a).

Bion, with the concept of reverie leading to alpha function, integrated Freud into an object-relations framework. This may well be Bion's greatest achievement. Mother's/analyst's reverie 'takes in' not just sense data from the object, but the baby's/patient's projective identifications. The change of terminology from 'sense data' (a non-intentional entity) to a projective identification (an impulse or a part of the baby/patient that seeks *intentionally* the object) makes reverie a new concept, but one that owes a great deal to Freud's free floating attention.

Mother's capacity for reverie (or lack of it) transforms both mother and baby, both container and contained, and can lead either to growth (or to negative growth). The transformation of Freud's free floating attention into 'reverie' within a Kleinian framework (possibly with the 'silent' influence of Winnicott) is one of Bion's lasting contributions to psychoanalysis. From this, the concept of alpha function follows as an attempt to give a name to the mysterious transformation that takes place between mother and baby or analyst and patient.

To summarise – I have traced most of Bion's new concepts to some influence of Freud's usually integrated into a Kleinian approach. Maybe this is no surprise to anybody as concepts like the mental apparatus, thinking, thought, dreamwork, myth and even K have their origins in Freud. What matters of course is the transformation of these concepts within a new framework. The importance of the scientific method as exemplified by the horizontal axis of the grid is a constant reminder of Freud's lasting influence. The concept of reverie, so much related to alpha function, arguably the most innovative of Bion's concepts, can be traced to Freud's free floating attention. It is less possible to trace concepts like O and F to Freud's influence. In these late concepts Bion seemed to want to expand psychoanalysis beyond the boundaries of Freud and Klein as if he wanted to go beyond Wittgenstein's famous words 'whereof one cannot speak, one must remain silent'. Yet he never abandoned the grid and in this he retained his allegiance to the scientific method.

This paper has been an attempt to show in some detail the extent and the scope of Freud's influence on Bion. The question whether Bion's innovative transformation of Klein through Freud constitutes a new paradigm is left to the reader, and to the future, to judge.

Appendix

Experiences in Groups

BION 141n/FREUD 'Totem and taboo' (1913)
BION 141n/FREUD 'Group psychology and the analysis of the ego' (1921)
BION p. 143/FREUD 'Formulations of the two principles of mental life' (1911a)
BION p. 153n/FREUD (1921)
BION p. 156/FREUD (1921)
BION p. 167/FREUD (1913)
BION p. 167/FREUD (1921)
BION p. 167/FREUD Civilization and its Discontents, 1930
BION pp. 174–180/FREUD (1921)
BION p. 184/FREUD (1921)
BION p. 187/FREUD (1921)

Second Thoughts

'Notes on the theory of schizophrenia'

BION p. 29/FREUD 'The unconscious' (1915a)

'Development of schizophrenic thought'

BION p. 36/FREUD 'Two principles of mental functioning' (1911a)
BION p. 36/FREUD 'Civilization and its discontents' (1930)
BION p. 38/FREUD (1911a)

'Differentiation of psychotic from the non-psychotic personalities'

BION p. 43/FREUD 'Two principles' (1911a)
BION p. 45/FREUD (1911a)
BION p. 45/FREUD 'Neurosis and psychosis' (1924)
BION p. 46/FREUD (1924)
BION p. 47/FREUD (1911a)
BION p. 49/FREUD (1911a)
BION p. 50/FREUD (1911a)
BION p. 54/FREUD (1911a)

'On hallucination'

BION pp. 81–82/FREUD 'Constructions in analysis' (1937)
BION p. 82/FREUD and Breuer Studies on Hysteria (1895)
BION pp. 82–83/FREUD 'pleasure principle', 'unburdening of the psyche' (implied): 'Two principles' (1911a)

'On arrogance'

BION's primitive catastrophe p. 88/FREUD archaeological metaphor

'Attacks on linking'

BION p. 99 'judgement'/FREUD reality principle 'Two principles' (1911a)

'A theory of thinking'

BION p. 112 capacity for toleration of frustration/FREUD 'Two principles' (1911a)
BION pp. 115–116 'consciousness'/FREUD 'Repression' (1915b)

Learning from Experience

BION pp. 4–5/FREUD 'Two principles' (1911a)
BION p. 7/FREUD *The Interpretation of Dreams* (1900)
BION p. 13/FREUD (1911a)
BION p. 25/FREUD 'Ego and the Id' (1923)
BION pp. 28–29/FREUD (1911a) (p. 29 modification of Freud – pleasure and reality principle co-exist)
BION p. 31 (modification of Freud continued)
BION p. 38/FREUD (1911a)
BION p. 48/FREUD (1911a)
BION p. 53/FREUD (1911a)
BION p. 56a/FREUD (1900)
BION p. 56b/FREUD (1911a)
BION p. 57a/FREUD (1900)
BION p. 57b/FREUD (1911a)
BION p. 61/FREUD (1900)
BION pp. 76–78/FREUD (theory of the Oedipus complex – no one paper implied)
BION p. 83/FREUD (1911a)

Notes

BION 2.1.1./FREUD 'Two principles' (1911a)
BION 2.2.1/FREUD *Interpretation of Dreams* (1900)
BION 2.3.1/FREUD (1911a)

p. 102

BION 12.8.1/FREUD *Interpretation of Dreams* (1900)

p. 103

BION 18.3.1/FREUD 'Two principles' (1911a)

p. 104

BION 19.3.1/FREUD *Interpretation of Dreams* (1900)

Elements of Psychoanalysis

BION p. 4/FREUD 'Two principles' (1911a)
BION p. 5/FREUD (Oedipus myth, no particular work implied)
BION p. 33/FREUD (1911a)

BION p. 45/FREUD (Oedipus myth)
BION p. 48/FREUD (attention) (1911a)
BION p. 19/FREUD (Oedipus myth)
BION p. 51/FREUD (Oedipus myth re-interpreted)
BION p. 59/FREUD (1911a)
BION p. 62/FREUD (1911a)
BION p. 66/FREUD (importance of myth as a fact finding tool/Oedipus myth)
BION p. 76/FREUD *Studies on Hysteria* (1895)
BION p. 86/FREUD 'Instincts and their vicissitudes' (1915c)
BION p. 92/FREUD (Oedipus myth/Oedipus complex – no one paper mentioned)

Transformations

BION p. 3/FREUD 'Fragment of an analysis of a case of hysteria' (1905a)
BION p. 18/FREUD 'Beyond the pleasure principle' (1920)
BION p. 36/FREUD 'Two principles of mental functioning' (1911a)
BION p. 39/FREUD (1911a)
BION p. 46/FREUD 'The unconscious' (1915a)
BION p. 59/FREUD 'Neurosis and psychosis' (1924)
BION p. 64/FREUD 'Group psychology and the psychology of the ego' (1921)
BION p. 79/FREUD 'Two principles' (1911a)
BION p. 98/FREUD 'Two principles' (1911a)
BION p. 107/FREUD *Interpretation of Dreams* (1900)
BION p. 115/FREUD (1900)
BION p. 120/FREUD The project of scientific psychology (1895)

Attention and Interpretation

BION p. 3/FREUD 'Group psychology and the psychology of the ego' (1921)
BION p. 17/FREUD 'Two principles of mental functioning' (1911a)
BION p. 28/FREUD (1911a)
BION p. 30/FREUD (1911a)
BION p. 43/FREUD Letter to Lou Andrea Salome
BION p. 44/FREUD (1911a)
BION p. 57/FREUD Letter to Lou Andrea Salome
BION p. 127/FREUD 'The ego and the id' (1923) (implied)

Two Papers: The 'Grid' and 'Caesura'

'The grid'

BION p. 6/FREUD 'Two principles of mental functioning' (1911a)
BION p. 7/FREUD Oedipus myth
BION p. 17/FREUD 'Letter to Lou Andrea Salome'
BION p. 22/FREUD 'Letter to Lou Andrea Salome
BION p. 24/FREUD 'Instincts and their vicissitudes' (1915c p. 125)
BION p. 25/FREUD 'Constructions in analysis' (1937)
BION p. 26/FREUD 'The future of an illusion' (1927b)
BION p. 27/FREUD (1927)
BION p. 29/FREUD (1937)

'Caesura'

BION p. 37/FREUD 'Inhibitions, symptoms and anxiety' (1926)
BION p. 38/FREUD 'Letter to Lou Andrea Salome'
Bion p. 39 'Letter to Lou Andrea Salome'
Bion p. 42/FREUD (1926)
BION pp. 47–48/FREUD (1926)
BION p. 49/FREUD (1926)

Notes

1 By *consciousness* Freud means a here and now consciousness of sense impressions and is not to be confused with the system Cs that exists in conjunction to the system Ucs.
2 The reader will no doubt recognise here Bion's horizontal axis of the grid (with the columns entitled notation, attention, inquiry, action) which examines the data in the analyst's possession – data to do with the session, with patient's utterances, formulations and behaviour and with the analyst's counter-transference.
3 Freud had already examined this in 'The project for scientific psychology' (1895).
4 Bion calls 'ideographs' visual images that preceded words and the combination of which forms the precursor of language. In this way Bion already postulated the *link* between ideographs (not the ideographs themselves) as the important factor in the development of language and of thinking. This is, of course, in accordance with the importance that Klein gave to the notion of integration.
5 Bion used the term *alpha function* specifically because it meant absolutely nothing prior to his use of it. 'The term alpha-function is intentionally devoid of meaning' he writes in Chapter 1 of *Learning from Experience* (1962), thus making sure that it is not to be confused either with Freud's 'thinking' or with Klein's projective identification.
6 Bion used Klein's notion of projective identification in combination with the idea that in normal development a container exists (the breast or mother's mind) to contain and transform the baby's projective identifications. He designated

'container' with ♀ and 'contained' with ♂. In normal development both container and contained are permeated by emotion. He saw normal development following the type of container that he named 'commensal' which he described as follows:

> By commensal I mean (♂) and (♀) . . . are dependent on each other for mutual benefit and without harm to either. In terms of a model the mother derives benefit and achieves mental growth from the experiences: the infant likewise abstracts benefits and achieves growth.
>
> (1962: 91)

7 Bion named sense impressions and raw emotions as 'beta elements'. Beta elements cannot combine with one another and therefore cannot be used for thinking or storing within the personality. They are fit only for evacuation. They need to be worked through by alpha function in order to be transformed into alpha elements capable of being stored within the personality.
8 Bion saw the beta screen as composed not of alpha elements, but not of beta elements either. Beta screen was composed of a 'reversal of alpha elements'. He writes: 'Reversal of alpha elements means the dispersal of the contact-barrier and is quite compatible with the establishment of objects with the characteristics I once ascribed to bizarre objects' (Bion 1962: 25). The bizarre objects, Bion continues, are beta elements plus superego traces. It is obvious from what follows that this kind of barrier does not allow the free exchange of elements between conscious and unconscious. I suggest that Bion's beta screen departs from Freud's pathological repression barrier and has the elements of a psychotic pathological organisation as developed by John Steiner, Rosenfeld and others. This point would necessitate a study of its own and I have not the space to pursue this here.
9 Bion attributed psychopathology to the creation of bizarre objects, beta-screen and minus K rather than to an unconscious rigidly cut off from the conscious.
10 Freud's *Wissentrieb* has been translated differently by different authors. Ronald Britton (1998) translates it as 'epistemophilic instinct'; Chris Mawson (2011) as 'drive for knowledge'; James Fischer (2011) also as 'drive for knowledge'.
11 Francesco Corrao has first noted this in 1981. Corrao writes: 'Psi (.) corresponds to an unknown factor in the personality, probably innate. It evokes the "Proton Psevdos" (Ysterikon)' (Corrao, 1981: footnote 3).
12 The term symmetry is used here in combination with the concept of 'construction'. In some cases, Bion maintains, interpretation is not enough and the 'symmetrical' situation needs to be stressed. He explains the concept of symmetry as analogous to bifocal vision in the domain of visual inquiry. For this, interpretation is not enough. Construction, that can be done with the help of the grid in relative isolation after the session, is the suitable instrument for the demonstration of symmetry and polyvalence. Polyvalence emerges through construction and the use of the C elements of the grid (myth, dreams). He comments: 'The C elements I have sketched out differ from the interpretation, which is usually monovalent, whereas the construction (C elements) is polyvalent' (Bion 1977 [1989]: 2).

Chapter 11

Thoughts, thinking, and the thinker

Bion's philosophical encounter with Kant

Kelly Noel-Smith

> The use I make of an existing theory may seem to distort the author's meaning; if I think so I have acknowledged it, but otherwise it is to be assumed that I believe I am interpreting the author's theory correctly.
>
> Bion, 1991, p. 3

> Do different readings of an author like Bion, whose writings are designedly so open textured, matter? Yes, surely, if they are misreadings. [. . .] Bion's writings are not sacred texts. They are open to criticism and his psychoanalytic writings belong not to any one of us but to the 'systematic ensemble' that is psychoanalysis.
>
> O'Shaughnessy, 2005, pp. 1526–1527

Bion did not formally study philosophy, but his work is peppered with allusions to philosophers: amongst others, to the ancient Greeks; to Descartes; to Hume; and, most of all, to Kant. Bion makes explicit references to Kant's notions of things-in-themselves, empty thoughts, and the primary and secondary qualities of phenomena. What I want to do here is look at both the use, and sometimes the misuse, of Kantian terms by Bion. I intend to show that care needs to be taken in drawing connections between Kant and Bion based on an assumption that Bion is using Kantian terms in a Kantian sense: for, despite Bion saying that he does, he sometimes does not. That said, I do not intend to criticise the *use* to which Bion put the Kantian terms he misappropriates. Bion's departure from Kant is an excellent illustration of a fundamental difference between philosophy and psychoanalysis: Bion, like Kant, looks at how knowledge of the world is possible; but he goes much further to show, as had Freud before him, how *different* minds, psychotic and neurotic, can create different worlds.

Bléandonu divides Bion's work into four 'seasons' which separate his work on groups, psychosis, epistemology and literary art (Bléandonu, 1994, p. 2). My focus is largely, in Bléandonu's categorisation, on the summer and autumn of Bion's productive life, from the mid-1950s to 1970, the period during which Bion produced his most important works on psychosis and on epistemology, including *Learning from Experience* (1962), *Elements of Psycho-Analysis* (1963), *Transformations* (1965), the collected papers and later commentary in *Second Thoughts* (1967) and *Attention and Interpretation* (1970).

How much of Kant did Bion read? Mrs Bion has confirmed, in a personal communication for which I am grateful, that the following books by and about Kant remain in Bion's library: two works by Kant: his *Critique of Pure Reason* and his *Groundwork of the Metaphysics of Morals*; and two commentaries, both by H.J. Paton: one on Kant's *Critique of Pure Reason* (Paton's *Kant's Metaphysics of Experience*); the other on Kant's moral philosophy (Paton's *Kant's Categorical Imperative: A Study in Kant's Moral Philosophy*). We do not know how critically Bion read the primary sources or how much he relied on Paton's commentary and that of Copleston's *History of Philosophy* which Sandler cites as a Kantian source in his paper, 'The origins of Bion's work' (Sandler, 2006). Sandler summarises Bion's sources in a table headed: *Confirmed (writings of Bion and the personal library of Wilfred and Francesca Bion)*. It names philosophers, their references in Bion's work and the use to which Bion put them. Sandler's entry for Kant, which strangely does not include three of the four works which Mrs Bion confirmed remain in Bion's library, refers only to Kant's *Critique of Pure Reason* and Copleston's *History of Philosophy*.

We know, also from Mrs Bion, that it was at Oxford where Bion first seems to have come into contact with Kantian philosophy.[1] There, Bion met Paton, the academic referred to above, an authority on Kant who taught at Oxford from 1917 (just before Bion's arrival) until 1922 (just after Bion left Oxford to begin work as a school teacher). In 1947, Paton produced *The Categorical Imperative: A Study in Kant's Moral Philosophy*, a copy of which remains in Bion's library. Francesca Bion's foreword to *The Long Week-End* tells us that: '[Bion] always recalled with gratitude the talks he had with H.J. Paton,[2] the philosopher' (Bion, 2005, p. 6); and, in 'The days of our years', Mrs Bion says: 'He also remembered with gratitude conversations with Paton, the philosopher, and regretted not having studied philosophy'.[3]

Bion, much more than Freud, acknowledged the importance of philosophy for psychoanalysis. In his commentary *Second Thoughts*, Bion says: '[a] psycho-analyst's experience of philosophical issues is so real that he often has a clearer grasp of the necessity for a philosophical background than the professional philosopher' (Bion, 1993c, p. 152). The critical difference between philosophy and psychoanalysis for Bion is that philosophy is of only theoretical use. The analogy Bion uses in *Learning from Experience* to describe the relationship between philosophy and psychoanalysis is that of pure maths to applied maths (Bion, 1991, p. 63). Kant might have disagreed with this: Kant's conclusion from his *Critique of Pure Reason* is that moral obligations follow from his analysis; and his *Critique of Practical Reason* puts forward the ethical considerations which follow from the first Critique and the Categorical Imperative which provides a well-known maxim as to how we ought to live our lives.

Bion specifically states in 'A theory of thinking' that he shares with philosophers a concern for the same subject matter, hence the resemblance he sees between his theory and philosophical theory (Bion, 1993b, p. 110). Sharing a concern for the same subject matter often includes sharing terms and this is where problems of meaning potentially arise. André Green sees these problems as inevitable:

> [Q]uoting from philosophers forces us, as psychoanalysts, to interpret their ideas to match them with our clinical experience. That is, to accept the fact that deformation of what they said can't be avoided. Kant was an important reference for Bion. But contemporary philosophers will probably complain of Bion's misunderstandings when interpreting Kant's conceptions for his own use
>
> (Green, 1998, p. 653)

There is an important difference between interpretation and deformation, however: deformation of ideas usually leads to confusion and loss of meaning and I am going to suggest that Bion's misunderstanding of some fundamental tenets of Kantian philosophy provides an example of this.

As it was David Hume's scepticism about causation which famously awoke Kant from his dogmatic slumbers and led to Kant's philosophical investigations taking a new direction, we need to remind ourselves what is was that Hume (1711–1776) concluded in his *Treatise of Human Nature and Enquiry Concerning Human Understanding* (Hume, 2004), a copy of which Sandler tells us is to be found in Bion's library (Sandler, 2006, p. 191). Hume asked how we can maintain the belief that we *know* certain things. How can we assume that we 'know' that every event has a cause: that, for example, we have knowledge that night will follow day? Hume argued that our experience only tells us what has happened, not what will happen. It is not analytically (in the philosophical sense) the case that the sun will rise tomorrow just because it has every day until now. We have no justification in our belief in causation but, nevertheless, our belief holds. Why? Because of what Hume describes as the 'constant conjunction' of event 'x' with event 'y'; the leap of faith we make that 'x' – say, day – having been succeeded by 'y' – say, night – in the past, will remain so connected in the future. This is belief, not knowledge, asserted Hume. Kant disagreed: and, in his *Prolegomena to Any Future Metaphysics that will be able to present Itself as a Science* (Kant, 1977), together with his *Critique of Pure Reason* (1929), Kant set out on an epistemological quest to establish what we know and how we know it. We need to look at this to understand the inferences Bion drew from his understanding of Kant.

Kant's quest begins with his contrasting four different types of propositions, into one of which all our statements of so-called knowledge must fall: analytic propositions; synthetic propositions; a priori propositions; and a posteriori propositions. An analytic proposition is one where the predicate is contained in the subject: Kant's example is 'all bodies are extended' (Kant 1929, p. 48, A7/B11); another common example is 'all bachelors are unmarried'. These statements cannot be anything other than true because an essential part of the definition of the subject is contained in the predicate. A synthetic proposition, on the other hand, is one where the predicate relates to, but is not an essential part of, the subject, for example: 'all bodies are heavy'; or 'all bachelors are happy'; or, arguably, 2 + 2 = 4 ('4' not being part of the definition of '2' or '+'). An a priori proposition is one which does not depend on experience at all. Most mathematical propositions fall within this category: you can argue that you need experience of number to understand what the symbols '2' and '+' represent, but you do not need experience to reason that the answer cannot be anything other than '4'. Finally, an a posteriori proposition is one whose validity depends on experience: 'all bachelors are happy', as well as being synthetic, is also an a posteriori proposition because its truth depends on having had experience of bachelors.

Kant looked at the possible combinations of these categories of propositions to structure the epistemological framework within which he then worked. He discounts analytic a posteriori propositions as being contradictions in terms, assumes the validity of analytic a priori propositions and synthetic a posteriori propositions, and then asks the big question: how can we know that our synthetic a priori judgments, a category into which Kant thought all metaphysical questions concerning God, freedom and the immortality of the soul fall, are true?

To answer this question, Kant argues that we need both the experience of the external world *and* the mental constructs to reason about that experience if we are to be able to make a judgement call about whether or not something is real or true. Only from that joint operation of experience and reason will knowledge follow: experience alone cannot be thought about; pure reason alone would have nothing to think about. Synthesis is achieved only when our mental concepts and our perceptions come together to give us knowledge and understanding. Thus Kant's much cited phrase: 'Thoughts without content are empty, intuitions without concepts are blind'. Kant goes on:

> It is, therefore, just as necessary to make our concepts sensible, that is, to add the object to them in intuition as to make our intuitions intelligible, that is, to bring them under conjunctions. [...] The understanding can intuit nothing, the senses can think nothing. Only through their union can knowledge arise.
>
> (Kant, 1929, p. 93 (A 51/B 75))[4]

The knowledge we gain from the union of experience and reason is not of what Kant calls the 'things-in-themselves' of the external world but of their phenomena (see below). The 'things-in-themselves' necessarily remain unknowable. The term 'thing-in-itself' is enthusiastically taken up by Bion and he agrees with Kant, and Freud, that things-in-themselves are unknowable. Freud said: 'Reality will always remain "unknowable"' (Freud, 1938, p. 196). Bion agrees. In, for example, the notes to *Learning from Experience*, Bion states that: 'The term "things-in-themselves" I hold with Kant to refer to objects that are unknowable to mankind' (Bion, 1991, p. 100). Bion follows Freud, too, in his extension of the unknowable to what constitutes the unconscious. Freud said:

> Just as Kant warned us not to overlook the fact that our perceptions are subjectively conditioned and must not be regarded as identical with what is perceived though unknowable, so psychoanalysis warns us not to equate perceptions by means of consciousness with the unconscious mental processes which are the object. Like the physical, the psychical is not necessarily in reality what it appears to us to be.
>
> (Freud, 1915a, p. 171)

And Bion agrees: 'Mental space [is] a thing-in-itself that is unknowable, but that can be represented by thoughts' (Bion, 1970, p. 11). Mancia *et al.*, in their consideration of Bion within a Kantian context, seem to suggest that a Kantian reading of the proto-mental, the phenomena of which are forerunners of Bion's later concept of beta-elements, is one which 'permits knowledge of external reality' (Mancia *et al.*, 2000, p. 1198). But this would, I suggest, represent a serious misreading: for Kant – and Bion says that he accords with him in this – external reality cannot be known.[5]

André Green suggests that the term 'thing-in-itself' is one 'borrowed from Kant but quite different in this psychoanalytic context' (Green, 1998, p. 657). And we see this difference in context in *Transformations*, where Bion tries to equate 'O' with the Kantian idea of the thing-in-itself: 'When I assigned O to denote the reality, the impressions of which the individual submits to the process T , I had in mind what Kant describes as the unknowable thing-in-itself' (Bion, 1965, p. 31). O signifies the ultimate reality in which Bion thinks analysts must have faith in his much-cited edict that: 'Every session attended by the psychoanalyst must have no history and no future' (Bion, 1967, p. 272) on the basis that, because memory is influenced by the unconscious and because desire distorts judgement, both mislead and both should be shunned in psychoanalytic practice. The required frame of mind is described in *Attention and Interpretation* as one of faith in O: 'It may be wondered what state of mind is welcome if desires and memories are not. A term that would express approximately what I need to express is 'faith' – faith that there is an ultimate reality and truth – the unknown, unknowable, 'formless infinite'. This must be believed of every object of which the personality can be aware: the evolution of ultimate reality (signified by O) has issued in objects of which the individual can be aware' (Bion, 1970, p. 31). The exclusion of memory and desire leads to the achievement of what Bion calls F: 'Through F one can "see", "hear", and "feel" the mental phenomena of whose reality no practising psycho-analyst has any doubt though he cannot with any accuracy represent them by existing formulations' (Bion, 1970, pp. 56–57).

This faith in an objective reality does not make Bion's concept of O an example of a Kantian thing-in-itself as Bion would have it: rather, it provides a very good example of what Kant calls the Ideal of Pure Reason. Kant thought that the scope of our powers of reason is such that we are driven to ask unanswerable questions. Kant's preface to the first edition of the *Critique of Pure Reason* begins:

> Human reason has this peculiar fate that in one species of its knowledge it is burdened by questions which, as prescribed by the very nature of reason itself, it is not able to ignore, but which, as transcending all its powers, it is also not able to answer.
>
> (Kant, 1929, p. 7 (A vii))

Reason is bound to lose itself in contradiction if it overreaches itself, if it tries to go beyond the limits of experience, and it was this realisation that caused Kant to make the paradigm shift in his epistemological quest from an examination of the objects of our knowledge to one of the process of knowing itself. Pure reason overreaching itself is exemplified in what Kant calls the 'Ideal of Pure Reason', which is the formation of an idea that there exists something which is 'really real': a total reality, the subject of all predicates, something which some people call 'God'. We can see this over-extension of reason in what eventually happens to Bion's musings on Freud's concept of 'evenly suspended attention' (see, for example, Freud, 1912, p. 111): a suggestion that faith in O should be the analyst's guiding principle.

Let us return to the agreement between Bion and Kant that things-in-themselves are unknowable. Kant asserts that these things-in-themselves give off 'noumena'. Kant takes the noumenon as constituting the necessary limit to our empirical knowledge (Kant, 1929, pp. 271–272 (A 253/B 310)). These noumena are unknowable, too. If we cannot know things-in-themselves, or their noumena, what can we know? Kant proposed that our encounter with the noumena is through our sensations of them which we perceive as phenomena. Phenomena have 'primary' and 'secondary' qualities: primary qualities correspond, in the case of an outer appearance, to extension and figure; secondary qualities to colour, texture etc. Bion says in his 1959 paper 'Attacks on linking': 'I use the term "phenomena" to cover what Kant called secondary and primary qualities' (Bion, 1993a, p. 100) but this is redundant: Kant had already provided the umbrella term.

Kant did not doubt that phenomena are the direct effect of things-in-themselves (Ward, 2006, p. 101) and proposed that we are able to intuit appearances in two pure forms: 'outer', which is the form of representation of extension and figure (so, space); and 'inner', which is the form of representation of succession and simultaneity (so, time) (Kant, 1929, p. 66 (A 21/B 35)).[6] Space is the a priori condition of outer appearances only; time is the a priori condition of all appearances, inner and outer.[7] Our conscious awareness of the external world is by way of these two 'pure intuitions': of space and, more fundamentally still, of time. In other words, space and time are the a priori forms of intuition through which experience of the phenomenal world is rendered possible. Kant's critical point is that these intuitions do not *follow* from experience; they are, instead, the necessary *preconditions* of experience.[8] As Scruton neatly puts it: 'experience contains intellectual structure' (1982, p. 34). Kant believed that the form of the appearance already exists in our mind.[9] But he did *not* think that particulars of extension or shape already exist in the mind. And this is an aspect of Kantian theory which Bion gets rather badly wrong. Bion's misunderstanding is most obvious in his 1962 paper, *A Theory of Thinking*, where Bion famously separates thoughts from thinking and then divides thoughts into preconceptions, conceptions and concepts. Bion says:

> 'Thoughts' may be classified, according to the nature of their developmental history, as pre-conceptions, conceptions or thoughts, and finally concepts; concepts are named and therefore fixed conceptions or thoughts. The conception is initiated by the conjunction of a pre-conception with a realization. The pre-conception may be regarded as the analogue in psycho-analysis of Kant's concept of 'empty thoughts'. Psycho-analytically the theory that the infant has an inborn disposition corresponding to an expectation of a breast may be used to supply a model. When the pre-conception is brought into contact with a realization that approximates to it, the mental outcome is a conception. Put in another way, the pre-conception (the inborn expectation of a breast, the a priori knowledge of a breast, the 'empty thought') when the infant is brought in contact with the breast itself, mates with awareness of the realization and is synchronous with the development of a conception. This model will serve for the theory that every junction of a pre-conception with its realization produces a conception.
>
> (Bion, 1993b, p. 111)

We can see in the above extract that Bion's explicit link to Kant is this: 'The pre-conception may be regarded as the analogue in psycho-analysis of Kant's concept of "empty thoughts"'. But are they analogous? 'Empty thoughts' meant for Kant the pure intuitions of time and space, which do not follow from experience but are its necessary preconditions. If Bion is saying that his idea of a preconception is analogous to Kant's idea of a thought without experience, then an innate preconception of a breast would be impossible. Kant would not permit a theoretical assumption of an innate idea of a specific object: this is precisely the idealism from which his philosophy represents a departure. Kant might, I think, say that we make sense of the sensations of hunger in terms of the temporally and spatially constructed experience of satisfaction of being fed: that is, in terms of experience of the breast. For Kant, using (without, I hope, distorting) Bion's terms, time and space constitute the container of the empty thought; the breast or no-breast is the experience which fills it. This accords, too, with Freud. Freud understood drives as being open-ended, directed towards whatever provides satisfaction and having no object until one presents itself. If the infant's hunger pangs are satisfied by the mother's breast, then, and only then, will the infant make the association between the object of satisfaction and his or her drive based on that experience of satisfaction. There is no a priori knowledge or pre-experience desire for a specific object. In this, Freud follows Kant. Bion, despite suggesting that he does, does not. The analogy Bion draws between what Kant meant by an empty thought and what Bion means by a 'pre-conception' is spurious. Bion's preconceptions are, in fact, more like Plato's Forms. Indeed, in *Transformations*, Bion says:

> I shall borrow freely any material that is likely to simplify my task, starting with Plato's theories of Forms. As I understand the term, various phenomena, such as the appearance of a beautiful object, are significant not because they are beautiful or good but because they serve to 'remind' the beholder of the beauty or the good which was once, but no longer is, known. This object, of which the phenomenon serves as a reminder, is a Form. I claim Plato as a supporter for the pre-conception, the Kleinian internal object, the inborn anticipation. Melanie Klein objected in conversation with me to the idea that the infant had an inborn pre-conception of the breast, but though it may be difficult to produce evidence for the existence of a realization that approximates to this theory, the theory itself seems to me to be useful as a contribution to a vertex I want to establish. Phenomena, the term being used as Kant might use it, are transformed into representations.
>
> (Bion, 1965, p. 138)

What are we to make of this? There is an interesting reference to Klein *not* taking the view that we have an innate preconception of a breast.[10] There is an incorrect reference to Kant's idea of phenomena – Kant did not include the extra step that Bion is suggesting he did: phenomena *are* the representations; it is noumena that get transformed. And there is the idea that preconceptions accord with Platonic Forms. If we follow the logic of this argument through, then we must acknowledge that the essence of a Platonic Form is its perfection. If we do have a preconception of the breast, prior to real experience of it, then this will be a perfect Form, a preconception not just of a breast but of a *perfect* breast, a template against which the real experience will be measured and inevitably found wanting. On that basis, we will begin our thinking life with an idea of lack rather than loss. Freud is, to me, much more compelling than Bion here: the integral component of Freud's theory of reality-testing is one of loss not lack. For Freud, reality-testing is the search to *refind* a lost object; an object of which we have had an initial experience which provided satisfaction. Like Bion, Freud gives the mother's breast as an example (Freud, 1895, p. 328) and maintains to the end that loss is the precondition of reality-testing and refinding the lost object its aim (for example, Freud, 1900b, p. 566; and Freud, 1925, p. 238).

We have looked at Kant's noumena, which we cannot know, and phenomena, which we can. Bion, with his concept of beta-elements, inserts an additional layer of non-conscious awareness between the noumena of the things-in-themselves and our consciousness of them as phenomena. Beta-elements are not thoughts but 'undigested facts' (Bion, 1991, p. 7), the concrete elements of psychotic experience (Bion, 1970 p. 9), existing in the domain of thoughts that has no thinker (Bion, 1993c, p. 313). Beta-elements can only be converted into material with which we can think by the operation of alpha function: without alpha function, sense impressions and emotions remain at the strange level of awareness where psychosis lies, where Bion says that 'beta-elements [are] felt to be things in themselves' (Bion, 1991, p. 6). The uneasiness one feels in trying to think about beta elements as things that cannot be known, and which are experienced neither consciously nor unconsciously as things that cannot be known, may well be a deliberate strategy by Bion to engender a particular state of mind but the strategy has risks attached. Bléandonu makes this point well:

> Another textual strategy much employed by Bion in his epistemological period is borrowing a technical term from another discipline, so that the word used in a psychoanalytic context remains surrounded by the 'associative penumbra' of its original context. This kind of thinking manages to convey the stranger aspects of reality but it may also create a sense of unease and suspicion.
>
> (Bléandonu, 1994, p. 90)

By using the Kantian term 'thing-in-itself' in this context, Bion risks misleading those of his readers who have a firm grasp of Kantian philosophy.

The possibility for misleading continues when Bion looks at the 'mating' of a preconception with a sense impression: the sense impression becomes contained by the preconception and the union gives rise to a conception. Repetition of this process sees the development of an apparatus for learning by experience. Bion is well known for his emphasis that thoughts come into existence first; the thinking apparatus follows to deal with them, claiming: 'thinking is a development forced on the psyche by the pressure of thoughts' (Bion, 1993b, p. 111). It is an important part of Bion's theory that we expect conceptions to be accompanied by the experience of satisfaction and it is the frustration of this expectation that triggers thought. He says, about the expectation of satisfaction:

> the pre-conception when the infant is brought in contact with the breast itself, mates with awareness of the realization and is synchronous with the development of a conception. This model will serve for the theory that every junction of a pre-conception with its realization produces a conception. Conceptions therefore will be expected to be constantly conjoined with an emotional experience of satisfaction
>
> (ibid.)

'Constant conjunction', we remember, is Hume's description of what gives rise to our unjustified belief in knowledge so here is a good use of a philosophical term capturing the idea of being brought up short by something we felt we *knew* would happen – say, the next feed – not happening and the change initiating something momentous in our mental structuring. Thought is what happens when an infant's 'expectation of a breast is mated with a realization of no breast available for satisfaction. The absent breast is the prototype for the first thought of a no-breast, or "absent" breast inside' (ibid.). The baby's expectation is unsatisfied: it is the negative of what is expected, namely, the experience to fill the empty thought. Thought is initiated not by satisfaction of an expectation but, rather, its frustration, the failure of the constancy of previous conjunctions.

We need to remember that, for Bion, a preconception is an innate idea, but *not*, as Bion claimed, something akin to a Kantian empty thought. Importantly, then, Bion's theory of psychic development works not in a Kantian framework but in one of which both Plato and Hume would approve: we have an innate idea of a breast; and an expectation of it providing satisfaction through the constant conjunction of ideas of hunger, breast and the satisfaction of hunger: failure of the constant conjunction leads to frustrated expectation and, as Bion shows so well, two divergent paths of development then follow from the frustrated expectation. Which path we follow depends on our critical decision between the evasion of frustration and its modification.

If things are to go well, the infant needs a personality where loving and creative impulses predominate and a mother capable of what Bion calls 'maternal reverie' who can receive her infant's projections and process them for the infant who will then be able to reintroject the now detoxified projections in a more manageable way (Bion, 1991, p. 36). When things do not go so well, our contact with reality can be disturbed and even destroyed. Evasion of frustration means that what could and should have been a thought becomes, instead, a bad object to be evacuated; and what could and should have been a developing thinking apparatus becomes instead the development of an apparatus for excessive and pathological projective identification (Bion, 1993b, p. 112). The bad objects are 'treated as if in-distinguishable from things-in-themselves' (ibid.) and are 'evacuated at high speed as missiles to annihilate space' (ibid.). Also attacked and evacuated are those parts of the psyche that structure reality temporally and spatially. The fragmentation and expulsion of the perceptual apparatus sweeps the baby out with the bath water: the expulsion takes with it not only the means to escape from the state of mind in which the patient then becomes trapped, but aspects of the patient's ego and superego which then surround and menace the patient. Real objects become suffused by the perceptual quality of the evacuated part of the psychic apparatus. Bion compellingly names these 'bizarre objects'.

> In practice it means that the patient feels surrounded not so much by real objects, things-in-themselves, but, by bizarre objects that are real only in that they are the residue of thoughts and conceptions that have been stripped of their meaning and ejected
>
> (Bion, 1991 p. 99)

In Bion's expressive turn of phrase: '[t]he patient now moves, not in a world of dreams, but in a world of objects which are ordinarily the furniture of dreams' (Bion, 1956, p. 346). What we have here is a nightmare creation, a negative Kantian world, in which the containing structure of the spatial and temporal intuitions through which we make sense of our experience has been destroyed.

Conclusion

When Bion uses his own terminology to describe his ideas, we are well served. Bion brings to life the idea of a world created and inhabited by a psychotic personality: of nameless dread, dream furniture and menacing bizarre objects and, in so doing, he highlights a fundamental difference between philosophy of mind and psychoanalysis: philosophy's concern is with mind; but the concern of psychoanalysis is with minds. Bion's use of Kantian terminology, on the other hand, is sometimes very misleading and does a disservice to his own work and to that of Kant. Bion seems to have failed to appreciate the essential difference between Hume, and his constant conjunctions, and Kant's departure from Hume. Further, Bion claims an analogy, where none exists, between what Kant meant by an empty thought and what Bion meant by a preconception. I suggested that, if this is taken into account, Bion's theory of psychic development does not work within a Kantian framework but does within one premised on the notion of innate ideas of which both Plato and Hume would have approved. There seems to have been an almost unquestioning acceptance that Bion understood Kant and used Kant's terms correctly (see, for example: Bléandonu, 1994; Schermer, 2003; and Sandler, 2006; but cf. Green, 1998, p. 653). Uncritical praise of Bion, as 'unsurpassed by any other analyst' (Symington and Symington, 1996, p. 26), and a 'hero' or 'wizard' (Grotstein, 1981, p. 502) brings with it the danger of taking for granted that, if Bion says something is so, then it is so. I have put forward the view here that, although Kant may have been one of Bion's inspirations, Bion misappropriates certain key Kantian terms, even when claiming a direct analogy between his use of the term psychoanalytically and Kant's use of the same term philosophically.

Notes

1 Failing his initial Oxbridge entrance examination after school, Bion later read modern history at Queen's College, Oxford, from 1918 to 1921, after active service in the First World War. He obtained a 'mediocre' result (Bléandonu, 1994, p. 37): a pass (no honours).

2 Paton (1887–1969) is well known as an authority on Kant and a translator of his works (Brown, 2004).

3 The text is from an address Mrs Bion gave in April 1994 in Toronto and Montreal. It was first published in *The Journal of Melanie Klein and Object Relations*, Vol. 13, No. 1, 1995 and is now published on the Institute of Psychoanalysis' website (www.psychoanalysis.org.uk/days.htm) (copyright Francesca Bion).

4 For an enlightening debate about Kant's confusion of predication with synthesis, and an account generally about the origins, nature and pretensions of epistemology, I recommend Rorty's *Philosophy and the Nature of the Mirror* (Rorty, 1979).

5 By 1977, Bion was claiming that 'In his mother's womb man knows the universe and forgets it at birth' (Bion, 1977) but, as I said, I am limiting this paper to Bion's earlier and more measured epistemological claims.

6 Hence, for Kant, the spatial relationships evident in geometry and the sequential, linear relationships evident in arithmetic.

7 Kant says:

> Just as I can say a priori that all outer appearances are in space, and are determined a priori in conformity with the relations of space, I can also say, from the principle of the inner sense, that all appearances whatsoever, that is, all objects of the senses, are in time and necessarily stand in time-relations
>
> (Kant, 1929, p. 77 (A 34/B 51))

8 Kant suggested that metaphysics consists of synthetic a priori propositions which can be reduced to 12 irreducible categories. Substance and causality are two examples. Each category can encompass many members. Not so, of course, for space and time: Kant thought that there is only one space; one time. Thus, space and time are *not* included in the list of categories. See further Paton (1931).

9

> Since, then, the receptivity of the subject, its capacity to be affected by objects, must necessarily precede all intuitions of these objects, it can readily be understood how the form of all appearances can be given prior to all actual perceptions, and so exist in the mind a priori
>
> (Kant, 1929, p. 71 (A26/B42))

And

> That in which alone the sensations can be posited and ordered in a certain form, cannot itself be sensation; and therefore, while the matter of all appearance is given to us a posteriori only, its form must lie a priori in the mind, and so must allow of being considered apart from all sensation
>
> (Kant, 1929, p. 65 (A20/B34))

10 Klein seems to take different views on whether we have a priori object images. In her earlier works on aggression, Klein's view is that the infant's earliest object relations are with body parts of which the infant has *innate* knowledge which generate images and sadistic phantasies against the mother's body, made up of 'breasts, penises, the womb, babies, perfection, poison, explosions and conflagrations' (Greenberg and Mitchell, 1983, p. 131). These take place without necessarily first encountering the (part) objects in reality and constitute the first relation to reality (see, for example, Klein's 1952 paper 'The mutual influences in the development of ego and id' (1997, p. 58). Klein's works on the depressive position, however, suggest that it is aspects of real objects in the external world which are introjected to people our inner world and then reprojected onto external figures (see, for example, Klein's 1935 paper 'A contribution to the psychogenesis of manic–depressive states' (Klein, 1998a) and her 1940 paper 'Mourning and its relation to manic–depressive states' (Klein, 1998b). Greenberg and Mitchell conclude:

> Klein's view of objects as phantastic and internally derived were developed during the period in which aggression was her major focus, while the view that objects are synthesised out of absorptions of experience with real others were developed during the period in which depressive anxiety and reparation were her major focus
>
> (1983, p. 135)

Chapter 12

Braithwaite and the philosophy of science

Bob Harris and Layla Redway-Harris

> How can something people feel be measured ... what about love and hate?
>
> Bion 1959, in 1992, p. 2

> Meaning is a function of self-love, self-hate or self-knowledge.
>
> Bion 1965, p. 74

Introduction

This chapter is about how and why Bion chose the relatively unknown British philosopher of science R.B. Braithwaite as one of the primary sources in his search to establish a scientific basis to his rapidly developing theoretical work. We discuss what Bion was attempting to understand about the nature of science and describe how Bion's reading and understanding of Braithwaite helped him to develop the significant concepts that underlay his own theories.

The British psychoanalytical movement, during the period between about 1950 to 1970, was undergoing massive internal upheavals, characterized by great problems in communication not only within the movement but also in relation to the external context. The golden years of psychoanalysis were beginning to come to an end. Bion, a central figure in the British Psychoanalytical Society and a renowned analyst in his own right, turned his mind to the bases of clinical and theoretical problems.

The development of Bion's theoretical work, which was markedly influenced by Braithwaite, both shaped and in turn was influenced by his extensive experience of clinical practice specifically, Braithwaite contributing theoretically towards his attempts to systematize and understand the clinical process of psychoanalytic sessions. This chapter explores and discusses the problems that Bion was attempting to address and suggests why and how Braithwaite, was a major influence on his thinking.

We also reflect on the outcome of this project to place psychoanalysis on a more 'scientific' basis.

In the beginning

Sigmund Freud abandoned his 'Psychology for Neurologists,' (later renamed 'Project for a Scientific Psychology' by his editor) in 1896 feeling that the goal of systematizing psychology into a scientific, physical 'biological' basis was beyond reach at that point. However, he did believe that this would be achieved at some future date. Current developments in neuroscience and neurobiology might, perhaps, be the fulfilment of this prediction. So Freud, somewhat reluctantly, diverted from neurology into working in a solely psychological sphere. Apparently, he remarked later that he was at his happiest when studying nerve cells in the laboratory. Bion could be thought of as taking up the fight again, but this time beginning in the psychological arena and staying there, trying to unearth and build a scientific basis in the dark and muddy fields and trenches of depth psychology rather than in the biological research laboratory. He attempted to use the illuminations of the philosophy of science to find a way to create a practical, meaningful and coherent foundation for psychoanalysis. Bion's 'laboratory' was the consulting room and the psychoanalytic session, and his dissections were of the discourse and communications between analyst and patient.

However, over the course of the early to mid-years of the 1960s, his preoccupations and search for ultimate meaning changed from the attempt to describe and work with the 'unknown' mathematically to an acceptance of 'unknowability' in its own terms. This is a profoundly important transformation.

Bion's contributions to theory

Bion made his major contributions to psychoanalytic theory over the period 1959 to about 1970, in a remarkable series of works. Early in this period, as a part of the genesis and preparation for this significant body of work, he set himself the task of developing an understanding of the psychoanalytic process in a scientific and logical format.

In order to do this in a coherent and systematic way that would be acceptable to scientists and educated lay people alike, he turned, appropriately, to a discipline that focuses on understanding and defining the nature and meaning of science itself: the Philosophy of Science.

What is philosophy of science?

The philosophy of science is the field of study that addresses how we get reliable knowledge, and assesses what kind of 'knowledge' we can trust by examining the basis of what we might accept as truth. It does this through investigating logical systems and the relationships that comprise these systems, testing assumptions and exploring the nature of relationships and communications.

This is very much the stuff of psychoanalytic interest; Bion was preoccupied over this period with the nature of relationships and communication – one of the reasons why his work is so influential today as there is an ever-increasing emphasis on the relational aspects of psychotherapy.

Philosophy of science[1] examines how knowledge is derived from the facts of experience, questioning the nature of the acts of observation and experimentation. It looks at the process by which resultant facts can become theories and makes conjectures about those theories' inner workings. The idea of scientific laws and their significance is considered as well as the relation of scientific endeavour to the truth. From a wider perspective, theories and methods are examined collectively in their historical context in order to chart their development and to make statements about the current context.

Emotional truth

Bion was very concerned with what, in his terms, constituted 'emotional truth' and the inherent difficulty of knowing anything for sure when dealing with human beings. When speaking of the analytic pair, termed *x* and *y*, he says 'The conviction that the scientific outlook prevails in the relationship ... is more easily maintained if *y* is inanimate and *x* can be made to seem to approximate to the inanimate' (Bion 1962, pp. 47–48). To try to emphasize and clarify this point he goes on to say 'Truth value is felt to inhere in the record(ing) of the human voice...' – by which he means that inanimate records are more likely to be taken and accepted as 'truth' than those made by human judgement, a viewpoint that may be of interest to those experiencing the current increasing emphasis on digitized and manualized forms of psychological intervention.

Early on in his quest for scientific validity, Bion seemed to be searching for some sort of certainty. Braithwaite, too, was especially interested in the nature of scientific 'laws', taking a less problematic view to other areas such as the nature of observation, which he did not find the need to investigate with such great rigour. Bion shared with Braithwaite similar ideas about what philosophical ideas carried the most significance to his science and found an inspiration in Braithwaite's work of philosophical elucidation. It seems that Braithwaite's search for the definition of scientific laws mirrored Bion's quest for certainty and scientific rigour in clinical psychoanalysis.

Relationships, conceptions and consequences

An important element of the logical systems used to establish truth is mathematical symbolism, and the symbols' relationships to one another. Here, Braithwaite was instrumental in highlighting the importance of calculus as a way of expressing these relationships and processing them in a meaningful way.

Bion's attempts to use calculus as a way of understanding the psychoanalytic relationship was both bold and paradoxical, as we shall see.

Logical systems

Logical systems are the structures by which we appraise our reality.

Conceptions, consequences, perceptions and experiences are all nodes within these systems. They are the points of entrance for empirical reality which we symbolically represent for the purpose of processing. The principles of calculus give the nodes' web of interconnections a comprehensible structure with an accuracy that standard mathematics can not quite reach. This is because it is able to deal with such concepts as layers and feedback loops as a whole, expressing formulas of far greater complexity than was previously possible.

A theory, then, can be seen as an expression of how the different nodes of a logical system *might* be connected, and a law is an expression of such connections that have been *empirically validated*. Importantly, a logical system possesses correlation and correspondence by virtue of its connections. Through understanding the location of such correspondence by using deductive reasoning, we are able to make a great many more working statements about reality.

In more basic terms this means that if we know one part of a logical system, then we can work out how to understand another part. Braithwaite saw this process as fundamental to the understanding of scientific endeavour, leaving a significant impression on Bion and the development of his thinking.

Relationships then, are a key constituent part of a logical deductive system.

A logical system becomes a scientific system when it is injected with empirical, that is, testable reality. A scientific system is then a tool we use to draw lines in order to bring fuzzy sensory experience into sharp, analytical, processable focus. This is exactly what Bion set out to try and achieve within the feelings-dominated and thus sensory world of psychoanalysis, inspired by the mathematical toolkit brought into form by Braithwaite. But here lay the paradox.

Science and logic

In the 1950s, 'science' and 'logic' was, and still is to a great extent, the dominant language of the field of medicine and in our attempts to understand and deal with the 'physical' world. This attitude has largely continued, and more than ever we demand 'scientific proof' and 'evidence' about the reasons for our behaviours and endeavours. The demand for and requirements of scientific explanations are still the dominant drive of our 'evidence-based' world.

The psychoanalytic unconscious – the obscure 'not-known' – only perceived through its manifestations and through the suspension of memory, desire, understanding and sense impressions is another matter entirely. Bion comments, following Freud's advice that the analyst 'blind himself'

> I include memory and sense perception with the properties to be eschewed ... the psychoanalyst is seeking something that differs from what is normally known as reality ... [this] does not indicate undesirability for the purpose of achieving contact with psychic reality
>
> (Bion 1970, p. 43)

At the time of his initial explorations of the philosophy of science, Bion's attitude was ambivalent about this; he both desired to create a logical and 'scientific deductive system', and at the same time doubted its usefulness and applicability to his purposes and understanding – intellectual and intuitive – of the nature of psychoanalysis.

Much later, after a great deal of hard, and one suspects, grinding work, Bion referred to the 'H' formulations in the section of the Grid; 'Calculus and 'Scientific Deductive System' as 'lacking body' (Bion 1970, p. 91).

Other philosophical sources

Primarily, his quest seems to have been to establish a workable scientific foundation for a clinical psychoanalysis that effected a transformative process in the patient. Calculus has been described as the mathematics of change, as a method of calculating problems that are continually evolving. Psychoanalysis is, after all, a clinical treatment for mental distress; originally developed by Freud on the theoretical basis of the primacy of sexuality. By the time of Bion's major scientific explorations between 1959 and 1967, the psychoanalytic community was still deeply divided following the 'Controversial Discussions' between the 'orthodox' Freudians and the followers of Melanie Klein. By the late 1940s, the British Society had split into three factions (King and Steiner 1991). Bion was analysed by Klein, and mentions her frequently in his writing. He also often cites Freud (Bion 1963, p. 4 fn. 1, 5, 18, 19, 33, 62, 86).

Over this period it is likely that he was reading and learning from a number of sources; Bradley and Popper certainly. He was also probably influenced by Alfred North Whitehead, a mathematician who journeyed a similar path to Bion from 'hard' science to philosophical, literary and metaphysical forms of exploration, although he appears not to be specifically mentioned in any of Bion's writings. Bion's longer-term trajectory took him into the mystical, autobiographical and poetical which, while fascinating, is beyond our current point of interest.

However, between 1955 and 1967, it seems that Bion turned largely to R.B. Braithwaite, and cites him a dozen or so times in his writings from this period. All citations are from Braithwaite's 1955 book *Scientific Explanation* (second edition), which is largely composed of re-writing and extensions of the Tarner lecture series that Braithwaite gave at Cambridge in 1946. It was published in its first edition in 1953.

Richard Bevan (R.B.) Braithwaite (1900–1990) was a British philosopher of science, working and writing in Cambridge during the 1930s and 1940s. He was part of a loose extended group of theoreticians and philosophers who would meet in various settings, notably the Cambridge 'Aristotelian Society', and discuss hot topics in philosophy and the philosophy of science, sometimes in very heated atmospheres. There is a story that an enraged Ludwig Wittgenstein, in an altercation with Karl Popper in Braithwaite's rooms at Cambridge, brandished a red-hot poker at Popper during a meeting of the venerable 'Moral Sciences Club' that Braithwaite was hosting. The whereabouts of Braithwaite's poker today is unknown.

Other less fiery philosophical influences are known to be H. Poincaré (Bion 1962, p. 72), David Hume (Bion 1965, pp. 64, 65), W. Heisenberg (Bion 1965, pp. 2, 45, 57) and Bertrand Russell (Bion 1992, pp. 21, 194). Partly through his readings of Braithwaite, he would also have been aware of Dampier and Eddington (Braithwaite 1955, p. 53).

Scientific explanations

It was largely between the years 1959 and 1967, that Bion was absorbed in investigating 'scientific method' and 'scientific explanations' with which to understand and describe the psychoanalytic relationship and the process of transformation. There are many references to this dogged search in *Cogitations* (1992), the collection of Bion's writings between 1958 and 1979 that forms a kind of background commentary to his writings, musings and research.

He became preoccupied with how scientists as a group communicated their evidence and convictions to each other, and Bion tried, one feels almost desperately, to find a way in which psychoanalysts could do the same or similar. His interest was in scientifically constructed communication and psychoanalytic analogy.

The latent and the manifest

Obviously, there are significant drawbacks in this attempt, not the least being the fact that you cannot see, hear, touch, taste or smell the obscure psychoanalytic object, the unconscious, in the same way that you can manage and manipulate objects in the 'real world'. In Newtonian physics (a classical use of calculus), for instance, the dropping of an object, say an apple, and its reliable and predictable acceleration (32 feet per second per second) is an example of this mathematical certainty and search for laws of nature.

Philosophy is an example of the 'manipulation' of things, ideas, that do not have a concrete presence in the world, and indeed the altercation with the concrete reality of the poker in Braithwaite's rooms was apparently to do with a vivid disagreement about the nature of philosophy itself, one of the protagonists, Wittgenstein, insisting that philosophy was just playing games with words, inferring that it is inconsequential.

Bion may have chosen Braithwaite because the philosopher of science did not himself hold the view that philosophy was just an inconsequential game. His view seems to be congruent with that of Bertrand Russell, whom Braithwaite, in a eulogy to Russell in 1970, quotes as saying 'The supreme maxim in scientific philosophising is this: *wherever possible logical constructions are to be substituted for inferred entities*' (Braithwaite, 1970, p. 1).

Bion's full-on attempt at scientific coherence eventually ran its course, and might be said to have exhausted or burned itself out by the time of his book *Transformations* which is an attempt to bring together his thoughts at that point, especially those contained and elucidated in *Learning from Experience* and *Elements of Psycho-Analysis* including the influence of philosophy and the philosophy of science. The problem of meaning (or in philosophy, *epistemology*), addresses the question 'what are the necessary and sufficient conditions of knowledge? What are its sources? What is its structure, and what are its limits'? (*Stanford Encyclopedia of Philosophy*, at http://plato.stanford.edu) These are also questions that the philosophy of science tries to answer, questions Bion was struggling with at that time which are perhaps encapsulated in a few lines from *Transformations*. 'Meaning is a function of self-love, self-hate, or self-knowledge. *It is not logically but psycho-logically necessary*' (Bion 1965, p. 73, emphasis added).

Shaky foundations

Bion may well have been more than intuitively aware in the late 1950s, when he began his most prolific period of writing, that the future of psychoanalysis was built on shaky foundations if the movement remained unable to link itself to a 'scientific' system that could not only achieve respect in the scientific community but also in the wider world of informed and educated people. These people demanded a 'scientific' and logically consistent underpinning to anything that claimed to be knowledge or truth, or indeed lay claims to be a clinical treatment for a physical or mental disorder. This was not so much about the demand for 'evidence based' outcomes in the way that we think about these matters today in 2013, but had to do with the search for a place in the scientific community and in a worldview that prized concrete appraisals and knowledge about how to deal with supposedly concrete realities.

Scientific institutionalization was then a vital end goal for psychoanalysis in Bion's eyes and through framing it within a logical system, Bion hoped to be able to achieve such an end.

However the psychoanalytic movement itself was riven by deep splits at the time, and the problem of communication amongst members of the psychoanalytic community must have preoccupied Bion in his role as director of the London Clinic of Psychoanalysis (1956–1962), and then president of the

British Psychoanalytical Society (1962–1965). Bion may have seen the application of scientific deduction not only as an essential framework for public acceptance in the scientific community, but also as a means of communication which might heal these rifts and bring about coherence to the divided world of psychoanalysis.

The wider social context of 'the Sixties'

But another force may have stepped on the gas. The seismic social and sexual eruptions of the psychedelic Sixties and the mind-jolting revelations and mysteries of quantum physics were a mere glimmer in the eye during the dog days of the late 1950s when Bion began to put his ideas together. Like the combative ex-rugby scrum half that he was, he threw himself headlong into the struggle to make sense of and use his internal experience to create links with and communicate with the most inaccessible areas of the psyche of his patients and himself. Like the ex-tank commander that he also was, he was not afraid to go into the unknown, where it was hottest, and not afraid to lead the troops into the darkness. At the front of the extended edition of *Cogitations*, produced by Francesca Bion (1994), there is a quotation from Henri Poincaré: 'Thought is only a flash between two long nights, but this flash is everything' and again, later, 'only facts worthy of our attention … introduce order into this complexity and so make it accessible to us'. It is our attention that creates order in the complexity rather than order being there already, just waiting to be discovered. It reminds us of Bion's advice to an anxious soldier on the battlefield who had just seen a single magpie and was worried that this would bring bad luck. Bion suggested that the soldier would be better off noting the positions of the enemy gun emplacements rather than spending his time looking for the magpie's mate.

Facts worthy of our attention

So, what are the 'facts worthy of our attention' (Braithwaite 1955, pp. 2–3) and how do we define, structure and use them? To what do we pay attention and why? Braithwaite pointed out that different disciplines in science tend to focus on facts relating to historical events relevant to their fields. Thus biologists focus on the origins of life, cosmologists on how the universe began and psychoanalysts on childhood and infantile experience.

Bion turned to Braithwaite to help him frame and formulate a system to organize psychoanalytical ideas and give a more structured justification for the questions psychoanalysis asks. In order to do so he needed to not only work out but also be able to express how a psychoanalytic ideational system develops into 'the scientific deductive system' (Bion 1992, p. 4) Unfortunately, to borrow an analogy initially applied to the work of Carl Linnaeus in the novel *The French Lieutenant's Woman* (Fowles 1969), Bion knew he was in a labyrinth, but what he did not appreciate was that the walls were constantly shifting.

The transformation of Bion's ideas

What really interested Bion was the emergence of the unknown and the action of the liminal areas between the unconscious and conscious that would enable transition and transformation of 'elements'. As evidenced above in the poker-waving episode, the academic discipline of philosophy of science was not a place of friendly and amicable agreement. Arguments were fierce and radical disagreement was common.

Bion was exceptionally drawn to Braithwaite because he was trying to understand the systems underlying psychoanalysis, and Braithwaite was trying to understand the systems underlying science. Both were attempting to identify relationships and to build a language in which to express them.

On a simple and prosaic note, it may also have been partly because Braithwaite was accessible and seemed to speak a similar language to Bion, literally as well as figuratively. Braithwaite was an English public schoolboy and Bion similarly was of an aspirant middle-class English background. Other philosophical and psychoanalytical friends and combatants had strong Germanic and Jewish backgrounds. There was a cultural similarity between them. Also, Braithwaite is fairly easy to read, and at times is almost avuncular.

But perhaps more importantly, Braithwaite, although counting himself to have been very fortunate to have studied with Wittgenstein, appeared to be sympathetic towards psychoanalysis. In the preface to *Scientific Explanation* we find him saying

> As the hierarchy of hypotheses of increasing generality rises, the concepts with which the hypotheses are concerned cease to be properties of things which are directly observable, and instead become 'theoretical' concepts – atoms, electrons, fields of force, genes, *unconscious mental processes* – which are connected to the observable facts by complicated logical relationships.
>
> (Braithwaite 1955, preface, emphasis added)

As a psychoanalyst, Bion was concerned with what went on between analyst and patient in the psychoanalytic session, in the to-and-fro of communication between the analyst and the patient, in the sequence and consequence of the patient's free associations and the analyst's response to them – especially unconscious mental processes – and 'hypotheses (that) cease to be the properties of things which are directly observable'.

Bion was asking himself the question; is it possible to describe the process by which an ideational system develops into a scientific deductive system? Can this chain of ideational deductive steps, these sequential and spatial ideational relationships, represented by the dialogue between analyst and patient, and the internal sequential dialogues of them both, be represented symbolically so that deductions can be symbolized and the correctness be checked by inspecting the relationships between the symbols?

It seems that, early in 1959, Bion had established in his mind, in a spirit of some optimism, perhaps, that

> we need to consider how the ideational system develops into the scientific deductive system. The ideational system I shall regard as relatively primitive and belonging principally to the mental dynamics by which ideas, related to objects, are formed

This seems to be the precursor to 'beta elements'

> The scientific deductive system I regard as more sophisticated and related to the permanent establishment of knowledge, or to the establishment of knowledge *in a form that is permanent and indestructible*

This seems to be the precursor to 'alpha elements'. Both quotes above are from *Cogitations* (Bion 1992, p. 4, emphasis added).

This is a somewhat lofty, some might say grandiose or omnipotent objective, Braithwaite quotes Sir William Dampier, who in 1944 wrote: 'the last trace of the old, hard massy atom has disappeared, mechanical models of the atom have failed, and the ultimate concepts of physics, it seems, to be left in the decent obscurity of mathematical equations' (Braithwaite 1955, p. 52 fn. 1). Braithwaite comments 'But a philosopher cannot allow obscurity to be decent, especially since the obscurity in question is not that of the pure mathematics concerned (which is abstruse but not obscure) but that of the application of the mathematics' (ibid., p. 52). He also goes on to quote Sir Arthur Eddington: 'I never discover what carbon really is. It remains a symbol. Carbon is a symbol definable only in terms of the other symbols belonging to the cyclic scheme of physics' (Eddington 1928, p. 269). The scientific deductive system is all about symbols' relationships to one another and the idea that once we go up levels in hypotheses, we are dealing with deductions *not* observations.

A conceptual match

In 1959/1960 this must have been music to Bion's conceptual ears. Psychoanalysis is concerned with that which is not accessible to the senses in the way that external objects are, or as Bion terms them, after Freud, 'external facts'. Psychoanalysis is concerned with the unconscious, the unknown.

Awareness of external facts is accessible by means of touch, smell, sounds and sight. As a psychoanalytic theoretician, Bion needed to find some way of describing that which could only be detected by its action or manifestation.

Like the atom, or 'carbon' could it be to able be described, annotated, symbolized, detected and tracked by its logical pathway and manipulated, thought about and its behaviour predicted in the same way that elements and combinations of elements can be in the periodic table which is of ubiquitous use in physics and chemistry. We remember the difference here between observation and the 'higher levels' of deduction.[2]

Intermission

At this point, you might like to take a look at Bion's famous grid, which is the tool he constructed to do the immensely complex job of attempting to frame the elements of a psychoanalytic session in the modality of a scientific deductive system. It takes some study to elucidate how successful an enterprise this actually is; it has not, to date, become the stock in trade of the jobbing analyst, although it does in my view repay patient study.

However, as a guide to the development and genesis of Bion's thinking it is very interesting; the more so once the underlying principles and driving forces are appreciated. Later, in 1968, Bion himself likened using the grid to limbering up with mental gymnastics before a session.

> The object of the grid is to provide a mental gymnastic tool ... it cannot do harm as long as it is not allowed to intrude into the relation between analyst and analysed and as by the elaboration of some theory about the patient which is then stored up and used as something which can be discharged like a missile in battle.
>
> (Bion 1989, p. 27)

The grid

It is of no co-incidence that the axis 'G' in Bion's 'grid' is called 'Scientific Deductive System,' and axis 'H' is termed 'Algebraic Calculus'. The co-ordinate for axis 'G' is 'alpha-elements', that is, 'not objects in the world of external reality but products of work done on the sensa believed to relate to such realities' (Bion 1963, p. 22). He is referring to purely mental objects and events, in other words.

The co-ordinate for axis 'H', Algebraic Calculus, is notably absent. Bion remarks that 'the scientific deductive system may also be represented by an algebraic calculus', and then emphasises that 'the signs have no properties other than those conferred upon them' (ibid., p. 24).

This seems to be Bion's aim; to create a purely mathematically logical construction of the psychoanalytic session, according to Braithwaite's rigorous scientific method, using the scientific deductive system as detailed in the philosopher of science's book 'Scientific Explanation' (1955).

Using the example of electrons, Braithwaite asserts that electrons are logical constructions whose presence can be detected from the action of observed events and objects. This is the equivalent of saying that the word 'electron' can be explicitly defined in terms of such observations. It is the job of the philosopher of science to show how the theoretical terms of a science can be explicitly defined by means of observable entities.

Therefore it would be the job of a psychoanalytical theoretician, Bion in this instance, to show how the theoretical terms of psychoanalysis can be explicitly defined and logically constructed by means of observable entities.

Braithwaite does seem to have been extremely influential in the construction of Bion's grid, his major attempt to formalize scientific explanations.

Here is a summary of Braithwaite's major contributions to the philosophy of science.

- Braithwaite asserted that scientific theory consisted of an initial hypothesis followed deductively by empirically testable generalizations. Explanation of a generalization means that it is implied by higher level generalizations in theory. Unobservable terms in a theory must be treated as formal calculi, that is, uninterpreted formulas. Then the meaning of the terms and structure of a theory can be understood.
- Complete interpretation of calculi is not possible, only lower generalizations can have full meaning. Therefore theoretical terms are partially and indirectly given meaning by an initial formula, because the formula makes a statement about the nature of the relationship of the theoretical terms.
- He divided initial postulates into either theoretical terms or dictionary axioms, which related theoretical terms to observational terms. He argued that theories containing theoretical terms were more able to encompass new information than ones with just identificationary terms. There was no particular advantage to these, however, as the same results would be got from the testable axioms. In a scientific model theoretical terms are replaced with something more tangible; therefore theory and model are different. Models are not necessary but they are helpful (at this point we might remember Sir Arthur Eddington's point about carbon, above).

The nebulous domain

In 'Notes on Ritual and Magic' (1968), in *Cogitations*, Bion writes

> I shall be concerned mostly with the discussion of ritual, but while I wish to preserve scientific rigour in discussion, I do not wish to give the impression that the rigidity imparted by the limitations of rigorous

> discussion has any counterpart in the nebulous domain that is the object of this discussion.
>
> (Bion, 1992 p. 297)

He then goes on to point out that at some periods in history the physical environment appears to have included spirits, good and bad, and that we assume that there is such a thing as a psyche that can be scientifically studied, but that 'to make such a claim for our investigations would be rash indeed, except as an assumption to be investigated' (ibid.). A philosopher of science might respond with a question: 'Is it really possible to investigate the existence of an object of investigation? Or does the very process of investigation create it? Could a psyche be a model, a tool to elucidate our theories of human feeling?'

However, in *Attention and Interpretation* Bion says

> Psycho-analytical events cannot be stated directly, indubitably or incorrigibly any more than can those of other scientific research. I shall use the sign O to denote that which is the ultimate reality, absolute truth, the godhead, the thing in itself ... its existence is conjectured phenomenologically.
>
> (Bion 1970, p. 26)

In spiritual terms this is the unrealized consciousness. In scientific terms it is a very fundamental realization that no matter how many layers of the onion we peel, we are in a growing onion. The necessary framework to deal with psychoanalysis needs this realization. The concept of calculus goes a significant way to understanding O, as O, just like Braithwaite said about calculus, cannot be described in its entirety and is used to express the ultimately unknowable which paradoxically we must know *about* in order to develop our overall knowing.

This is the distillation of a very important idea that has as it were, been running through a series of minds, from the scientific to the spiritual, over a great deal of time. *Nodal points extending through time, resulting in what we have today in terms of theory.*

In her observations about Bion's contact and communication with the inspirational teacher and poet Roland Harris and the development of Harris' radical pedagogy, Meg Harris Williams remarks that

> the central conviction, later hallowed in Bion's concepts of 'learning from experience', was that the kind of learning which transformed a person into a professional worker had to be rooted in the intimate relations with inspired teachers, living and dead, present and in books
>
> (Harris Williams 2010b, p. 176)

At the time of writing, there is something of a revolt in the zeitgeist against the dominance of the commodification of experience, obsession with things, preoccupation with the acquisitive nature of consumerism, preoccupation with money and inanimate objects. Bion remarks that the emphasis on scientific investigation is limited, by human inadequacy

> to those phenomena which have the characteristics of the inanimate. We assume that psychotic limitation (to the world of things) is due to an illness, but that of the scientist is not.... Confronted with the complexities of the human mind the analyst must be circumspect at following even accepted scientific method; its weakness may be closer to the weakness of psychotic thinking than superficial scrutiny would admit.
>
> (Bion 1962, p. 14)

The unknown to the unknowable ... 'O' ... the scientific to the poetic...

Bion found in Braithwaite a method of systematization which fitted very well with his needs because they shared points of interest. However, what started as his main tool, the expression of the unknowable in a symbolically manipulable mathematical form, influenced by Braithwaite's use of calculus, also became his downfall as it prevented him from developing a finite frame within which a mutually agreeable language could grow. Instead he got lost in the infinite world of detail, unable to bring back to the surface the nuggets of insight and importantly, certainty, needed for the permanent institutionalization of his discipline that he so desired.

Whilst Bion may have fallen short of his holy grail, like Newton and many great thinkers before him, his personal failure to create a fully realized scientific system for psychoanalysis was not a failure at all. Bion may not have been able to contain his concept of O (in its nature, uncontainable) in a neat enough package to pass through the bureaucratic gates of orthodox mental health treatment, but he still hit on a very important idea, revealing a fundamental truth about science and knowledge that many have only been able to scrape the surface of. Indeed, his problems could have been just as much due to the conceptual language into which he was forced to frame his ideas to suit his clinical and academic audiences as with the subject matter. Perhaps he hoped that philosophy of science might afford him some middle ground.

Notes

1 For a relatively easy introduction to the philosophy of science, see Chalmers (1999). For a much deeper adventure, see Curd and Cover (1998).

2 *The Periodic Table* is also the title of a well-known book by the chemist Primo Levi, who tried to understand his observations and experiences in Auschwitz (translated by Raymond Rosenthal and first published in the UK in 1995 by Michael Joseph).

Chapter 13

Notation, invariants and mathematical models

William J. Massicotte

It is a fact that Bion did use notation to express some of his key ideas and since this will be with us for the long term within psychoanalysis, I believe facilitating a better understanding of his readings in the history of mathematics is warranted. My purpose is to explain certain notions found in Bion and to review selected books that Bion is known to have read and used. By actually reading some of the books Bion read a number of astonishing things come quickly to light, which might be helpful. The first is that mathematicians have written many books that are very accessible and easily read, with profit, by analysts. They are not arcane and overloaded with so much notation and formulas as to be in a foreign language; rather they write much like us and an astonishing number of better mathematicians had an explicit concept of the unconscious which they employed for their work. I also want to show how Bion's work in this area could be expanded, followed up and extended, partly by supplying references for future reading. However, first and foremost, I want to pique your curiosity about this truly fascinating world. As a side effect, we will cast a better understanding on 'model,' 'selected fact,' 'intuition,' 'invariance' and the mind liberating phenomena of 'notation.'

Preliminary overview

It is incumbent upon us to employ the logical principle of charity when assessing Bion's excursion into notation, etc. This means, we try to get the best and most accurate reading of it with a sympathetic eye, before criticizing it or dismissing it as a failure. Since Bion was convinced that psychoanalysis formed part of science, he held that, like virtually all parts of science, expressing core notions in notation, preferable algebraic notation, would aid in communicating views between psychoanalysts themselves, and also fix some of these discoveries for all time. It is true that he was writing for posterity, the distant future, which is right, since psychoanalysis is not merely young, but a neonate at only 100 years old, whereas the other areas like mathematics and philosophy have had millennia to develop with dozens of *true* geniuses along with hundreds of the merely brilliant. While off to a great sprinting start, it is far too early to consider if psychoanalysis can aspire to being on the Royal Road to Truth, an expression used at Oxford to mean the conjunction of mathematics, physics and philosophy.

If psychoanalysis is 'a permanent cultural acquisition', to borrow Husserl's fortuitous characterization of the discovery of geometry, then we may have to wait for something analogous to Descartes' world-changing discovery which added notation and algebra to geometry, a feat which changed the world of mathematics forever (making possible Newton, Leibniz, Boole, etc.). Without Descartes and Boole (the logician of Boolean search fame and the first to notice invariance which Bion borrows from) computers would not yet be possible, to cite but one trivial example.

Bion borrows in a perfectly respectable way from the history in science. To wit, many discoveries are made by noticing an analogy between something known in one area and applying it to another; for instance it often has happened that knowledge in economics is used to make observations in physics. Therefore, when Bion extracts *analogies*, he is simply not obliged to use the notions of transformation, invariance or notation in precisely the same way as they are used in mathematics. Perhaps it would help if I showed how to understand the precise nature of an analogy (not only for Bion, but also for Freud who was a master in the use of analogies, and also to understand our patients' analogies.) Every analogy whatsoever can be understood as fitting into a four-box grid, like this:

Within the four boxes, put in any term used analogically, lower left and upper right box and the two areas compared in the upper left and lower right column. So, it now looks like this, with the analogical terms in italics:

Math	*Invariant*
Invariant	*Psychoanalysis*

We could read it as 'the term invariant in Math is analogous to the term invariant as used by Bion for psychoanalysis.' Let me generalize and say that for any term, we think of it as analogous when it is proportionate in the sense of Euclid. So, using two columns for the proportionate, then ½ is as ²⁄₄, right? Using Euclid's notation of two colons to mean proportion we can then rewrite it as ½ :: ¾, and we note that proportion and analogy are not distinguished by Euclid. With only a slight leap to letters we arrive at the general form a/b :: b/c. This is the same grid as before, where **b** stands for the common term.

a	b
b	c

By extension, if you want to specify the constants within psychoanalysis, across schools and across individual analytic practices, we could call these the invariants under the heading psychoanalysis, as Bion does. Again, by extension to individual instances which might confuse us more easily, a patient may say as one of mine did 'I am a worm. So low, I do not even see daylight. Maybe lower than a worm.' 'I am a worm' is the metaphoric expression of an analogy, since every metaphor has the form 'a is c' and does not explicitly state the common element **b**, but silently implies it. When we make our interpretation as in 'You felt so useless and undervalued that to express it to me, you state that you are **lowly** like a worm,' we are supplying one version of the common element expressed analogically. Whereas, if we hear any metaphor, more effort in searching for the unexpressed common element must exerted, as in an instance of '**a** is a **c**' when hearing someone say 'A beautiful woman is a sunset.' Since we know it is an analogy with a silent common term of comparison, our intuition might be on structural grounds, that the unsaid component is something like 'both are soothing and fascinating to watch' or 'draw the eye' or something more specific to the speaker. It becomes then fairly easy to intuit the candidates for silent common term **b**, and usually we do this quite automatically.

I have belabored this simple point to illustrate that we can use algebra to understand the structure of what we hear. Hence, the argument is sometimes raised that what Bion sought to do in his excursions into notation is simply impossible, on a priori grounds. Since I have just shown it can be done on a minor topic, it implies that it is possible to do it. That is, 'is' strictly implies 'can' if we have respect for the facts.

Now if Bion is judged in terms of making a contribution to mathematics in those works where he employs notation, it would be a failure. However, since the topic of focus is psychoanalysis and the clinical events analysts experience, then we would not find it a shortcoming or failure that nothing of what he wrote could be submitted to a mathematics journal as a potential contribution to mathematics. However, is it a contribution to psychoanalysis? If we find that while analysts have not found it efficient to generally adopt his proposed notation and also if his notation does not enable us to think more complex thoughts in one operation (Descartes' idea) then it might be considered a failure so far. But on the other hand if even parts are found to be useful, such as the distinction between K and −K, then we have preliminary indication of potential success and the possibility of further success at some far distant date. This also applies to his borrowing ideas from formal logic (cf. Tarski below). There is nothing that could be submitted to a logic journal as a potential contribution to logic, which merely highlights that he intended to make a contribution to psychoanalysis, not to logic, and to do so by accurately employing analogy. Since logic has progressed exponentially since his time, it is possible there already exist proper tools to better formulate the embryonic ideas Bion left us with. If we happen to attract a few logicians who wanted to train as psychoanalysts we might one day see some of this; or, if some became curious about Bion's work, we may see it even if they do not train. (And this could go beyond transcribing associations into formal logic, which could be done now; and to more sharply formulating some of Bion's claims, which could also be done now.) The same is true of mathematicians, but perhaps more so, since they have powerful tools available.

Also, Bion was *too old* when he entered Oxford at the age of 25, to become mathematically sophisticated since the solving of math problems and seeing new theorems is almost exclusively a young person's domain. Bell (1937 p. 441) mentions how astonishing it was that Boole published his important work at 39, although his intuition was obtained as a teenager. Older people do become more efficient in their thinking and senior mathematicians do write very comprehensible books, but only young ones solve the problems. Mathematicians are, in effect the Olympic power lifters of the mind since math takes astonishing force and youth. There also can be intense emotional suffering while enduring the agony of waiting to see if the work will pay off, as exemplified by Farkas Bolyai (1820). He discouraged his son János from any further attempt at the parallels problem, by writing to his son who was getting curious about Euclid's work on parallels, the key to non-Euclidean geometry, 'Do not try the parallels in that way: I know that way all along. I have measured that bottomless night, and all the light and all the joy of my life went out there.' Indeed. Since they use their minds in ways few can imagine, it is not surprising that just as champion athletes come to know subtleties about the body, so too, mathematicians often come to know subtleties about the mind. Poincaré whose curiosity about his mind's workings enabling him to observe detailed aspects of its unconscious properties exemplifies this. He judged these to be important enough to publically deliver and later publish in *Science and Method*. Bion derived his use of the 'selected fact' notion from reading that volume.

Henri Poincaré: intuition,[1] selecting facts and the psychology of mathematical discovery

Poincaré (1854–1912) was quite probably the last person to understand all branches of mathematics since it is now too complicated, hence Bell called him the last universalist. By 1908, when he was elected to the Académie Française, he had 1,300 publications. Bion is known to have studied his work and credits his and now our use of 'selected facts' to Poincaré. As I dove into Poincaré's work while researching this chapter, I could not help but be struck by numerous similarities between his views and those of Bion. But let us first examine how Poincaré sees the notion of selected fact within his philosophy of science and his, I use this term advisedly, psychoanalysis of mathematical discovery.

For Poincaré every science uses selected facts as a matter of course, for to observe every instance of the facts under one sub-domain of science is impossible both in terms of time and the task of getting to the essence of the matter. For instance, if we were to observe every star before undertaking astronomy, we wait perhaps a few billion years before beginning to form astronomy – indeed if ever, since it would require some sort of unimaginable space travel which in turn would require some knowledge of astronomy in the first place. Hence we have to select among the things we observe. Meaning, we have to select from among a few observations that strike us as important or odd. This applies to every science and also to mathematics. So, therefore, when psychoanalysts use selected facts they are not doing anything special scientifically and, in fact, if something purporting to be a science does not use selected facts it might be an indication we should be suspicious about its claims to being a science. How we make such selection in math requires *talent*. The mathematicians are not embarrassed by the fact that they use a subjective talent involving an *aesthetic* element (Poincaré) in the process of making a discovery for once it is proven, the fact that it used a subjective element to get there does not diminish in any way the truth arrived at. Discovery requires selection (Poincaré, 1907 [1914], p. 51), aesthetic sense and a taste for *elegance*.

To explain mathematical intuition further let me say that it is a common understanding that mathematicians have different abilities. One of these abilities is having what we could call a nose for the truth, which here specifically means they have a hunch as to where the solution to a math problem lies. Therefore, they do not mechanically exhaust each avenue open to them simply with brute force, but look only in certain places. Since it is subjective, they can be wrong but the proof of the pudding is in the eating, that is, if one of them develops a track record of success, after the fact, we see that he or she had good mathematical intuition, or this special talent. Given this, Poincaré gets curious about his own mind and sees that he relies on unconscious processes (so named by Poincaré, 1907 [1914], pp. 55–63). By analogy, when psychoanalysts select certain facts within a session which helps an idea form spontaneously in the mind, they too should not expect this to be a guarantee of success, for they too have varying degrees of this required subjective talent, or psychoanalytic intuition. We should in no way be defensive about using this talent, and honing the talent, and in trying to cultivate it in others, just as the mathematicians do without apology.

In an effort to augment mathematic talent Poincaré hit on many things psychoanalysts take for granted. For instance, he pays attention to the transitional space between sleeping and waking (ibid., p. 56) since that is where ideas often gel, in the semi-somnolent state. He independently observed that the unconscious ego continues to work during sleep and is superior to the conscious ego (p. 57). He confirmed by independent scientific observation Freud's idea that the majority of the ego was unconscious. It is also clear that he basically 'dreams the problems' before him by letting his mind drift and looks at things with a peripheral point of view, not necessarily employing disciplined secondary thought processes. This supplies the 'liberty' (p. 63) to allow the absence of discipline to rule over thoughts, he says, coming very close to recommending that we use free floating attention and reverie to attempt to solve math and science problems. There is also resistance to an idea, which may occur, and he recommends 'forgetting' (Hadamard, 1973, p. 33) to enable a more open mind to operate while also advocating having respect for sleep and its role in maintaining what could be called the 'mental mathematical instrument' which is analogous to the psychoanalysts' 'analytic instrument.'

When he put these ideas together he delivered them to the Société de Psychologie in Paris in 1907; confident that psychologists would find them most interesting for these question have great significance for science and humanity (Poincaré 1907 [1914], p. 63). It seems that psychoanalysts failed to hit on a prime opportunity he presented, which was to show an independent confirmation of many psychoanalytic views by an accomplished scientist. Some of his views were also independently arrived at by means of a Swiss mathematical journal's survey conducted and published in 1912, but of which Poincaré was unaware until after his research (Bell, 1937 p. 547). I suspect their sophistication was lower than Poincaré's penetrating insights.

That Poincaré noticed aspects about unconscious processes, albeit usually (but not always) in a more cognitive and impersonal way than the familiar psychoanalytic mode has overlooked significance. For when Poincaré correctly anticipated aspects of relativity theory and was cited by Einstein, this was a rather big deal in the history of science (Pyle's introduction to Poincaré 1907 [1914], p. xi) for consistency and continuity with other scientific discoveries is an important mark of scientific plausibility. While Bion does not harp on this, he immediately goes on to *apply* some of Poincaré's ideas.

Among these is Poincaré's intuitionalism, which is different from mathematical intuition. Intuitionalism is a general picture of the nature of mathematics which is diametrically opposed to formalism, in that it claims math should be comprehensible to an individual mind in a way that is consistent with common sense and such comprehension is directly accessible by an individual human mind whereas formalism holds that mathematics is an artifact of formal systems only and common sense is actually the enemy of real understanding (Hersh, 1997). In the strongest way, I am personally opposed to formalism and favor intuitionalism, as a goal towards which mathematics should aspire since I believe not to do so cuts it off from our true understanding and limits the freedom of mind achievable by mathematical thought. This strong preference is also favored by Bion, implicitly, since he has deep respect for common sense,[2] and saw that within science and within psychoanalysis, some people simply see further even when the required conceptual tools have yet to be devised. In mathematics, most of the truly talented people favor both intuition and are intuitionalists with respect to their picture of mathematics in general, including Poincaré. This is also true of E.T. Bell and as Bell highlights, of many people. A clear example not cited by Bell, but spoken of by the great historian of mathematics Hadamard (1973) in his classic follow up to Poincaré's psychological inquiries is Fermat. Fermat had an accurate intuition of a relation within math, called his last theorem,[3] the solution of which required the invention of mathematics of which there was not conception at the time and he wrote down his famous conjecture (Hadamard, 1973, p. 117). To put it simply, they have the clear idea, it is accurate, but the math has to be invented in order to even begin to state the proof and this process can take centuries. On the Poincaré/Hadamard reading such exceptional intuitive grasping indicated even deeper unconscious work:

> If, in some exceptionally intuitive minds, ideas may evolve and combine in still deeper unconscious layers than in the above-mentioned cases, then even important links of the deduction may remain unknown to the thinker himself who has found them. The history of science offers some remarkable examples. [e.g. Fermat]
>
> (Hadamard, 1973, p. 116)

You will notice in this quote that the expression 'links' occurs, which plays such a central role Bion's thought. Such links are unconsciously made among people with vision, to whom Bion sometimes somewhat misleadingly refers as 'mystics' etc. What they actually are is clear: people posing great mathematical-type intuition who are more often than not intuitionalists with respect to the nature of mathematics. It is not mystical but rather the better use of the unconscious combined with a perpetrator phase of hard, disciplined work using secondary processes. Poincaré was fond of saying that his unconscious mind was obviously more intelligent than his conscious mind for even with monumental amounts of drudgery the solution does not come about on problems that the unconscious solves without apparent effort.

Of course, Poincaré annoyed a lot of people with his apparent ability to grasp so many things so quickly and without apparent effort, and they are understandably envious dismissals of his views, but Bion could not be counted among the envious dismissors.[4]

Of the many commonalities I see between Bion and Poincaré, apart from the habit each had of not referencing their sources and a talent for very brief poignant expression, I would include many things beyond the use of the selected fact notion. These include: the notion of links; dreaming the session, which is similar to dreaming the math problem; respect for the mind as an instrument; trying to develop a theory of thinking; and the psychoanalysis of their respective areas. That is, just as Poincaré was engaged in the psychoanalysis of mathematical discovery so too Bion recommended a psychoanalysis of psychoanalysis (although a better term might be metapsychoanalysis). If it was respectable for Poincaré to do this with respect to math and science then Bion's attempt to do it with psychoanalysis perhaps should be taken as a normal part of scientific reflection. Further, Poincaré was preoccupied with how we attend to a thing, all things, including math and our own minds. So too, Bion wrote in this epoch a work on attention (Bion, 1970). Both were concerned with a kind of illumination, which on Poincaré's reading points to 'obvious indications of a long course of pervious unconscious work' (Poincaré, 1907 [1914], p. 55). Both were also concerned with freedom of mind and how the ability to think freely could be aided with, of all things, algebraic notation. The reason is that with notation we are able to think (K) complex thoughts at a glance and communicate better with each other in the end. They were not alone, and now I will turn to the book by E.T. Bell, which further throws light on Bion's preoccupations and is also surprisingly consistent with Bion's work.

E.T. Bell (1883–1960): the astonishing lives of the mathematicians, a subtle aspect of the psychology of science

It is hardly surprising that we know Bion had E.T. Bell's classic work on psychology and lives of the mathematicians, *The Men of Mathematics: The Lives and Achievements of the Great Mathematicians from Zeno to Poincaré* in his library. This book is a masterly examination of the subtle factors that enable people to go from merely enduring math courses to grasping the idea that you can actually become a mathematician since it is real people who do this. Some have objected to his being 'picky' about the personal lives of these people and being less than stellarly accurate on all details; but that is to miss the key point: The biographies of greats show both what hindered or interfered with their creative potential and communicating this can help build a different order of interest in math. This is consistent with Heisenberg's view that it is real people who do science, an all too obvious fact that is often forgotten (Heisenberg, 1962, which Bion cites). Bell was successful in inspiring people to become mathematicians and it is quite possible that it forms a source of Bion's turning to notation. I could feel the effect on my own interest being stimulated while reading this contribution to the history of science, yet it is only cited twice in the PEP database (e.g. Nandy, 1979). It opens a world to people.

E.T. Bell is a fascinating person himself, perhaps worthy of a psychoanalytic study. He was ashamed of his family background in shipping and hid it from everyone including his children and colleagues. He even hid the fact that his mother took an undergraduate degree in math. A *bon vivant*, he spent his last days flirting with his nurses while sipping Scotch and enjoying cigars. It took a great biographer, Constance Reid (1993), to succeed in tracking down his story long after his death; whose sister read Bell and was so changed that she became the first woman mathematician elected to American Academy of Science. Bell himself succeeded in becoming president of American Mathematical Society and also winning their Bôcher Memorial Prize. But now to the book proper which insightfully extracts the essence of math and therefore poses a difficulty in our task to extract its own essence. This book was written under the encouragement of his friends, the Hubbles of Hubble telescope fame, and we will skip his excursions into inventing plausible science fiction under his pseudonym of John Taine.[5]

Bell, like Poincaré, emphasizes the unity of scientific thought across the ages, quite unlike the revolution model popular with fans of Thomas Khun, even though both are revolutionaries despite themselves. Both favor intuition, both are men of science and literary men of note, favoring in contemporary terms the views of Steve Jobs over those of Bill Gates. (Jobs said success comes by combining art and science whereas the more narrow-minded Gates favors virtually eliminating all but a narrow focus in education of engineering.) But whereas Poincaré was a member of the elite within French society, Bell came from a modest background which he lied about, almost playing the role of an impostor. Yet he turned this to a keen eye for the role backgrounds and foibles played in the formation of intellectual giants, thus extending Poincaré's psychoanalysis of mathematical discovery in very interesting way, with a keen non-envious eye towards intergenerationality. Since he had a keen eye the sole consolation in facing death was the hope that someone even better could come after oneself. He was very disappointed that his two children became physicians and that he failed to tempt them towards a higher order of scientific calling. Part of his preparation was sparing them exposure to religion, which Bell found an unhelpful obstacle in the path of mathematics, resulting in his child once asking (roughly), 'What's that building with the giant plus sign on the roof?' (Reid, 1993, p. 194).

Every chapter in his work can be read independently; if we start with Poincaré we see Bell noting that Poincaré did not take notes when attending math classes since his poor eyesight did not permit seeing the blackboard, but simply *listened* and let his mind drift, almost implying that free floating attention has been found to be efficient here too. And also how social events deeply helped form his personality, such as his being traumatized by witnessing the Prussian occupation of Nancy, France, when he was 16. While it is known that Bell took an elective in the history of math while doing his PhD, he really does not aspire to write simple history. The point is: Bell sees clearly that personal and psychological details matter enormously. Hence, Bell notes their foibles and how incredibly stupid these people occasionally are, as in Bion's notion, 'Have you ever come across people who you feel must be extremely intelligent in order to be so stupid? (Bion, 1980, p. 101). That is, there are duels (one who almost solved Fermat, died in a duel), passions (male mathematicians are notorious womanizers),[6] misplaced idealization of royalty (Descartes), unbecoming political ambition (Leibniz) and envy (Gauss). Gauss's inability to generously acknowledge the monumental accomplishment of the young János Bolyai, who published in an appendix to his father's book the first non-Euclidian geometry without which relativity theory would have been impossible inclined Gauss to withhold praise since he had seen something similar but was hording his precious position for posthumous publication (like Gollum holding on to his precious ring in the children's book). Envy of either youth or accomplishment often destroys the inspiration of mathematicians,[7] which happened in part with Bolyai who fell into a depressive non-productive funk following Gauss's destructive remarks.

Such envious destruction of potential ability is a problem all of our faculty at psychoanalytic institutes also face, so there are subtle lessons that can be extrapolated from Bell's work here too. Now shifting to the opposite, Bell also identifies some very astonishingly wise teachers of math who intuited exactly what was required, and who share the Poincaré-type respect for sleep, dreams and the role of intuition. One is found in Bell's Chapter III where he gives his account Descartes's father who 'wisely let him [Descartes] do as he liked' (p. 36) but even more tellingly, investigated schools and found a sagacious rector of a Jesuit school who assessed the young boy's capabilities with an insightful eye and instructed him to stay in bed all morning and join the class at noon if he felt like it (p. 37). It was during these meditations in bed that the young Descartes developed the idea (paradoxically) not to accept anything on mere authority, which inclined him to eventually develop a method for clear thinking. The import of the method was shown to mathematicians in his illustrating it with a mere example, published as an appendix to his *Method*, i.e. his analytic geometry. While Bell discloses that although he really tried he could not quite understand Descartes's method (which I find strangely telling since I find it rather transparent and have long thought any capable person could profitably read it), he makes it clear that with the discovery of Descartes's use of how to use algebraic notation in geometry, a true revolution occurs without which the rest of the history of math is scarcely imaginable (p. 52). Even though I had studied and taught Descartes I failed to grasp just how important this feat was for mathematicians until I read Bell's account. Bell highlights that Descartes arrived at his insight via his dreams and falsely assumes that 'No doubt the Freudians have analyzed these dreams' (p. 39); falsely, because I think a respectable paper on Descartes's dreams has yet to be written.[8]

Using Bell's work to track down invariance, transformation and function

There are endless fascinating details in this one book of Bell's but let us skip ahead to see if what he discovers can help us extrapolate a better working knowledge of some of the notions Bion used in his excursions. Here too we are presented with a further opportunity to follow our theme of the psychological aspects of great mathematical work, not as an a priori expectation, but rather because, in fact, it is clearly present with respect to these topics also.

Again, without making any pretense to understanding even a fraction of the ways invariance has productively shaped mathematics, it is clear that Boole (1815–1864) first discovered it, although as often happens, he failed to grasp the significance of this discovery. Carly (1821–1895), another Brit, took it much further. To look just at the sources' psychology of discovery to shed further light on Bion's analogous use of the expression 'invariants'[9] by which he means constants we see within it but he thinks he is not *usually* presenting an alternate theory which he takes to be the set of ideas found in Freud, Klein, Bowlby etc. (Category F). Boole's idea is that it is a constant,[10] which is similar to Bion's. By discovering how to do formal logic, Boole, on Bell's reading, made the revolutionary invention of the 'algebra of logic' (Bell, 1937, p. 444) which enabled thinkers to avoid getting lost in the details which is the *exact* point of good logic. Throughout Bell's and other people's work a key theme emerges: that is, no individual person has enough memory or intelligence to work with words or with arithmetic. Therefore to go from the *mud* of arithmetic (their common expression) to the freedom of algebra is the key. Just as in psychoanalysis, no one has the ability to remember all their own clinical experience, it is impossible even though people like to read clinical examples since they feel more at home there. But we cannot see the commonality across all clinical experience, our own and that of others, without representing it. Such representation could be done with algebra, say right now, by calling it C. Then say, in C, I notice F is a constant, where F stands for Frustration. If frustration is ubiquitous within clinical experience, either its avoidance or tolerance, then you only have two choices as to how to organize F within C, under either avoidance or tolerance. Here, I am just giving you an example, for understanding what Bion is up to most likely is marked by an emergent ability to extend the categories he proposes and modify them; and not by mere exposition. With frustration considered as the impetus for developing a mind and concepts to hold that frustration; as in, if Mother is not there, does not come, we can see the concept of negation (usually written ~ in logic) developing for the first time. And if such core logical concepts are foundational for understanding math, this is quite serious.[11]

Now, the amazing thing about the history of math, when I followed up Bell's leads while trying to retrace Bion's reading, taking Bell's book as more or less a 'blood sample' to determine what else is going on in his thinking just as we determine what is going on within a person's body by taking a blood sample (analogy practice here), we find that human *freedom* and a preoccupation with the unconscious is a constant theme. Taking Boole as an example, it is easy to discover that he attributes his discoveries to the unconscious and says it came to him in a flash at the age of 17 or so. His wife, who has quite inappropriately been related to a footnote within the history of math, but who is more than that, is also mentioned by Bell,[12] so I obtained a selection of her writing in her books and read them (Boole, 1972). Therein we see that the Booles took the unconscious seriously and she perhaps even more seriously. She devoted her life after his untimely death, to the reform of the teaching of math and other things along the lines Bell privately told her about, but proceeds in such a startlingly modern way, that it reads like a sophisticated twenty-first century psychoanalytic social worker, looking for how freedom is hindered by pedestrian teachers. Mary Boole (1832–1916) tried to reform other areas of society as well, using his ideas about the importance of algebraic notation as a means to prepare the mind to study science and also acquire freedom (again freedom). She even sought to develop a program to lessen the toxic effects bad teaching had on students where envy and the, to use her exact expression, the 'teacher lusts' help destroy students' minds. Both the Booles were out to capture the nature of the mind itself, that is why that called it the 'laws of thought.' How does this bear on Bion? He too was out to discover the laws of thought in a different way, that is not only K and –K but how disturbances in thinking in general can be seen and how the mind grows to contain thinking and experience.

The Booles saw that math is only properly understood when algebra is introduced. It works this way: let us say you are trying to learn multiplication. It starts with examples and practice, which is fine. But it is only understood when you see relations expressed in a general form by means of algebra, for instance if A times B is expressed in the common way as AB, and if we know it works in both directions, then we can grasp the (invariant) expression AB = BA. This is invariant and we now truly understand multiplication for the first time. On Mary's view, such things are not trivial for they enable people to be free from authority and think for themselves, see things for themselves, and have freedom in a real sense. It frees the mind to see more and have clear ideas that are not dependent on books, teachers, authority or toxic emotions. It is, in short, the capacity to think one's own thoughts and to claim the right and freedom to do so even when under pressure. Although this is incomplete, let me turn to transformation now.

From what I can track down, a transformation is a change of shape within a definite pattern. Again, it is infinitely complicated but we need to bring this to intuitability right here, so it becomes useful. A transformation is a change within an object that is predicable and describable in a precise mathematical manner. For instance, imagine a cylinder. Now, imaging a large building, a modern high-rise which has been constructed in the shape of a cylinder of, say, 120 floors in height. That building will inevitably be subjected to wind force strong enough to cause the building to sway and therefore bend and slightly distort in a twisting manner. This building is now no longer a cylinder, strictly speaking, but something like a cylinder. Now if we squash that building by dropping, say a cubic kilometer of iron ore on it, and it now becomes a disk, we might not then continue to call it a cylinder which has been distorted. If now apply this to Bion's notion of H or hate, then H can be distorted by defensive reorganization into its erotic version by means of sadomasochistic transformation of H into the erotic version of H. If you wanted to, I suppose this could be elegantly formalized. Since transformation occurs under a function and the function defines the, in this case, geometrical object in the first place, which is the object in our example being transformed.

Function was introduced to the world by Leibniz in 1694 (Bell, 1937, p. 98, in Bell's Chapter VI on Leibniz), but in a fuzzy way. Since Bion uses a version, let us summarize it. If $y = f(x)$ means that no matter what, whenever a numerical value is assigned to x, there is a resultant numerical value to y. (For simple, one-valued or uniform functions.) Therefore we can know the solution when we know one bit of information, since the function determines the other bit. From this simplification we could see that there are functions everywhere, including within the clinical data and experience the psychoanalyst is exposed to every day. From this we are on our way to Bion's model, or psychological instrument. If people do not learn from their own experience, which I think is true other than in rare cases, rather they repeat and accumulate multiple instances of emotional experiences but do not stop repeating or do not start learning, then what? Under the special condition if the analyst's mind performs a certain function, then some new 'learning' can occur, but we are not really in the education business, but rather the 'changing the patient' business, hence let us call it the transformation business. If we call designate that strange set of things the analyst has, that is those who can function as actual analysts, Alpha, where this alpha is left fairly non-specified on purpose (non-saturated in other words), then the micro change within a micro slice of the analytic encounter is a function of Alpha. Of course, we cannot give a numerical value to this, but our freedom of mind now being augmented by algebra, allows us to see the general pattern at a glance. This is very consistent with Descartes and Newton, who said he stood on the shoulders of giants, meaning Descartes, Kepler and Galileo, to see further (Bell, 1937 p. 93). But now we just stand on Bion's shoulders to see a bit further ourselves.

We see that I have given a perspective[13] on the idea of function and the idea of transformation being intrinsically related. There is not a determinate set of psychological functions that the analyst uses or that we see in patients. Therefore, there is the possibility of further work to help better specify more of these functions. So too, the types of transformations we see in ourselves and in others we listen to, are rather large in number and it might be worthwhile, as part of the ongoing research project of psychoanalysis to start to track down and record more of these.

Tarski, models and the model of the functioning analyst's mind

We know that Bion read a few of the logicians and selected elements that caught his attention, here too using the method of selecting facts. They include Aristotle (on names and naming), Quine (on logical connectors,[14] like that for 'and' which is written as either a dot or a horseshoe pointing down), and others, including Tarski who he cites. Therefore, I tracked down the work on the pages cited by Bion in Tarski's short work (1956) on basic logic. It casts some light on Bion's expressions 'model' and 'intact model.' It is clear that Bion very quickly moves to thoughts about what could be understood as our 'working analytic instrument.'

While seemingly daunting, since Tarski as a whole is complicated, it is pretty simple since Bion used only two pages and then goes on. The essence of the matter is that Tarski wanted to provide a mathematical model of sentences (or statements) we might make in such a way that equivocation was eliminated, that they have sufficient specificity so they were about something definite and they category mistakes. In other words, you could know if it was true or false or nonsense. Bion wanted to use this to form a template basically, where an analyst could have a model with blank sections and fill in the specific content when organizing clinical material about specific patients in order to say clear and true things about it, i.e. more scientific.

I will try to illustrate this with things a psychoanalyst might say to make it more transparent. If a psychoanalyst says *x* is a patient, while since we do not know who or what *x* is, we simply cannot determine if it is true that *x* is a patient. If we say, Ms. Dora is a patient, this is true if in fact Ms. Dora is actually a patient. If we say, the green armchair is a patient, this is false, since green arm chairs cannot be patients by definition (somewhat like $1 \div 2$ cannot be an integer). By extension, such basic model theory applies not only to integers and patients, but to anything the psychoanalyst might try to observe, experience, think about, or form a psychoanalytic theory about. This, therefore, casts some initial light on how Bion is using the expression 'model.' Now, it is obvious that we understand metaphors, we do not relegate them into the dustbin. So if a mathematician patient says, for example, 'psychoanalysis is peacock and about as important to science,' we are not lost. We can translate the metaphor into an analogy, determine which parts are true or false, and also, more importantly 'know how to go on' to use Wittgenstein's phrase. Here meaning we understand how to proceed clinically.

One further problem is that Bion also seems to talk about keeping the 'model' *intact* (which is both his mind and a mode of organizing the clinical material). When he does this he seems not to be speaking in exactly the same domain but rather to be talking about keeping our minds functioning as psychoanalysts or keeping our 'analytic instruments' intact. Clarity helps, or again, keeping our Alpha functions working and available. We know our mind can be attacked not only by patients but also by others.

In applying this dual-zone understanding of 'model' in Bion, we could say that there are several drafts of a model with which we could generate 'articulate speech' and talk to each other as psychoanalysts. Such better ways of talking might include abstract categories, such as the grid as but one draft attempt, where what we say can be judged to be either true or false rather than just babble. However, the zone of a 'model' is a working, internalized way of actually hearing what our patients are saying, without becoming insane ourselves and also without corrupting our mind to the point where confusion dominates. The last part might be included under 'transformations' and 'links.' Such models have yet to be fixed for all time and we have yet to 'data mine' Bion to extract various usable elements of his model so that we can discuss it. An element that has yet to be discussed is that, on his view, the reaction to frustration can be taking the emotional turmoil that results and developing logical thought as a result. Given that I have known some truly crazy (near psychotic) logicians along with some who are just neurotically tortured, it seems initially implausible that logic could in any way help produce sanity. But Bion does see something here about higher mental functions emerging to contain turmoil, which would entail a distinction between the flight to higher order thought as a comfort zone and the better use of it to gain mastery by being able to think our own thoughts. He correctly observes that with some psychotic people, aspects of logical intellect maybe nearly all that still functions; whereas the capacity for emotional transformation and the functions required to understand people are virtually non-existent. (I have had this experience clinically with an autistic-type mathematician female and an articulate schizophrenic male who was responsible for the development of a new department within universities.) So there is both a flexible sane sort of higher order algebraic thought and a rigid, insane version, which we might one distant day be able to better clarify for both ourselves and even eventually for mathematicians.

An endnote on the occupational hazard of Platonism

I want to end by briefly mentioning these two issues, first Plato, who, while not known as a mathematician, has loomed in the minds of every mathematician. Platonism is a view that mathematical relations, numbers and knowledge must exist prior to any human discovering it. Therefore, numbers and the like exist in a realm, which is apart from and above normal reality. Virtually every math student, engineer and many others are eventually tempted by Platonism since, given the vividness with which mathematical ideas present themselves and their enduring truth, it seems implausible that they are 'invented' rather than 'discovered.' If discovered, they must have already existed. Such a proclivity is an occupational hazard of the talented, much like carpal tunnel syndrome is an occupational hazard for people who type too much at a computer. It is raised by Bion with his 'O' and more so in discussions of 'O' by others.

Plato (who Bion also read) himself was, on the best reading, not a Platonist, at least not towards the end of his life. In one of his last dialogues, the Theaetetus, where Socrates discusses knowledge with the mathematician Theaetetus, he does not employ the use of pre-existing forms. Actually, Plato was old by that time, eighty-ish, and his students were getting bored by Plato always saying the same old thing (the same thing happened to Bion in England), hence he tried a different approach. Instead of relying on the pre-existence of mystical math entities, he argues that it emerges as result of a human interactive process (which is actually quite similar to the model of the interactive psychoanalytic session). It seems that Platonism and the pre-existing forms were introduced merely as a pedagogical device to help his students climb up the ladder towards being able to think for themselves. If we draw an analogy with Bion's 'O' then it would be advisable not to reify this along the lines of Platonism. Rather, O is that thing which the patient is actually talking about of which we get only an approximation and also, those things going on in the mind of the analyst, of which we also only get an approximation of (Massicotte, 1994, 2005). It is decidedly *unhelpful* to understand 'O' and his idea of intuition as part of God or the Godhead or some sort of mystical entity. Rather, it just trying to get to what is going on, or the real stuff, which we call the things-in-themselves, just as the mathematician turned philosopher, Husserl, did.

Thus we end and tolerate numerous omissions hoping someone else will become curious. If the hallmark of being an analyst is to develop the capacity to be curious about everything how can we then say, 'anything *but* math?' Bion did retain his curiosity about how to best apply his extrapolations of the essence of mathematical thinking towards improving psychoanalytic thinking even in his last writings. Therefore, he himself did not consider it a failed effort to be discarded.

Notes

1 Others have arrived at a similar take '*Science and Method* is one long argument in praise of both psychological and mathematical intuition, [quoting Poincaré] "... what the true scientist alone can see is the *link* that unites several facts which have a deep but hidden analogy"' (Gruber and Bödeker, 2005, p. 210, emphasis added).
2 Cf. Bion common sense, e.g. 'Common sense is only rarely in fashion. "Real" common sense, in contrast to cosmetic common sense, tells too many uncomfortable things.' (Bion, 1975/1979 [1991], Part III, p. 526).
3 Again, when aged just ten, Andrew Wiles who solved it, dreamed he would crack it.
4 Cf. McLarty, 1997, proposing numerous distinctions, proposing intuitionism divides into the banal, expansive and restrictive, etc. but seems to miss the overall point.
5 Bell was ahead of his time here since recent developments indicate that science fiction is non-trivial for the exercise of the scientific imagination. Bell's term for it was 'Fantascience' (Reid, 1993, p. 268). He wrote of time travel in 1931 and helped foster the genera of plausible science fiction which eventually led to Professor Freud appearing on *Star Trek* to explore the question of whether androids like Data can dream. The title of Bion's book *A Memoir for the Future*, seems to play on science fiction themes and prefigures films which would later appear (e.g. *Back to the Future*).
6 The pleasure of doing math is extreme, as many point out. I have heard from the couch the expression 'mathgasm' for the pleasure experienced in solving a problem. It can occasionally result full physical orgasms when solving a problem.
7 Bell shows the very wise council given to Poincaré that he hide his true ability from his examiners and appear both more stupid and conventional (p. 434). This is but one example of Bell's acute insight into how to survive.
8 Although the analyst Sheldon Roth wrote an interesting paper, not on Descartes but on the general problem, 'Dreams as the Royal Road to Unconscious Solutions,' it showed solutions to math problems might be dreamt. But the dream censor still applies, so the dreamer might not see the solution contained in the dream (Roth, 2005).
9 Isolating the invariant features of psychoanalysis to improve communication of psychoanalytic ideas and their teachability was an organizing idea I previously used (Massicotte, 1994, 1995).
10 A proposition, or P, is the carrier of truth since it cannot be any one expression of P in a natural language; say English or French, since both expressions must be equivalent lest translation of mathematical thought be impossible. Common examples of constants in math are π and e.
11 The origin of negation in a frustrated wish is also found in Husserl's *Logical Investigations* (1921 [1970], in a manner that does not fall prey to the fallacious pitfall of psychologism (for then there would be no foundation).
12 Cf. Mary Boole (1902) *Boole's psychology as a factor in education*. Colchester, Benham and Co. – see Boole 1972 for an excerpt.
13 I am leaving out vertex and vertices since they are just the points were lines meet, hence a triangle has three vertices. Therefore, it is a perspective when brought to the intuitive level and similar to the expression 'perspectival viewing' in Husserl, meaning we can look at it from a certain angle.
14 Cf. 'It would be useful to take a leaf out of the mathematical logician's book and consider concepts such as, "breast", "penis", etc. as conjunctions, or the emotions as connectives, or whatever else was thought to be most accurate' Bion (1992, p. 256).

Chapter 14

Investigating Bion's aesthetic turn

A Memoir of the Future and the 1970s

Matt ffytche

Research into Bion's work of the mid-1970s, and in particular the trilogy of 'postmodern' novels collected as *A Memoir of the Future* (1991) – *The Dream* (1975); *The Past Presented* (1977); *The Dawn of Oblivion* (1979) – is the least developed area of Bion scholarship. The relative neglect of this period in the psychoanalytic journals, taken in conjunction with his stepping down from the presidency of the British Psychoanalytical Society in 1965 and his departure for Los Angeles in 1968, has helped create the perception that the later 1960s and 1970s constitute a major break with the epistemological phase of Bion's work and with the British psychoanalytic establishment – a mental transition to a new and foreign territory (see, for instance, the criticisms raised in O'Shaughnessy, 2005). Advocates of the late work, such as Grotstein (2007) and Harris Williams (2010a), have in their own way confirmed this assumption by locating it as a 'turn' towards the aesthetic – implying, variously, a greater degree of interest in poetry, creativity, dream or mysticism.

This poses some interesting questions in terms of sources. It can lead naturally to the assumption that Bion was reading new authors and discovering new ideas which were inflecting the epistemological work of the 1960s in an entirely new direction. Various influences have been proposed in passing, including the impact of the Californian environment and the spirit of 1970s counter-culture; the long-term influence of Bion's 1930s analysis of Samuel Beckett (Connor 1998); the encouragement of another analysand, Roland Harris (Harris Williams 2010a, p. 28); and another long-range influence, C.J. Jung, whose work Bion had encountered at the Tavistock lectures in 1935. Moreover the aesthetic element in Bion's work can be conceived in various ways: as a shift from the conceptual to the sensuous; as an exploration of aesthetic pattern (Harris Williams 2010a, p. xi); as a 'poetic' model of the unconscious (Reiner 2008; Harris Williams 2010b); as a turn towards autobiography; or as a greater concern with myth and mystical experience (Grotstein 2007; Symington and Symington 1996).

For the purpose of this brief review of sources, I want to begin by reframing this debate in simpler terms, which is a question of whether we are witnessing the modelling of a new determining principle within Bion's approach to psychoanalysis (for instance, a 'poetic' or 'aesthetic' model displacing the previous epistemological work) or whether the major transition is one of expression or presentation – the use of an aesthetic form. It may be that ultimately these factors cannot be so easily separated, but in the first instance I want to make the case that nearly all the key theoretical ideas expressed in works such as *Memoir* are either extensions, or sometimes close repetitions, of propositions or tendencies put forward already in the work of the 1960s; what changes more radically is the mode of expression. I am therefore going to proceed by examining first the ideas that might have led to shifts in Bion's epistemological approach, and will then consider the influences on Bion's style of writing as a separate question. I will end with a brief consideration of 'dreaming' in the work of the 1970s.

Aesthetics and epistemology

Reviewing the contents of *Memoir* it is striking how many of its recurrent ideas are repeated from the 'epistemological phase' of the 1960s: alpha- and beta-elements; preconceptions; thoughts without a thinker; growth; constant conjunction; primitive thinking as an alimentary canal; binocular vision; transformation; O; L-, H- and K-links: these are ideas that were certainly all present in 1965, with many of them reaching back to 1962. In addition, a key preoccupation of the novels is the behaviour of groups under stress (the main ensemble of characters in *The Dream* – Alice, Rosemary, Roland, Robin and Tom – form erotic pairs, fight and take flight) showing continuities with the work of the 1940s. Projective identification is also an explicit theme: 'she had herself become the home of feelings that might have belonged to someone else' (Bion 1991, p. 14). For Donald Meltzer (1985) *Attention and Interpretation*, which might be taken as inaugurating this late phase, with its comparisons to Christian mysticism and Platonism, is very much 'an outgrowth of the earlier work' (Meltzer 1985, Part 3, p. 97) – and indeed, even these reference points had already emerged in *Transformations.* The implication is that one of the key sources for the theoretical ideas evident in the late work are concepts and formulations developed from *Learning From Experience* onwards.

This is particularly evident in Bion's turn away from scientific method, perceived as being inadequate for the object of investigation, and the initiation of a search for alternative ways of modelling psychical processes, as well as a growing emphasis on the 'unknowability' or 'ineffability' of experience. In many ways this characterises people's perception of the later work's concern with poetry and mysticism. In *Memoir* Bion presents psychoanalytic theory as vitiated by its commitments to 'classical logic' (1991, p. 265); 'We shall fail – if you think the problems can be solved in a framework where things happen in time and space' (p. 188). But the warning was already given in *Learning From Experience*, where 'the analyst must be circumspect in following even accepted scientific method; its weakness may be closer to the weakness of psychotic thinking than superficial scrutiny would admit' (Bion 1962, p. 14), and remains a continuous feature of his 1960s psychoanalytic writings.

There are two reasons why Bion finds existing scientific methods inadequate for psychoanalytic work. One arises from his speculative proposition of 'beta-elements' (1962) which radicalised Freud's notion of unconscious memories, and Klein's notion of unconscious phantasy, in that it evokes primary units of experience which fall beyond the range of human representation. They are 'infra-sensuous' and cannot themselves be experienced as phenomena, but must be inferred from the negative effects they produce on thought and symbolisation. Thus 'beta-elements are not felt to be phenomena, but things in themselves' (Bion 1962, p. 6); envy 'does not smell; it is invisible, inaudible, intangible' (Bion 1970, p. 54). There is a second, broader form of inadequacy, which seems to affect the whole of the psychoanalytic domain, and this is the sense that we lack an apparatus for representing psychical experience per se. Bion argues: 'there are no sense data directly related to psychic quality, as there are sense data directly related to concrete objects' (Bion 1962, p. 53); 'what the absolute facts are [of a session] cannot ever be known' (Bion 1965, p. 17); 'I am thus postulating mental space as a thing-in-itself that is unknowable, but that can be represented by thoughts' (Bion 1970, p. 11).

Such arguments, running through the work of the 1960s, establish the theoretical basis for *Memoir*'s exposition of psychoanalytic thinking, and lead directly to its preoccupation with a dark, ineffable core of experience: it is 'as difficult to see the centre of one's own personality' as it is to view the centre of the galaxy (Bion 1991, p. 254). In *Transformations* Bion linked this structural problem of 'unknowable' dimensions of experience to Kant's 'thing-in-itself' and to Plato's theory of forms, and established the term 'O' to designate 'unknowable ultimate reality' (Bion 1965, p. 140). This is in turn linked to representations of the unknowable in Dante, and the Christian mystics Meister Eckhart and St John of the Cross (Bion 1965, pp. 138–9). All these reference points are carried over into *Memoir* – in particular, allusions to Kant's noumena and Platonic forms. At the opening of *The Dream* Bion promises to confront facts 'as near to noumena as the human animal is likely to get' (Bion 1991, p. 4). However, this seems less a call to reorient psychoanalysis around a new philosophical or religious framework, which would represent the 'source' of Bion's late ideas, than a set of passing analogies for Bion's argument that certain elements of psychoanalytic experience may be unapproachable by the tools of thought. (There is a direct analogy here with Theodor Adorno's critiques of epistemology and instrumental reason in *Negative Dialectics*, also from the mid-1960s, which also led to a renewed engagement with aesthetic theory.)

The same might be said for many of the literary allusions Bion makes in *Memoir* (to Milton, Horace, Hopkins and so on) some of which date back to previous works, and recur in the South American lectures given in the mid-1970s, as well as the notes gathered in *Cogitations*. They help give rise to the perception that Bion is soliciting a new aesthetic dimension. In *Transformations* Bion suggested at one point: 'I cannot support this conviction by evidence regarded as scientific. It may be that the formulation belongs to the domain of the Asethetic' (Bion 1965, p. 38). However, the more general case Bion so often makes in the later work is not that there is a more useful, alternative model to be found in art, literature or poetry, but that Bion finds in such writers metaphors of 'darkness' and 'formlessness' of use in his own attempts to describe 'unrepresentable' dimensions of experience. After quoting these words from Milton

> The rising world of waters dark and deep
> Won from the void and formless infinite

Bion stresses 'I am not interpreting what Milton says but using it to represent O' (Bion 1965, p. 151). Lines of poetry here are a placeholder for an idea, not the invocation of a new foundational literary mode of analysis. The description is repeated in both volumes one and two of *Memoir*.

This more limited view of the role of the aesthetic in Bion's late work is borne out in the way in which he continues to locate it as one paradigm, or vertex, amongst others – the scientific, the religious, the mystical – all of which create different perspectives on truth, but none of which are adequate substitutes for the methodology that psychoanalysis should itself evolve. 'Psychoanalysis is not scientific, religious or artistic' (Bion 1970, p. 62); 'I do not expect the art [of psychoanalysis] to be analogous to music, painting, literary expression, sculpture or quantum mechanics' (Bion 1991, p. 88). It might be closer to Bion's intentions to suppose that he alludes to aesthetic models in order to disrupt some of the existing associations of psychoanalytic discourse, but not necessarily to privilege the aesthetic itself. In fact, the aesthetic is already potentially vitiated by its overt dependence on notions of sensuous experience, and vocabularies attached to sensuous representation (for instance, metaphor), whereas what is often sought by Bion is a language adequate to mental experience that is non-sensuous. From early on in the 1960s a goal of Bion's work is to purge the psychoanalytic vocabulary of the penumbra of concrete associations that language brings with it, because this encourages rogue emotional projections – the term alpha-function is, 'intentionally, devoid of meaning' (Bion 1962, p. 3); *Transformations* uses grid categories 'in order to escape from the trammels imposed by the penumbra of associations' possessed by certain terms (Bion 1965, p. 138). In this respect, the works of the 1970s continue to privilege the mathematical as a model for ridding terminology of its sensuous accompaniment (Bion 1991, p. 99). In *Memoir* lengthy passages are devoted to the model of Cartesian co-ordinates, or the possibility of an irrational mathematics (p. 50), or one freed 'from the fetters exposed by its genetical links with sense' (p. 30).

And yet, on the other hand, the failure or absence of sensuous or aesthetic dimensions of thinking is also conceived by Bion as a danger, in that alpha-function is tied to the sensuous. The lack of alpha-function, involving the 'absence of mental visual images of points, lines and space' (Bion 1970, p. 12) constitutes the conditions for psychosis. The possibility that something *closer* to alpha-function might be required is important, as it may form a basis for the decision to write *The Dream*. I will discuss this possibility below. But there is a further criticism levelled at epistemology I want to raise first, which has to do with a split between the search for knowledge, and the therapeutic task of establishing an emotional relation, or promoting growth within the analysand. The grid is the most obvious product of Bion's attempt to meet the demand, speculatively voiced in *Learning from Experience*, that psychoanalysis be rationally organised, using symbols which were 'part of a system of reference that was applied uniformly and universally' (Bion 1962, p. 38). Later it is 'an instrument for classifying and ultimately understanding statements' (Bion 1965, p. 13). At the same time, Bion was clear from early on that this kind of approach may be 'adequate when the problems are associated with the inanimate, but not when the object for investigation is the phenomenon of life itself' (Bion 1962, p. 14). *Learning from Experience* implicitly makes the comparison between a scientific outlook, which is 'more easily maintained in the relationship xKy if x uses a machine' (Bion 1962, p. 47), and psychotic attacks on alpha-function where 'live objects are endowed with the qualities of death' (p. 9).

The question arises then as to whether the grid is a transformation or evasion of emotional experience (substituting a painless relation for a painful one); or worse, an annihilation of its object. It is this perception which is key to the *Memoir*, because, though the grid itself is now absent from its flyleaf, one could argue that this is only because its negative effects are thematised all the more dramatically within the pages of *The Dream*. Its opening subject matter is a group of people whose 'normal' lives are subjected to invasion and the imposition of an alien authority which threatens their existence as personalities: 'Are you alive? ... All Alice's belongings were neatly ticketed, parcelled, labelled – though she could not see the labels – and removed' (Bion 1991, p. 18). The women undergo medical examinations which are 'minute and thorough. The wishes of the two girls were of no consequence' (p. 28). The substitution of classificatory relations for those of love or hate leave Alice 'naked, incongruous, without a point of reference that made sense' (p. 27). Elsewhere reference is made to 'the living who might as well be dead for all the thinking they do' (p. 59).

To sum up so far, ideas relating to the aesthetic in the *Memoir* can most often be related to one of the following concerns:

- psychoanalysis is its own paradigm, comparable to but ultimately unlike those of aesthetics, science or religion;
- poets (and religious mystics) have given powerful metaphorical descriptions of truth beyond expression, or ineffable levels of reality, and psychoanalysts need to learn to tolerate the same kind of idea (though not necessarily in the same terms);
- in order to render an account of internal life that doesn't eviscerate it by converting it into knowledge one might have to draw on forms of exposition closer to reverie or myth.

This last point seems crucial in the turn to the novelistic form which can be conceived both as an illustration of the existing ideas (from the 1960s) via a fictional dramatic form, and as an attempt at a new methodology, insofar as theoretical exposition is replaced by something more hallucinatory that gets closer to the very experience to be understood. 'Is it possible through psychoanalytic interpretation to effect a transition from knowing the phenomena of the real self to being the real self?' asked Bion in *Transformations* (1965, p. 147).

Poetry and literature

In the remainder of this chapter I will consider briefly some of the sources at Bion's disposal for the mode in which he cast his literary exposition of psychoanalysis (that is, not the theoretical content, but the 'aesthetic' style he chose), and, second, the place of the 'dream' in the *Memoir*. Just as the 'grid' emerged as a strategy to assemble, organise and contain Bion's thinking on psychoanalysis in the epistemological phase, so the 'science fiction novel' is the form chosen to represent many of the same ideas in the aesthetic phase. One of the implications of this decision may be that Bion recognised that, if the goal of psychoanalysis was not specifically an item of knowledge, but instead the ability to foster the tolerance of difficult experiences, abstraction and conceptualisation should be abandoned in favour of forms of representation capable of containing a greater degree of incoherence: narrative, mutilated narrative, or writerly free association.

The move towards the 'fictitious account of psycho-analysis' (Bion 1991, p. 4) was anticipated in a number of ways. In *Second Thoughts* Bion noted the distortions he was required to make in order to conceal the identity of his analysands – if they are effective, 'the narrative must be regarded as fiction'. Moreover, 'If the narrative were a work of art it might be reasonable to regard it as more nearly representative of truth than any literal transcription' (Bion 1967a, p. 120). In *Attention and Interpretation* Bion further loosened the boundary between fiction and fact by asserting that 'in any situation where a thinker is present the thoughts when formulated are expressions of falsities and lies' (Bion 1970, p. 117). The implication is that all psychoanalytic exposition is already fictional – both on the part of the analysand *and* the formulations of the analyst. In holding to this position, Bion was in fact not so far removed from similar arguments being put forward by postmodern philosophers such as Jacques Derrida in the 1970s, and Richard Rorty in the 1980s, though these must be seen as parallel developments, rather than sources. Observations made in *Learning from Experience* that 'the writing of this book is a realisation of K' (Bion 1962, p. 66) also raise the possibility that one could write a book from a different grid position, which would be not a realisation of K, but some other act – –K, or alpha-function.

The question of sources for the form and style of *Memoir of the Future* is important, as the most notable change is a stylistic one. The publication of *Cogitations* in 1992 has supplied much incidental evidence of Bion's day-to-day reading in the 1960s and 1970s (including of poets, mystics, religious and scientific texts) although none of this quite prepares one for the radically experimental and heterogeneous style of *Memoir.* Meg Harris Williams captures something of the impossibility of pinning down what genre the work belongs to when she characterises it as 'a mixture of dream-poem, Socratic dialogue, Shavian or Beckettian drama, Orwellian or Dodgsonian parable, and "pornographic novel" ' (2010a, p. 30).

Much of the writing on Bion's later work uses the epithets 'dream' and 'poetry' (Grotstein 2007; Reiner 2008; Harris Williams 2010a, 2010b), which is backed up by the frequent allusions to Keats, Shelley or Milton in the later writing as a whole, and by Francesca Bion's 'Envoi' to *All My Sins Remembered* which argues that 'poetry was of central importance to him all his life'. She also mentions his intention to compile an anthology of poetry for psychoanalysts (Bion 1985, p. 240). However, too great a stress on the 'literary greats' or on the British Romantic tradition – Bléandonu suggests 'Virgil, Dante and Milton' as antecedents (2000, p. 256); Harris Williams emphasises Blake, Keats and Shelley (2010a, 2010b) – can lead to a slight distortion in the representation of what Bion actually produced. What disturbs this view is the extreme experimentalism of the novels, which are as much 'anti-poetic', as they are poetic. I mean by this the lengthy passages in which the writing is fragmentary, or obtuse, or intentionally banal or bathetic. *Memoir* makes great efforts to resist conventional sentimentality, and to challenge conventional notions of 'aesthetic' beauty, in favour of forms of writing that correspond more to psychotic mechanisms, or at least convey as much hate and envy as they do love and regenerative capacity: 'These are scraps of a conversation destroyed and fragmented by a jealous, hostile, curious and destructive ... personality' (Bion 1991, pp. 120–121); 'voices resemble but are not a conversation; it is inchoate, it is not past. It is "minus k" ' (p. 155).

This dimension has been relatively neglected in commentary on *Memoir* – the ubiquity of sentences such as 'come ... come ... my beamish boy ... come. Not in terror like Ozymandias, but kind and good, like Hitler who chortled in his joy. Is that you Cap'n?' (Bion 1991, p. 41), which might be described as doggerel – a tissue of disjointed and trivial bits and pieces of quotation, and poor puns ('it is human to Ur ... Toot and come again' [Tutenkhamen] (Bion 1991, p. 51). Such patches of writing are linked to Bion's theorisation of paranoid-schizoid mechanisms, in which the normal grammar of thinking has been attacked. In *Attention and Interpretation*, he describes the impact of projection on language: 'the sentences were mutilated ... important parts of speech were missing' (Bion 1970, p. 22). Early in *The Dream* we are told that the characters 'were having dreams – mutilated dreams' (Bion 1991, p. 33).

There is good reason to suppose that this writing was drawing on acquaintance with work by James Joyce and Ezra Pound – that is, modernist examples such as the 'Night-town' sequence in *Ulysses*, Pound's *Cantos*, or the even more advanced semantic dislocation of *Finnegan's Wake. Memoir* not only contains many passing references to Joyce and Pound (for instance to Joyce's concept of *idée meres*; or, 'Fin i gain ... Alph where's Om?' Bion 1991, p. 135), but links their work in turn to psychotic mechanisms: 'It is like being bombarded with chunks of feeble puns, bits of Shakespeare, imitations of James Joyce, vulgarizations of Ezra Pound' (Bion 1991, p. 51) is voiced by the character P-S; in the Rio lectures, Bion notes that 'Ezra Pound has frequently been regarded as psychotic; his poems have been said to be rubbish' (1975, p. 39) (rubbish being routinely the subject of projection or evacuation). He also identifies Joyce's radicalism with Freud's (Bion 1991, p. 228). The point in characterising such writing as psychotic is not to denigrate it, but perhaps to test the reader's ability to tolerate frustration – which is a rather different model from that suggested by Romantic theories of aesthetic organicism, or the autonomous creativity of the imagination. In *Memoir* far more shock, danger and dislocation is involved in the writing, theorisation and organisation of material.

A parallel point concerns Bion's preference for demotic, or 'low-brow' genres of writing. Yes, there are frequent references in the text to 'Pope, Brooke, Shakespeare, Milton, Gita, Jesus, Eckhart' – but often these are a shorthand for the accumulations of wisdom in human culture as a whole, as these are debated (and subverted) by characters in the novels. Such allusions are at least matched by quotations and personae drawn from Conan Doyle (Sherlock and Mycroft Holmes), Gilbert and Sullivan, First World War trench songs ('We are Fred Karno's army'), *Diary of a Nobody* (Mr Pooter), and so on. Reference to Keats' 'negative capability' is balanced on the same page by one to 'Mister Toad' from Kenneth Grahame's *Wind in the Willows*.

If there is romanticism in Bion's turn to literature, then, it is closer to the German Romantic conception of the novel, which aimed not so much at coherence, as heterogeneity, irony and a shattering of conventional form – the novel as the container in which any kind of writing or experience could be incorporated (Friedrich Schlegel demanded novels that would be original, eccentric, fantastic, grotesque and 'a colourful hodgepodge of sickly wit' (Schlegel 1799) which seems a closer analogue to Bion's writing). Another example of a book which bursts its generic container might have come through Bion's encounter with Melville's *Moby Dick* (the encounter being itself memorialised in *Memoir*, p. 88). But the most explicit presence of a source text, pushing the novel form towards fantasy, paradox and eccentricity, is Lewis Carroll's Alice books. The Mad Hatter's tea-party was already cited in *Second Thoughts* to convey the destruction of the experience of time in the psychotic universe; in *Memoir* there are running allusions to the Cheshire Cat as personalities start to dematerialise, and *The Dream* itself is framed as the continuing adventures of Alice, who seemingly wakes up from Wonderland into an even more hallucinatory confusion of dream and reality. It seems that Carroll, Melville and Joyce most clearly influence the marked 'postmodernism' of Bion's own fictional style.

Finally, Bion also evidently drew on his own experience of scraps of psychotic conversation from his clinical encounters (many of the works of the 1960s already contain fictional dramatisations of psychoanalytic sessions). So that what one gets in the more literary parts of the novel (as opposed to those sections given over to debate and theorisation) is probably a merging together of experiences in sessions with imitations of Joyce and Carroll, as well as snatches of Bion's own memories and free associations.

Dream and biography

This leads to a final set of points about the centrality of dreaming in the late work, attested to by Grotstein, Meltzer, Harris Williams and others. Again it is important to consider tendencies developing over a longer period than just the 1970s. Already in 1962 Bion radically extended the implications of the 'dream' as a conceptual tool within psychoanalysis. It forms both a partial model for alpha-function and is intimately connected with the notion of 'reverie'. Most significantly, Bion framed the very differentiation of conscious and unconscious around the new concept of 'contact barrier', so that a process akin to dreaming, operating in sleep and waking, transforms beta-elements into symbolically perceptible elements (thus controlling the exclusion of certain kinds of emotional data, and constituting forms of symbolic narrative central to the existence of personality). A person converting impressions into alpha-elements 'is able to remain "asleep" or unconscious of certain elements that cannot penetrate the barrier represented by his "dream"' (Bion 1962, p. 15). Viewed in this light, a central preoccupation of *The Dream*, and *Memoir* as a whole, is an analysis of the way in which experience might move from a state in which alpha-function fails or is gradually evolving ('fact and nightmare were indistinguishable from hallucination,' 1991, p. 22) towards the possibility of primitive relationships ('a dream about violence and murder', 1991, p. 3), through mutilated conversations, to actual conversations, and towards debate and analysis. One of the models for the more constructive levels of experience attained by the characters (particularly in *The Past Presented*) is Plato's *Symposium*, in which characters from different walks of life meet to debate their understanding of love and human nature.

Various other dream texts are echoed throughout the writing of the novels – including *Alice in Wonderland*, *Finnegan's Wake* and sundry quotations from Shakespeare (*The Tempest*, *Hamlet*). One source, which is understated, but crucial as a model, is Freud's *Interpretation of Dreams*, and this comes through in a number of different ways. First, Freud provides the model for a book about dreaming which also forms the original core of the psychoanalytic enterprise; its foundational work. Second, it provides an example of a work that is both technical/conceptual and autobiographical, in that, though disguised, Freud's work was also an interpretation of *his own dreams* and therefore the product of a crucial stage in his own self-analysis. *Memoir* not only contains some of Bion's actual dreams (one of them a recurrent nightmare) but also reworks his own autobiography (retold more conventionally in *The Long Week-End* (1982) and *All My Sins Remembered* (1985)) *as* a dream, so that we are treated to a complex of theory evolved in response to his own experience, along with free associations to that material, and hallucinatory and fictional reworkings of it. Dream, one might say, for both Freud and Bion, was the most instructive point of entry into the life of the psyche, the evolution of the self, *and* the construction of psychoanalytic theory. The links between *Memoir* and the pair of autobiographical works have been ably traced by Harris Williams (2010a), who also points out the close relationship between many recurrent metaphors in Bion's work and the visual and structural features of key episodes in his life – 'the escape from the burning tank images the birth of thought itself' (2010a, p. 13). It is clear that *Memoir* is constantly working through both sides of this equation – the corpus of Bion's previous conceptualisations and metaphorical models from *Experiences in Groups* onwards, and their ramifications and anticipations in his own experiences, memories and dreams. Arguably, this brings a further dimension of self-reflection to the bridging of theory and subjectivity already pioneered in *The Interpretation of Dreams*.

This has been a necessarily abbreviated account of influences and arguments informing *Memoir*, which remains monumental, and relatively unabsorbed both by psychoanalytic and literary scholarship. As the continuities with the critical arguments of the earlier works become more established, it may be that *Memoir* ceases to function, as it now often does, as the repository for the unwanted aspects of those earlier arguments. O'Shaughnessy (2005), for instance, characterises the late work as defective for its 'less disciplined' thinking, and this may be so; but that also seems intimately connected with Bion's analysis of 'the instinct to know', which she finds 'of such notable psychoanalytic significance'. That is, Bion's theory of knowledge is hard to separate from his concern that the 'discipline' of thinking may evade something within the experiences that are to 'be known'. As Sandler (2004) suggested, Bion's greater distance from psychoanalytic officialdom in Britain may have enabled a freer development of these ideas – may have brought them prodigally, outrageously into the open, from where they had been hiding in the crevices in Bion's terser locutions of the 1960s. But the *Memoir* is not an entirely different country, and itself remains an important source for understanding the implications (theoretical and emotional) of some of his more widely heralded concepts.

Chapter 15

Conclusion

Bion's nomadic journey[1]

R.D. Hinshelwood and Nuno Torres

Bion spent his lifetime trying to make sense of human experiences. He could be said to be driven by considerable desire. Not only that, but it seems fair to say he was driven by memories he could not lay to rest. Not least were the experiences he suffered in 1917 in the First World War, when he commanded a unit in a tank battle at Amiens. He spent his lifetime trying to make sense of human experiences. And moreover, he struggled endlessly to understand the actual process of making the sense. In a paper to the British Psychoanalytical Society, titled 'Negative capability' (not published under that title) in 1967, Bion (1967b) developed his idea of memory and desire being an interference to understanding others, an interference to reverie. This was responded to in a letter by Winnicott, saying

> When I got home Clare reminded me again that the phrase memory and desire, which you have used before, is a quotation from T.S. Eliot, and she was able to give me the whole poem, and for some reason or other I accept memory and desire as naturally interrelated in the poem. At the same time in the application of the same idea to psycho-analytic work I cannot help finding myself using the word intention and not feeling desire to be correct. As you said, we each have to find the word that fits for oneself.
>
> (letter from Winnicott to Bion, 5 October 1967 in Rodman 1987, p. 196)

It is not clear if Bion had used the phrase in the way Eliot had intended. Eliot describes memory and desire as stirring dull roots, and with spring rain. All of this seems to imply a generative or regenerative function. (The crucial lines are numbers 4–5 of T.S. Eliot's *The Waste Land* (1922), also at: www.bartleby.com/201/1.html for those who want to check the actual wording.) Eliot's more fruitful inference to memory and desire throws doubt on whether Bion had in fact taken the phrase from Eliot or intended any reference. Of course, it is most likely Bion would have been aware of Eliot's despairing poem, written in 1922, just as he was attempting to recover from his own war experience.

Bion's memory and desire are interferences, to refer not merely to the distorting effect on the psychoanalyst's subjectivity when at work, but also the restlessness of his own predicament, the baggage he carried all of his life. By the time he was fifty-four, when he qualified as a psychoanalyst he had begun to make some progress with making sense. He made up for his late start with a varied and powerful contribution over the next twenty-five years, to making sense of psychoanalysis, and of the picture of the human mind that comes from it.

In this book we have taken certain territories that Bion hunted in to find the wherewithal to satisfy his need to understand. The territories we have picked may not seamlessly cohere together. This is, we would suggest, because Bion was in practice nomadic, settling in one intellectual place for a time, and then in another. In the course of his one life he travelled between history, literature, psychiatry, psychoanalysis, art, religion, philosophy, mathematics, politics, economics ... and no doubt others. To some extent this resembled Freud, but whereas Freud wrote in a linear narrative style, accumulating his points and his evidence and informing the reader with careful referencing and quotations, Bion wrote in a non-linear, labyrinthine and enigmatic style, purposely concealing and overlooking many of his sources, allegedly to achieve fresh outlooks, different vertices of reality, unsaturated with memory, and uncontaminated from intellectual prejudice.

We started the book by referring in our introduction to his daughter's curiosity about the breadth of varied reading in his library. And we have been provoked by that curiosity. At present thorough research into his library is not possible, and this book is limited by that restriction. If access is possible in the future, no doubt a very different book will be compiled. For the time being, we can make do with tracking down the sources of the influences on Bion's thinking, from his published works, including *Cogitations* (1992) which is the posthumous publication of his rich notes, logging his thinking, and in many cases the works by others from which those ideas of his sprang. There is no doubt that when he took ideas from elsewhere, and harnessed them for his own purposes, the ideas were inevitably sharpened or blunted in various ways, as he needed. This is only to be expected. But it is of course important that we should be aware of how the fate of concepts has fared in passing through Bion's own mind, and employed on his own projects. This is not to complain that he changed concepts he took up, merely that we are obliged to recognise not only the original concept, but the creative use made of it to form an enhanced (or even mutant) form of the idea.

There is no claim that we have exhaustively plotted all the origins of Bion's thinking, nor all the stretching and moulding of ideas that Bion undertook, wittingly or unwittingly. What is important is that Bion was faced with questions that crop up in psychoanalytic work, and he never shied away from facing the puzzles and having a go at solving them.

Did he solve those questions, inherent in the psychoanalytic project? Many different people will have a wide variation of different answers. There are many different Bions out there for all of us to construct our own version. But intriguingly, if the question were to have been asked of Bion himself, it is not clear he would have answered with any satisfaction that he had accumulated some answers. In fact one could conclude that Bion was never very satisfied, and that one of the reasons for his digging in so many domains of knowledge, was because of his dissatisfactions, a pressure to move on to find some more satisfactory answers. We want to suggest that this pattern of packing up and moving on, recurred through his professional life as an analyst.

Bion's caesuras

Bion's journey was to make sense of his life experiences, his patients', and of psychoanalysis in general. In the final phase of his search, he seemed to become resigned to seeking something unknowable, what he called 'O'. In this Conclusion about his journey, the three phases prior to the Los Angeles (from 1968) one were, first, in the 1940s when he researched groups and reality; then the 1950s was the schizophrenia decade; and third, in the 1960s he tried to squeeze together psychoanalysis, science and mathematics.

When his book *Attention and Interpretation* was published in 1970 he had finished all that, and he was on the cusp of his move from London to Los Angeles, and on the cusp of whatever the *internal* changes that went along with, and provoked, that geographical relocation. In a sense, each of the three phases I mentioned ended by running into the buffers as it were. Bion then moved onto the next phase. As Meltzer described it, Bion became familiar with caesuras from his own experience, 'the quality that distinguished Wilfred Bion, and which marks his passing from us with such serious consequences for psychoanalysis – perhaps for the world – was his capacity to tolerate caesura after caesura, to weather what he called "Catastrophic Change"' (Meltzer 1981, p. 13). When he moved on from his group work at the end of the 1940s, he simply started on the schizophrenia project with Klein, and with Segal and Rosenfeld, and others, with hardly a look over his shoulder. I say 'hardly' because there was a kind looking back, but it was a particular kind. It was not nostalgic. What he did when he reviewed his group work, was to take it as material with which he could then re-examine in the light of the new interest he was working on with colleagues of the 1950s. In other words he looked again at his group thinking but now with a framework of Klein's concepts of primitive (or psychotic) mechanisms. Arguably that same kind of reviewing of the schizophrenia years (Phase 2) occurred in the next, epistemological, phase (Phase 3), and then again in his fourth phase (in California) he appears to review his epistemological work in the same kind of way. Each of Bion's phases, apart from the first, includes a text that does this reviewing job I have just described – taking his recent observations and theories, and subjecting them to the enthusiasm he was developing for a new idea (maybe to be called a 'selected fact'). There are therefore three of these reviewing texts. They interleave, but are not bridges: they are reviews. They take a new perspective (a new vertex) on the work he has left behind. The caesuras, and the reviewing he did of each phase can be summarised as

Phase 1: Group work,

Phase 2: Schizophrenia, including, 'Group dynamics: a review' (1952/1955),

Phase 3: Epistemology, including the review text, 'Commentary' to *Second Thoughts* (1967a),

Phase 4: Intuition, including the review text, *Attention and Interpretation* (1970).

These phases correspond to those marked out by Bléandonu (1994).

The phases, the caesuras, and the review texts give Bion's body of work as a whole that sense of restlessness, which destroys any impression of smooth progress. The three texts mark disjunctions. The stopping places are discontinuous and Bion himself felt the need to theorise discontinuities of that kind. In 1977, at the end of his life, he wrote his paper titled 'Caesura', a term taken from Freud who wrote, 'There is much more continuity between intra-uterine life and earliest infancy than the caesura of the act of birth would have us believe' (Freud, 1926, p. 138). Each of Bion's characteristic moves was therefore performed with a specific strategy; the move (1) revises the work of the earlier phase; and (2) does so in the terms of the later phase.

We want here to concentrate on the reviewing texts, one for each of the three phases we mentioned. These are the paper called 'Group dynamics: A review', written in 1952 and revised in 1955; the lengthy Commentary at the end of *Second Thoughts* (1967a), which reviews his work on schizophrenia; and *Attention and Interpretation*, in which Bion rewrites his work on the philosophy of science and mathematics.

Group dynamics: a review (1952/1955)

This paper was first written in 1952 when he was still in his analysis with Klein, but he rewrote it in 1955 (Sanfuentes 2003; the 1955 version was republished in the collection of group papers in 1961). This paper indicates a radical disjunction in his group ideas, but he made a valiant attempt to create a joined-up review. The new perspective on groups is however from his *second* phase, analysing schizophrenics and their psychotic mechanisms.

In the reviewing text, he changed his theory of basic assumptions rendering it in terms of the Kleinian theory of primitive splitting mechanisms that cope with experiences of disintegration and annihilation. For instance, 'The impulse to pair may now be seen to possess a component derived from psychotic anxiety associated with primitive Œdipal conflicts working on a foundation of part-object relationships' (Bion 1955, p. 457), he is indicating the conversion of a basic assumption – pairing – to the functioning of the part-object level of the Oedipus complex.

Whereas basic assumptions were part of the inherited disposition of the individual, selected as an evolutionary advantage of the species, à la Trotter, he speculated in 1952, that being in a group is a psychotic experience defended against with the primitive mechanisms of splitting and projection that interrupt the proper appreciation of reality, just like psychosis in the individual. There is little doubt that disrupting experience was very familiar to Bion from his war service, and maybe earlier, his separation from home at the age of eight to go to an English boarding school.

He took the rather tired analogy of the social group as a surrogate family, and completely regenerated it by arguing that the group is experienced as a mind in pieces trying to get the pieces into some tolerable relation to each other:

> The more disturbed the group, the more easily discernible are these primitive phantasies and mechanisms; the more stable the group, the more it corresponds with Freud's description of the group as a repetition of family group patterns and neurotic mechanisms. But even in the 'stable' group the deep psychotic levels should be demonstrated, though it may involve temporarily an apparent increase in the 'illness' of the group.
>
> (Bion 1955b, p. 458)

He sees the pieces trying to get into relation with each other – either the pieces of a group, or the splits and part-objects of psychosis. His group theories from Phase 1 were reviewed in terms of the theories of the second phase.

Commentary in *Second Thoughts* (1967)

Now, moving on to a similar caesura after the second phase, the republication of his clinical papers on schizophrenia (in 1967) carried a commentary of 10,000 words, but this was in his third phase, the epistemological one. So, when faced with republishing the papers, he had reflected in 1967, in the context of his new preoccupations. The book contained all the papers on schizophrenia, but included other clinical work as well (his first was 'The imaginary twin', 1950, his membership paper for the Psychoanalytical Society; and 'On arrogance', 1958a). The body of the work is on the clinical phenomena of schizophrenia, and the disruption of two kinds of links: first, the link with reality which succumbs to an attack as Freud described, and second, the inward link between mental contents, or the links that hold together the 'constant conjunctions' a phrase used by Hume to denote the basic associations that constitute a mind. But the commentary no longer used these clinically inspired ideas to advance the understanding of schizophrenia. Instead, he was following his new interest, in Phase 3, the epistemological ones. So when he took the first of the papers, on the imaginary twin, and discussed it at length – in fact a third of the commentary – he was investigating the problems of writing a case history. The point of writing a case history is to communicate to other psychoanalysts. The problem is the linking between two professional analysts. This led him to consider the whole conception of the nature of science, and of a body of knowledge to be passed on, and passed around. What sort of links go on in one mind that can be transmitted with a conviction of truth through a link to another mind? In a sense the purpose of science is to link the knowledge and minds of separate researchers. But that purpose depends so much on the nature of knowledge, and its formulation in some sort of notation such that it may be transmitted with precision and conviction.

So, the commentary on his Phase 2 paper, in the midst of Phase 3, is doing the epistemological work of Phase 3, not adding to the clinical work of Phase 2. He took those schizophrenia papers as exemplars. The disorders of thought were used to investigate the nature of knowledge and science. From the disorders, Bion attempted to create a model of *properly* ordered thinking, and of linking through intellectual and scientific communication. Bion's reconsideration of the schizophrenia papers therefore reviewed the kind of knowledge which is to be expected from psychoanalysis.

Transformations (1965)

It is worth taking a slight detour from the series of reviewing texts which I have set myself, in order to consider the book, *Transformations* (1965). It addresses directly a concern for apparently incompatible points of view, or vertices. Through the mathematics of transformation, Bion discovered a powerful conceptual tool for understanding the relation between different points of view. The idea he drew on from the mathematical work of Cayley and Sylvester (see Bell 1937) was that changing a point of view can still carry across something common to both. A drawn circle on a piece of paper, if turned to an angle appears as an ellipse. However, something of the circle remains. A map is different from the geography it is a map of, but the relation of distances from London to New York compared with the distance from London to Los Angeles, is the same *ratio* on a map as on the ground. A painting of poppies in a field continues to bear a relation to the real thing, the poppy-field. The theory of transformation says there is some 'invariant' that is carried from one point of view to the other. If an invariant exists then the move from one to the other is a transformation

Therefore Bion's brilliant application was that if the problem with psychoanalytic debate is that people occupy different points of view, then we need to communicate about the invariants in those different points of view. Likewise a patient's conviction in the voices he hears, and the analysts 'take' on this as a hallucination, are different points of view, but there is an invariant, a content of meaning that the psychoanalyst can make constant between his view and the patient's. As president of the Psychoanalytical Society, between 1962 and 1965, he was literally presiding over, and inevitably functioning as an organisational bridge between, great theoretical differences.

At the same time, Bion could use the same principle in a more personal way. He appeared to be making sense of his own various different fields of study – groups, psychoanalysis, science and human communication (private and public). It is tempting to consider, and quite possibly true, that his research into transformations between points of view (vertices) was prompted by his need to string his own separate phases of thinking into a more integrated corpus. The notion of an invariant that is constant between quite diverse points of view may have been heartening for him personally as well as for his Society. In fact quite possibly he found it more satisfactory to try to integrate his own thinking, than to quell the clamour of the resolutely inharmonious groupings of the British Society. At this point perhaps quite explicitly he could consider these reviewing texts as trying to find the invariants between his own diverging points of view as he passed through a caesura between two phases.

Attention and Interpretation (1970)

In the course of the epistemological investigations in the 1960s, notably *Learning from Experience* (1962), and *Elements of Psycho-Analysis* (1963), Bion was concerned that psychoanalysis is not about hard facts, like material science. Psychoanalytic facts are not gained by sensuous experience. What the psychoanalyst deals with is non-sensuous; he can only *intuit* his patient, not sense or feel him/her, no measurement, and no objectivity. The caesura that disrupted the epistemological phase and put an end to it was the failure to tie psychoanalysis into a standard form of knowledge.

So in the next and final phase, in Los Angeles, psychoanalysis had to be severed from any continuity with other disciplines. Psychoanalytic knowledge is excitingly unique if it is discovered properly, and proper discovery is by intuition, rather than perception. Such realisations specific to the psychoanalytic setting may resemble hallucinations, he says, not ordinary observations. As Grotstein summarised, 'the truth drive functions in collaboration with an "unconscious consciousness" that is associated with the faculty of "attention", which is also known as "intuition"' (Grotstein 2004, p. 1081). The invariant, that which is known only from different perspectives, is a powerful conceptual tool for integrating apparently diverse perceptions and conceptions. If the invariant is only known from perspectives, it is essentially unknown in itself. This led Bion to explore the possibility of a collection of comparable concepts – the invariant, Kant's 'thing-in-itself', and also the ineffable which the religious mystics contemplated. He began to use the term 'O' to represent that 'unknown': that which cannot be perceived, only intuited.

So he had to review his work on the mathematical and scientific pillars of psychoanalysis, by reviewing them in terms of his new interest in intuition. This is the problem with which he started *Attention and Interpretation*. Like the previous review–summaries, *Attention and Interpretation* has its context rooted in the next phase, that beyond 1968, that occupied him in his new home in Los Angeles (from 1968). His new explorations concerned what he regarded as a distinct form of knowledge which only psychoanalysis can capture. Whilst he retained the 'grid', his mathematical/scientific creation, as his end-pieces to the book, he was in effect reviewing the epistemological work on knowing and thinking.

He began the book with a contrast between science (he chose medical science) and psychoanalysis. In particular, he discussed the difference between pain felt in the body, and psychic pain. One has to be cured, and the other needs a very different approach; *psychic* pain, for example a bereavement, has to be 'suffered'.

> Suppose the patient complained not of physical but of mental pain; no one doubts the existence of anxiety or sees any incongruity in seeking help to cure it. We find it necessary to differentiate between the pain of a broken leg and, say, bereavement; sometimes we prefer not to, but exchange mental for physical pain, and vice versa. Physician and psycho-analyst are alike in considering that the disease should be recognised by the physician; in psycho-analysis recognition must be by the sufferer too.
>
> (Bion 1970, pp. 5–6)

This puts a completely different complexion on things, captured in the ringing phrase, 'the abandonment of memory and desire'. Psychoanalytic 'observations' do not derive directly from the perception of the senses, and therefore strictly speaking are not empirical, he argued. What memory and desire do is that they employ empirical sensation that conceals and distracts from intuition. In his example, as clear as crystal glass, he gets us to recognise that suffering a bereavement is a quite different activity from the scientific treatment of a broken leg. Whether 'intuition' is the correct term is a moot point. What is clear is the difference in the point of view, in the *intention* as Winnicott put it.

So, the analogy between psychoanalysis and science became more and more difficult for Bion to sustain. The modality of psychoanalytic attention is not sensuous, emphasised when he said he preferred this term ['intuited'] to 'observed' or 'heard' or 'seen', as it does not carry the penumbra of sensuous association (Bion 1967a): 'I propose to use the term "intuit" as a parallel in the psychoanalyst's domain to the physician's use of "see", "touch", "smell", and "hear"' (Bion 1970, p. 7). The question then was how to optimise the function of intuition. So, in the book, he reiterated the short paper, 'Memory and desire' (Bion 1967b) dealing with a technique clearly akin to Freud's free-floating attention. But by maximising intuition he drew psychoanalysis as far from science as he could achieve. That meant towards art, aesthetics and mysticism. And to underline that, he quoted St John of the Cross, Keats and others.

All through the third, epistemological, phase of the 1960s, Bion had used the initial 'K' to indicate knowledge, the desire for knowledge, and the complex relationship with knowledge. However, in the fourth phase he claimed to find it incomprehensible. In introducing the compilation of the epistemological texts, *Seven Servants*, published in 1977, he wrote in typical ironic vein:

> I must have understood what I meant when I wrote it, but I do not understand what it means now. As the poet replied when asked what he meant by *Sordello*, 'Once God and Robert Browning knew, now, only God knows'.
>
> (Bion 1977, p. ii)

At this point in his fourth phase in Los Angeles during the 1970s, he gradually established another initial – 'O'. At the limits of 'K', there begins 'O'. The 'O' has allusions to the Kantian 'thing-in-itself'. It is what we perceive from a perspective, and thus distort. But for Bion, the psychoanalyst, 'O' means the experience of another person, knowable only by approximation through intuition. He now considered psychoanalysis as no longer about cure, but an attempt to know something inherently unknowable, 'O'. And human endeavour in general and psychoanalysis in particular are aligned as one on that project. But, he stumbled into the problem of what sort of a knowledge is created by a formal discipline that studies the unknowable.

Attention and Interpretation is a kind of summation of the conclusions on learning from experience, plus the problems that led to abandoning it. Perhaps the telling contrast between a broken leg and a bereavement indicating the vast gulf between the sensuous knowledge of science, and the experiential knowledge of psychoanalysis, is Bion's greatest legacy. It requires the suspension of memory and desire to allow the play of intuition. And only through intuition can we pursue the inner state of 'suffering' an experience. The prize of discovering the faith one must have in untrammelled intuition was a delicate formula that had taken all of seventy years and more to slowly wend his nomadic path towards.

Bion's words can make us feel enriched or disarmed, enlightened or confused, motivated or despairing. The reader is either critical of him or a devotee; or maybe we are more likely to be undecided and ambivalent, confused with *all* these different attitudes. Perhaps however, let us remain calmer in the face of the most precious of Bion's legacies; this is his overarching dismissal of simplistic intellectual arrogance and defensive certainty, combined with a faith, a hope, and an admiration for the human mind. That impelling openness is expressed clearly in his words from *Taming Wild Thoughts* written in the spring of 1977:

> This somewhat long-winded description is to draw attention to the fact that when you see your patient tomorrow, I do not know whom you will see and nor do you. It might be anybody. I am sure we have to have respect for that mind or personality; that seems to me the most valuable thing about the whole of psycho-analysis – the suggestion that the human mind and its products are worthy of attention. I am not suggesting you are going to see William Shakespeare; I am not suggesting that you are going to see the writer of *Baghavad Gita* or some famous painter or sculptor or composer, a Mozart – we don't know. But I do suggest that you will not know unless you are able to respect the actual experience made available to you when the patient goes so far as to spend time and money coming to see you.... It may turn out to be very worthwhile because the patient has gifts that have so far not been revealed or, have been dismissed on the grounds that he or she is stupid, or psychotic or crazy. The same thing may apply to ourselves.
>
> (Bion 1997 [1977], pp. 42–43)

Bion was open to many sources in his professional and personal quests. These sources, both explicit and implicit, were selected by a demanding mind that travelled widely; they are a sophisticated cuisine from which we may savour many dishes to feed our mental digestive system. They were chosen from the best ingredients and intellectual products of human thought available in our culture. The mental 'digestion' might be difficult, but if indigestion is not avoided, but suffered, then the eventual satisfactions are priceless and rewarding, they do not just inform us, but they will 'grow' us. Everyone must find the word that fits best. It is the need to travel the road in the dark. Bion might have agreed with a contemporary, Leonard Woolf (1969), that 'the journey not the arrival matters'. That could describe Bion's nomadic life, alighting at various points to savour what he can find, only to find the need to move on. Did he achieve his goal and make sense of his troubled life, or was his journey, in his own words, 'making the best of a bad job'?

Note

1 Much of the material in the concluding chapter, was part of a presentation at the First Annual Bion Conference of the Psychoanalytic Centre of California, in February 2011 by R.D. Hinshelwood.

References

Ackland, M., Choi, B. and Puska, P. (2003) Rethinking the terms non-communicable disease and chronic disease, *Journal of Epidemiology and Community Health*, 57(11): 838–839.

Adorno, Theodor W. (1990) *Negative Dialectics*, London: Routledge.

Alexander, F. (1936) Addenda to 'The Medical Value of Psychoanalysis', *Psychoanalytic Quarterly*, 5: 548–559.

Alexander, F. (1939) Psychological aspects of medicine, *Psychosomatic Medicine* 1(1): 7–18.

Alexander, F. and Pollock, G.H. (1968) *Psychosomatic Specificity. Vol. I: Experimental Studies and Results*, Chicago, IL: University of Chicago Press.

Allport, G.W. (1948 [1951]) Foreword to the 1948 edition, in G.W. Lewin (ed.) *Resolving Social Conflicts. Field Theory in Social Science*, Washington, DC: American Psychological Association, pp. vii–xiv.

Armelius, K. and Armelius, B.A. (1985) Group personality, task and group culture, in M. Pines (ed.) *Bion and Group Psychotherapy*, London: Routledge and Kegan Paul, pp. 255–273.

Armstrong, D. (1980) Madness and coping, *Sociology of Health and Illness*, 2(3): 293–313.

Atmanspacher, H. (2004) Quantum theory and consciousness: an overview with selected samples, *Discrete Dynamics in Nature and Society*, 2004(1): 51–73.

Baldwin, T. (2003) *The Cambridge History of Philosophy 1870–1945*, Cambridge: Cambridge University Press.

Ball, W.W.R. (1908) *A Short Account of the History of Mathematics*, New York: Dover Publications.

Béguin, A. and Thévenaz, P. (1943) *Henri Bergson: Essais et Témoignages Inedits*, Neuchatel: A La Baconniere.

Bell, D. (2011) Bion: the phenomenologist of loss, in C. Mawson (ed.) *Bion Today*, London/New York: Routledge.

Bell, E.T. (1937) *The Men of Mathematics: The Lives and Achievements of the Great Mathematicians from Zeno to Poincaré*, New York: Simon and Schuster.

Bergson, H. (1896 [1911]) *Matter and Memory*, London: George Allen and Unwin. Republished by Zone Books, New York, 1991.

Bergson, H. (1901[1920]) Dreams, in H. Bergson (ed.) *Mind-Energy*, London: Macmillan, pp. 84–108.

Bergson, H. (1903 [1912]) *An Introduction to Metaphysics*, Cambridge: Hackett Publishing Company.

Bergson, H. (1907 [1911]) *Creative Evolution*, New York: Henry Holt and Company.
Bergson, H. (1911 [1920]) *Mind-Energy: Lectures and Essays*. London: Macmillan.
Bernfeld, S. (1944) Freud's earliest theories and the school of Helmholtz, *Psychoanalytic Quarterly*, 13: 341–362.
Bion, F. (1995) The days of our years, *The Melanie Klein and Object Relations Journal*, 13(1): 1–25.
Bion, W.R. (1918 [1997]) Diary 1918, in F. Bion (ed.) *War Memoirs 1917–1919*. London: Karnac Books, pp. 72–197.
Bion, W.R. (1940) 'The war of nerves': civilian reaction, morale and prophylaxis, in E. Miller and H. Crichton-Miller (eds) *The Neuroses in War*, London: Macmillan.
Bion, W.R. (1946) The leaderless group project, *Bulletin of the Menninger Clinic*, 10: 77–81. Republished 1996 *Therapeutic Communities*, 17(2): 87–91.
Bion, W.R. (1948) Psychiatry at a time of crisis, *British Journal of Medical Psychology*, 21(2): 81–89.
Bion, W.R. (1948a [1961]) Experiences in groups: I, in W.R. Bion (1961) *Experiences in Groups and Other Papers*, London: Routledge, pp. 29–40.
Bion, W.R. (1948b [1961]) Experiences in groups: II, in W.R. Bion (1961) *Experiences in Groups and Other Papers*, London: Routledge, pp. 41–58.
Bion, W.R. (1949a [1961]) Experiences in groups: III, in W.R. Bion (1961) *Experiences in Groups and Other Papers*, London: Routledge, pp. 59–76.
Bion, W.R. (1949b [1961]) Experiences in groups: IV, in W.R. Bion (1961) *Experiences in Groups and Other Papers*, London: Routledge, pp. 77–92.
Bion, W.R. (1950a [1961]) Experiences in groups: VI, in W.R. Bion (1961) *Experiences in Groups and Other Papers*, London: Routledge, pp. 115–126.
Bion, W.R. (1950b) The imaginary twin, in W.R. Bion (1967) *Second Thoughts*. London: Heinemann.
Bion, W.R. (1950c [1961]) Experiences in groups: V, in W.R. Bion (1961) *Experiences in Groups and Other Papers*, London: Routledge, pp. 93–114.
Bion, W.R. (1951 [1961]) Experiences in groups: VII, in W.R. Bion (1961) *Experiences in Groups and Other Papers*, London: Routledge, pp. 127–137.
Bion, W.R. (1952) Group dynamics: a review, *International Journal of Psycho-Analysis*, 33: 235–247 [revised 1955 – see below].
Bion, W.R. (1954) Notes on the theory of schizophrenia, *International Journal of Psycho-Analysis* 35: 113–118. Expanded as Language and the schizophrenic, in Melanie Klein, Paula Heimann and Roger Money-Kyrle (eds) (1955) *New Directions in Psychoanalysis*, London: Tavistock. Republished in W.R. Bion (1967) *Second Thoughts*, London: Heinemann.
Bion, W.R. (1955) Group dynamics: a review, in Melanie Klein, Paula Heimann and Roger Money-Kyrle (1955) (eds) *New Directions in Psychoanalysis*. Reprinted 1961 in W.R. Bion, *Experiences in Groups*, London: Tavistock.
Bion, W.R. (1955a [1985]) Letter to Francesca, 25 July, in *All My Sins Remembered and Another Side of Genius*, Abingdon: Fleetwood Press.
Bion, W.R. (1955b [1985]) Letter to Francesca, 26 July, in *All My Sins Remembered and Another Side of Genius*, Abingdon: Fleetwood Press.
Bion, W.R. (1956) Development of schizophrenic thought, *International Journal of Psycho-Analysis* 37: 344–346. Reprinted 1967 in W.R. Bion, *Second Thoughts*, London: Heinemann.
Bion, W.R. (1957) Differentiation of the psychotic from non-psychotic personalities,

International Journal of Psycho-Analysis, 38(3/4): 266–275. Reprinted 1967 in W.R. Bion, *Second Thoughts*, London: Heinemann.

Bion, W.R. (1958a) On arrogance, *International Journal of Psycho-Analysis*, 39(2): 144–146. Reprinted 1967 in W.R. Bion, *Second Thoughts*, London: Heinemann.

Bion, W.R. (1958b) On hallucination, *International Journal of Psycho-Analysis*, 39(5): 341–349.

Bion, W.R. (1959) Attacks on linking, *International Journal of Psycho-Analysis*, 40, 308–315. Reprinted 1967 in W.R. Bion, *Second Thoughts*, London: Heinemann.

Bion, W.R. (1961) *Experiences in Groups and Other Papers*, London: Routledge.

Bion, W.R. (1962) *Learning from Experience*, London: Heinemann.

Bion, W.R. (1963) *Elements of Psycho-Analysis*, London: Heinemann.

Bion, W.R. (1965) *Transformations*, London: Tavistock.

Bion, W.R. (1966) Catastrophic change, *Bulletin of the British Psychoanalytic Society*, no. 5, London: British Psychoanalytic Society. Reprinted as Chapter 12 in W.R. Bion (1970) *Attention and Interpretation*. London: Tavistock.

Bion, W.R. (1967a) Notes on memory and desire. *Psychoanalytic Forum*. 2: 271–280. Reprinted in E. Bott Spillius (ed.) *Melanie Klein Today, Vol. 2: Mainly Practice*, London: Routledge, 1988, pp. 17–21.

Bion, W.R. (1967b) *Second Thoughts*, London: Heinemann.

Bion, W.R. (1970) *Attention and Interpretation*. London: Tavistock.

Bion, W.R. (1975/1979 [1991]) *A Memoir of the Future*, London: Karnac Books. [Three volumes collected 1991.]

Bion, W.R. (1975) *Bion's Brazilian Lectures 2*, Rio de Janeiro: Imago Editoria.

Bion, W.R. (1975 [2000]) Contributions to panel discussions: Brasilia, a new experience, in F. Bion (ed.) *Clinical Seminars and Other Works*, London: Karnac Books.

Bion, W.R. (1977 [1989]) The grid, in F. Bion and M. Patterson (eds) *Two Papers: 'The Grid' and 'Caesura'*, London: Karnac Books.

Bion, W.R. (1977 [1997]) *Taming Wild Thoughts*, London: Karnac.

Bion, W.R. (1977) *Seven Servants: Four Works by Wilfred R. Bion*, London/New York: Jason Aronson.

Bion, W.R. (1978 [1994]) Transcription of a tape recording, in F. Bion (ed.) *Cogitations: New Extended Edition*, London: Karnac Books.

Bion, W.R. (1997) *War Memoirs 1917–1919*. London: Karnac Books.

Bion, W.R. (1979 [2000]) Making the best of a bad job, in F. Bion (ed.) *Clinical Seminars and Other Works*, London: Karnac Books.

Bion, W.R. (1980) *Bion in New York and São Paulo*, Strath Tay: Clunie Press.

Bion, W.R. (1982) *The Long Week-End*, Abingdon: Fleetwood Press.

Bion, W.R. (1985) *All My Sins Remembered and Another Side of Genius*, Abingdon: Fleetwood Press.

Bion, W.R. (1989) *Two Papers: The Grid and Caesura*, London: Karnac Books.

Bion, W.R. (1991) *Learning from Experience*, London: Karnac.

Bion, W.R. (1992) *Cogitations*, London: Karnac.

Bion, W.R. (1993a) Attacks on linking, in W.R. Bion, *Second Thoughts*, London: Karnac Books.

Bion, W.R. (1993b) A theory of thinking, in W.R. Bion, *Second Thoughts*, London: Karnac Books.

Bion, W.R. (1993c) Commentary, in W.R. Bion, *Second Thoughts*, London: Karnac Books.

Bion, W.R. (1994) *Cogitations: New Extended Edition*, London: Karnac Books.

Bion, W.R. (2005) *The Long Week-End 1897–1919: Part of a Life*, London: Karnac Books.

Bion, W.R. and Rickman, J. (1943 [1961]) Intra-group tensions in therapy, in W.R. Bion (1961) *Experiences in Groups and Other Papers*, London: Routledge, pp. 11–26.

Bion Talamo, P., Borgogno, F. and Mercai, S.A. (eds) (1998) *Bion's Legacy to Groups*, London: Karnac Books.

Bion Talamo, P., Borgogno, F. and Mercai, S.A. (eds) (2000) *W.R. Bion: Between Past and Future*, London: Karnac Books.

Bjelland, A.G. (1981) Čapek, Bergson and proto-mentalism, *Process Studies*, 11(3): 180–189.

Bjelland, A.G. (1987) Durational succession and proto-mental agency, in A.C. Papanicolaou and P.A.Y. Gunter (eds) *Bergson and Modern Thought Towards a Unified Science*, Chur: Harwood Academic Publishers, pp. 19–28.

Bléandonu, G. (1994) *Wilfred Bion: His Life and Works 1897–1979*, London: Free Association Books.

Bléandonu, G. (2000) *Wilfred Bion: His Life and Works 1897–1979*, New York: Other Press.

Bloom, D.E., Cafiero, E.T., Jané-Llopis, E., Abrahams-Gessel, S., Bloom, L.R., Fathima, S., Feigl, A.B., Gaziano, T., Mowafi, M., Pandya, A., Prettner, K., Rosenberg, L., Seligman, B., Stein, A.Z. and Weinstein, C. (2011) *The Global Economic Burden of Noncommunicable Diseases*, Geneva: World Economic Forum.

Bolyai, Farkas (1820) Letter (4 April) to his son, János Bolyai, in J.J. O'Connor and E.F. Robertson, 'Farkas Wolfgang Bolyai' (March 2004), web article in MacTutor, online, available at: www-history.mcs.st-andrews.ac.uk/Biographies/ Bolyai_Farkas.html.

Boole, M.E. (1972) A Boolean anthology: selected writings of Mary Boole on mathematical education, compiled by D.G. Tahta, Nelson: Association of Teachers of Mathematics.

Boris, H.N. (1986) Bion re-visited, *Contemporary Psychoanalysis*, 22: 159–184.

Bornstein, P.L. (1996) *Against the Gods: The Remarkable Story of Risk*, New York: John Wiley and Sons.

Bowlby, J. (1988) Development psychiatry comes of age, *American Journal of Psychiatry*, 145(1): 53–62.

Braithwaite, R.B. (1953) *Scientific Explanation: A Study in the Function of Theory, Probability and Law in Science*, Cambridge: Cambridge University Press.

Braithwaite, R.B. (1955) *Scientific Explanation: A Study in the Function of Theory, Probability and Law in Science*, 2nd edition, Cambridge: Cambridge University Press.

Braithwaite, R.B. (1970) Bertrand Russell as philosopher of science, *The British Journal for the Philosophy of Science*, 21(2): 129–132.

Britton, R. (1998) *Belief and Imagination: Explorations in Psychoanalysis*, London: Routledge.

Bronfenbrenner, U. (1979) *The Ecology of Human Development: Experiments by Nature and Design*, Cambridge, MA: Harvard University Press.

Bronfenbrenner, U. (2005) *Making Human Beings Human: Bioecological Perspectives on Human Development*, Thousand Oaks: Sage Publications.

Brown, L. (2011) *Intersubjective Processes and the Unconscious: An Integration of Freudian, Kleinian and Bionian Perspectives*, London: Routledge.

Brown, J.A.C. (1964) *Freud and the Post-Freudians*, London: Penguin.
Brown, S. (2003) Preconception and realisation: a constant conjunction of theory and measurement, in R.M. Lipgar and M. Pines (eds) *Building on Bion: Branches. Contemporary Developments and Application of Bion's Contributions to Theory and Practice*, London: Jessica Kingsley, pp. 285–300.
Brown, S. (2004) Paton, in *Oxford Dictionary of National Biography*, online, available at: www.oxforddnb.com./view/article/65672 [accessed 1 November 2010].
Brown, T.M. (2000) The rise and fall of American psychosomatic medicine, talk given at the New York Academy of Medicine on 29 November 2000, online, available at: http://human-nature.com/free-associations/riseandfall.html.
Cannon, W.B. (1914) The emergency function of the adrenal medulla in pain and the major emotions, *American Journal of Physiology*, 33: 356–372.
Cannon, W.B. (1932) *The Wisdom of the Body*, New York: W.W. Norton.
Cannon, W.B. (1935) Stresses and strains of homeostasis, *American Journal of Medical Science*, 189(1): 1–14.
Cannon, W.B. (1942) Voodoo death, *American Anthropologist*, 44(2): 169–181.
Čapek, M. (1971) *Bergson and Modern Physics: A Reinterpretation and Re-evaluation*, Dordrecht-Holland: D. Reidel.
Carlson, N.R. (1994) *Physiology of Behaviour*, 5th edition, Boston, MA: Allyn and Bacon.
Cartwright, D. and Zander, A. (1953) *Group Dynamics: Research and Theory*, London: Tavistock.
Cassel, J. (1964) Social science theory as a source of hypothesis in epidemiological research, *American Journal of Public Health*, 54(9): 1482–1488.
Chalmers, A.F. (1999) *What is This Thing Called Science?* Buckingham: Open University Press.
Choi, B., Hunter, D., Tsou, W. and Sainsbury, P. (2005) Diseases of comfort: primary cause of death in the 22nd century, *Journal of Epidemiology and Community Health*, 59(12): 1030–1034.
Clarke, Graham (2006) *Personal Relations Theory: Fairbairn, Macmurray and Suttie*, London: Routledge.
Clifford, W.K. (1874) *Lectures and Essays*. London: Macmillan.
Cohen, R.A. (1999) Philo, Spinoza, Bergson: the rise of an ecological age, in J. Mullarkey (ed.) *The New Bergson*, Manchester: Manchester University Press, pp. 18–31.
Connor, S. (1998) Beckett and Bion, online, available at: www.stevenconnor.com/beckbion.
Corning, P.A. (2002) The re-emergence of 'emergence': a venerable concept in search of a theory, *Complexity*, 7(6): 18–30.
Corrao, F. (1981) Bion's model of transformation of thoughts, *Riovista di psicoanalisi*, 27(3/4): 684–694.
Crichton-Miller, H. (1920a) Physical etiology, in H. Crichton-Miller (ed.) *Functional Disease: An Epitome of War Experience for the Practitioner*, Oxford: Oxford University Press, pp. 3–13.
Crichton-Miller, H. (1920b) The mother complex, in H. Crichton-Miller (ed.) *Functional Disease: An Epitome of War Experience for the Practitioner*, Oxford: Oxford University Press pp. 115–128.
Crichton-Miller, H. (1933) *Psychoanalysis and its Derivatives*, London: Thornton Butterworth.

Crichton-Miller, H. (1935) Psychotherapy clinics in fact and fancy, *British Medical Journal*, 1935(1): 1205–1208.

Crociani-Windland, L. (2009) How to live and learn: learning, duration and the virtual, in S. Clarke and P. Hoggett (eds) *Researching Beneath the Surface: Psycho-Social Research Methods in Practice*, London: Karnac Books, pp. 51–78.

Curd, M. and Cover, J.A. (1998) *Philosophy of Science: The Central Issues*, New York: W.W. Norton.

Damasio, A. (2000) *The Feeling of What Happens: Body, Emotion and the Making of Consciousness*, London: Vintage.

Dampier, W. (1944) *A Shorter History of Science*, Cambridge: Cambridge University Press.

Darwin, C. (1871) *The Descent of Man*, online, available at: http://darwin-online.org.uk/EditorialIntroductions/Freeman_TheDescentofMan.html.

Davidson, L. (1985) The strange disappearance of Adolf Meyer, *Orthomolecular Psychiatry*, 9(2): 135–143.

de Board, R. (1978) *The Psychoanalysis of Organizations*, London: Tavistock.

De Maré, P. (1985) Major Bion, in M. Pines (ed.) *Bion and Group Psychotherapy*, London: Routledge and Kegan Paul, pp. 108–112.

Descartes, R. (1628/1647 [1911]) *The Philosophical Works of Descartes, Volume I*, London: Cambridge University Press.

Deutsch, F. (1939) The choice of organ in organ neuroses, *International Journal Of Psycho-Analysis*, 20: 252–262.

Dicks, H.V. (1970) *Fifty Years of the Tavistock Clinic*, London: Tavistock.

Double, D.B. (2007) Adolf Meyer's psychobiology and the challenge for biomedicine, *Philosophy, Psychiatry, and Psychology*, 14(4): 331–339.

Dunbar, H.F. (1935) *Emotions and Bodily Changes: A Survey of Literature on Psychosomatic Interrelationships*, New York: Columbia University Press.

Dunbar, H.F. (1943) *Psychosomatic Diagnosis*, New York: P.B. Hoeber, Inc.

Eastman, T.E. and Keeton, H. (2004) *Physics and Whitehead: Quantum, Process, and Experience*, New York: State University of New York Press.

Eddington, A. (1928) *The Nature of the Physical World*, Cambridge: Cambridge University Press.

Edelman, G. (1992) *Bright Air, Brilliant Fire: On the Matter of the Mind*, New York: Basic Books.

Eidelson, R.J. (1997) Complex adaptive systems in the behavioral and social sciences, *Review of General Psychology*, 1(1): 42–71.

Eliot, T.S. (1922) The waste land, *The Criterion*, 1: 50–64.

Engel, G.L. (1977) The need for a new medical model: a challenge for biomedicine, *Science*, 196: 129–136.

Fenichel, O. (1946) Nature and classification of the so-called psychosomatic phenomena, *Psychoanalytic Quarterly*, 14: 287–312.

Ferro, A. (2006) Clinical implications of Bion's thought, *International Journal of Psycho-Analysis*, 87(4): 989–1003.

Ferro, A. (2011) Clinical implications of Bion's thought, in C. Mawson (ed.) *Bion Today*, London/New York: Routledge.

Fisher, J. (2011) The emotional experience of K, in C. Mawson (ed.) *Bion Today*, Abingdon: Routledge.

Fowles, J. (1969) *The French Lieutenant's Woman*, London: Jonathan Cape.

Franck, G. (2008) Presence and reality: an option to specify panpsychism? *Mind and Matter*, 6(1): 123–140.

Freud, S. (1888) Some points for a comparative study of organic and hysterical motor paralyses, *The Standard Edition of the Complete Psychological Works of Sigmund Freud, Volume I*, London: Hogarth, pp. 157–172.

Freud, S. (1890) Psychical (or mental) *treatment*, *The Standard Edition of the Complete Psychological Works of Sigmund Freud, Volume VII*, London: Hogarth, pp. 281–302.

Freud, S. (1891) *Zur Auffassung der Aphasien*, Leipzig: Deuticke.

Freud, S. (1895 [1950]) Project for a scientific psychology, *The Standard Edition of the Complete Psychological Works of Sigmund Freud, Volume I*, London: Hogarth, pp. 281–391.

Freud, S. (1900a) The interpretation of dreams, part I, *The Standard Edition of the Complete Psychological Works of Sigmund Freud, Volume IV*, London: Hogarth, pp. 1–338.

Freud, S. (1900b) The interpretation of dreams, part II, *The Standard Edition of the Complete Psychological Works of Sigmund Freud, Volume V*, London: Hogarth, pp. 339–625.

Freud, S. (1905a) Fragment of an analysis of a case of hysteria, *The Standard Edition of the Complete Psychological Works of Sigmund Freud, Volume VII*, London: Hogarth, pp. 3–124

Freud, S. (1905b) Jokes and their relation to the unconscious, *The Standard Edition of the Complete Psychological Works of Sigmund Freud, Volume VIII*, London: Hogarth, pp. 9–236.

Freud, S. (1908) 'Civilized' sexual morality and modern nervous illness, *The Standard Edition of the Complete Psychological Works of Sigmund Freud, Volume IX*, London: Hogarth, pp. 177–204.

Freud, S. (1910) The psycho-analytic view of psychogenic disturbance of vision, *The Standard Edition of the Complete Psychological Works of Sigmund Freud, Volume XI*, London: Hogarth, pp. 209–218.

Freud, S. (1911a) Formulations on the two principles of mental functioning, *The Standard Edition of the Complete Psychological Works of Sigmund Freud, Volume XII*, London: Hogarth, pp. 213–226.

Freud, S. (1911b) Psychoanalytic notes on an autobiographical account of a case of paranoia (dementia paranoides), *The Standard Edition of the Complete Psychological Works of Sigmund Freud, Volume XII*, London: Hogarth, pp. 3–82.

Freud, S. (1912) Recommendations to physicians practising psycho-analysis, *The Standard Edition of the Complete Psychological Works of Sigmund Freud, Volume XII*, London: Hogarth, pp. 109–120.

Freud, S. (1913) Totem and taboo, *The Standard Edition of the Complete Psychological Works of Sigmund Freud, Volume XIII*, London: Hogarth, pp. 1–162.

Freud, S. (1915a) The unconscious, *The Standard Edition of the Complete Psychological Works of Sigmund Freud, Volume XIV*, London: Hogarth, pp. 159–215.

Freud, S. (1915b) Repression, *The Standard Edition of the Complete Psychological Works of Sigmund Freud, Volume* XIV, London: Hogarth, pp. 141–158.

Freud, S. (1915c) Instincts and their vicissitudes, *The Standard Edition of the Complete Psychological Works of Sigmund Freud, Volume XIV*, London: Hogarth, pp. 109–140.

Freud, S. (1920) Beyond the pleasure principle, *The Standard Edition of the Complete Psychological Works of Sigmund Freud, Volume XVIII*, London: Hogarth, pp. 1–64.

Freud, S. (1921) Group psychology and the analysis of the ego, *The Standard Edition of the Complete Psychological Works of Sigmund Freud, Volume XVIII*, London: Hogarth, pp. 65–144.

Freud, S. (1923) The ego and the id, *The Standard Edition of the Complete Psychological Works of Sigmund Freud, Volume XIX*, London: Hogarth, pp. 3–68.

Freud, S. (1924) Neurosis and psychosis, *The Standard Edition of the Complete Psychological Works of Sigmund Freud, Volume XIX*, London: Hogarth, pp. 149–156.

Freud, S. (1925) Negation, *The Standard Edition of the Complete Psychological Works of Sigmund Freud, Volume XIX*, London: Hogarth, pp. 233–240.

Freud, S. (1926) Inhibitions, symptoms and anxiety, *The Standard Edition of the Complete Psychological Works of Sigmund Freud, Volume* XX, London: Hogarth, pp. 75–176.

Freud, S. (1927a) Fetishism, *The Standard Edition of the Complete Psychological Works of Sigmund Freud, Volume XXI*, London: Hogarth, pp. 149–156.

Freud, S. (1927b) The future of an illusion, *The Standard Edition of the Complete Psychological Works of Sigmund Freud, Volume XXI*, London: Hogarth, pp. 3–58.

Freud, S. (1930) Civilization and its discontents, *The Standard Edition of the Complete Psychological Works of Sigmund Freud, Volume XXI*, London: Hogarth, pp. 59–145.

Freud, S. (1937) Constructions in analysis, *The Standard Edition of the Complete Psychological Works of Sigmund Freud, Volume XXIII*, London: Hogarth, pp. 255–270.

Freud, S. (1938) An outline in psycho-analysis, *The Standard Edition of the Complete Psychological Works of Sigmund Freud, Volume XXIII*, London: Hogarth, pp. 141–296.

Freud, S. (1938 [1940]) Splitting of the ego in the process of defence, *The Standard Edition of the Complete Psychological Works of Sigmund Freud, Volume XIII*, London: Hogarth, pp. 271–278.

Freud, S. and Breuer, J. (1895) Studies on hysteria, *The Standard Edition of the Complete Psychological Works of Sigmund Freud, Volume II*, London: Hogarth.

Friedman, M. (1985) Toward a reconceptualization of guilt, *Contemporary Psychoanalysis*, 21(4): 501–547.

Gillespie, W.H. (1942) The inter-relationship of mind and body, *International Journal of Psycho-Analysis*, 23: 45–46.

Gillespie, W. (1979) Ernest Jones: the bonny fighter, *International Journal of Psycho-Analysis*, 60: 273–279.

Glover, J. (1924) Problems in dynamic psychology: review of John T. MacCurdy's 'A Critique of Psycho-Analysis and Suggested Formulations', *International Journal of Psycho-Analysis*, 5: 379–385.

Godwin, R.W. (1991) Wilfred Bion and David Bohm: toward a quantum metapsychology, *Psychoanalysis and Contemporary Thought*, 14(4): 625–654.

Goudge, T.A. (1949) Editor's introduction, in H. Bergson (1912 [1949]) *An Introduction to Metaphysics*, Cambridge: Hackett Publishing Company, Inc. Originally published in French in 1903.

Granqvist, P., Mikulincer, M. and Shaver, P.R. (2010) Religion as attachment: normative processes and individual differences, *Personality and Social Psychology Review* 14(1): 49–59 [special issue on 'Religiosity: perspectives from social and personality psychology' edited by C. Sedikides].

Green, A. (1998) The primordial mind and the work of the negative, *International Journal of Psychoanalysis*, 79: 649–665.

Greenberg, J.R. and Mitchell, S.A. (1983) *Object Relations in Psychoanalytic Theory*, Cambridge, MA: Harvard University Press.

Gregg, A. (1953) The place of psychoanalysis in medicine, in F. Alexander and H. Ross (eds) *20 Years of Psychoanalysis: A Symposium in Celebration of the Twentieth Anniversary of the Chicago Institute for Psychoanalysis*, Oxford: W.W. Norton, pp. 28–49.

Grotstein, J.S. (1981) Wilfred R. Bion: the man, the psychoanalyst, the mystic a perspective on his life and work, *Contemporary Psychoanalysis*, 17(4): 501–536.

Grotstein, J.S. (2004) The seventh servant: the implications of a truth drive in Bion's theory of 'O', *International Journal of Psychoanalysis*, 85(5): 1081–1101.

Grotstein, J.S. (2007) *A Beam of Intense Darkness: Wilfred Bion's Legacy to Psychoanalysis*, London: Karnac Books.

Gruber, H.E. and Bödeker, K. (eds) (2005) *Creativity, Psychology and the History of Science*, Dordrecht: Springer, Series: Boston Studies in the Philosophy of Science, Vol. 245.

Guillemin, R. (1977) Peptides in the brain: the new endocrinology of the neuron, Nobel lecture, 8 December, in: J. Lindsten (ed.) (1992) *Nobel Lectures in Physiology or Medicine 1971–1980*, Singapore: World Scientific Publishing Company, pp. 364–397.

Hadamard, J. (1973) *The Psychology of Invention in the Mathematical Field*, Princeton, NJ: Princeton University Press.

Hadfield, J.A. (1917) Mind and brain: A discussion of immortality from the standpoint of science, in B.H. Streeter, *Immortality: An Essay in Discovery*, London: Macmillan.

Hadfield, J.A. (1952) *Mental Health and the Psychoneuroses*, London: Allen and Unwin.

Hadfield, J.A. (1954) *Dreams and Nightmares*, Harmondsworth: Penguin.

Halliday, J.A. (1948) *Psychosocial Medicine: A Study of the Sick Society*, London: Heinemann.

Harris Williams, M. (2010a) *Bion's Dream: A Reading of the Autobiographies*, London: Karnac Books.

Harris Williams, M. (2010b) *The Aesthetic Development: The Poetic Spirit of Psychoanalysis: Essays on Bion, Meltzer, Keats*, London: Karnac Books.

Harrison, T. (2000) *Bion, Rickman, Foulkes and the Northfield Experiments: Advancing on a Different Front*, London: Jessica Kingsley.

Hart, B. (1912) *The Psychology of Insanity*, London: Cambridge University Press.

Hayward, R. (2009) Enduring emotions: James L. Halliday and the invention of the psychosocial, *Isis*, 100(4): 827–838.

Heaton, J. (1989) Review: 'The Origins of Love and Hate', by Ian Suttie, *Free Associations*, 1S: 128–133.

Heidelberger, M. (2005) Naturphilosophie, in E. Craig (ed.) *The Shorter Routledge Encyclopedia of Philosophy*, London/New York: Routledge.

Heisenberg, W. (1962) *Physics and Philosophy*, New York: Harper and Row.

Hersh, R. (1997) *What is Mathematics, Really?* Oxford University Press.

Hinshelwood, R.D. (1987) *What Happens in Groups: Psychoanalysis, the Individual and the Community*, London: Free Associations.

Hinshelwood, R.D. (1989) *A Dictionary of Kleinian Thought*, London, Free Associations.

Hinshelwood, R.D. (1995) Psychoanalysis in Britain: points of cultural access, 1893–1918, *International Journal of Psychoanalysis*, 76(1): 135–151.

Hinshelwood, R.D. (1997) *Therapy or Coercion: Does Psychoanalysis Differ from Brain-Washing?* London: Karnac Books.

Hinshelwood, R.D. (1999) How Foulkesian was Bion? *Group Analysis*, 32(4): 469–488.

Hinshelwood, R.D. (2001) *Thinking about Institutions: Milieux and Madness.* London: Jessica Kingsley.

Hinshelwood, R.D. (2003) Group mentality and having a mind, in R.M. Lipgar and M. Pines (eds) *Building on Bion: Roots*, London: Jessica Kingsley, pp. 181–197.

Hinshelwood, R.D. (2004) Two early experimenters with groups, *Group Analysis*, 37(3): pp. 323–333.

Hinshelwood, R.D. and Chiesa, M. (2001) *Organizations, Anxiety and Defence*, London: John Wiley.

Hoch, P.H. (1952) Psychosomatic problems: methodology, research material and concepts, *Psychoanalytic Review*, 39(3): 213–221, online, available at: www.pep-web.org/document.php?id=psar.039.0213a.

Hollway, W. (2008) The importance of relational thinking in the practice of psycho-social research: ontology, epistemology, methodology and ethics, in S. Clarke, P. Hoggett and H. Hahn (eds) *Object Relations and Social Relations*, London: Karnac Books, pp. 137–162.

Hume, D. (1758 [1996]) An enquiry concerning human understanding, in D. Appelbaum (ed.) *The Vision of Hume*, Shaftsbury: Element, pp. 94–130.

Hume, D. (1779) *Dialogues Concerning Natural Religion. The Second Edition.* London: Entered in Stationers Hall according to Act of Parliament.

Hume, D. (2004) *Treatise of Human Nature and Enquiry Concerning Human Understanding*, Harmondsworth: Penguin Classics.

Humphrey, N. (2000) *How to Solve the Mind–Body Problem*, Thorverton: Imprint Academic.

Husserl, E. (1921 [1970]) *Logical Investigations, Vol. 2*, trans. J.N. Findlay, New York: Humanities Press.

Huxley, T. (1870) *On the Physical Basis of Life*, New Haven, CT: Charles C. Chatfield.

Imbasciati, A. (1998 [2006]) *Constructing a Mind: A New Basis for Psychoanalytical Theory*, Hove/New York: Routledge.

Imbasciati, A. (2002) A psychoanalyst's reflections on rereading a cognitivist: toward an explanatory theory of relationship, *Psychoanalytic Review*, 89(5): 595–630.

Jarvie, I.C. (1993) Obituary: J.O. Wisdom, *The Independent*, 4 March, online, available at: www.independent.co.uk/news/people/obituary-j-o-wisdom-1495568.html.

Jones, E. (1940) Wilfred Trotter, *International Journal of Psycho-Analysis*, 21: 114.

Jones, E. (1942) The concept of a normal mind, *International Journal of Psycho-Analysis*, 23: 1–8.

Jones, E. (1945) Reminiscent notes on the early history of psycho-analysis in English-speaking countries, *International Journal of Psycho-Analysis*, 26: 8–10.

Kant, I. (1783) [1983]) *Prolegomena to Any Future Metaphysics that will be able to present Itself as a Science*, Indianapolis, IN: Hackett.

Kant, I. (1788 [1997]) *Critique of Practical Reason*, Cambridge: Cambridge University Press.

Kant, I. (1929) *Critique of Pure Reason*, translated by Norman Kemp Smith. London: Palgrave (A: 1781 (first edition) B: 1787 (second edition)).

Karterud, S.W. (2000) The group emotionality rating system, in A.P. Beck and C.M. Lewis (eds) *The Process of Group Psychotherapy: Systems for Analyzing Change*, Washington, DC: American Psychological Association, pp. 113–134.

Karterud, S.W. and Foss, T. (1989) Group emotionality rating system: a modification of Thelen's method of assessing emotionality in groups, *Small Group Behavior*, 20(2): 131–150.

Khaleelee, O. and Miller, E. (1985) Beyond the small group: society as an intelligible field of study, in M. Pines (ed.) *Bion and Group Psychotherapy*, London: Routledge and Kegan Paul, pp. 354–385.

King, P. (2003) Introduction: the rediscovery of John Rickman and his work, in P. King, *No Ordinary Psychoanalyst: The Exceptional Contributions of John Rickman*, London: Karnac, pp. 1–68.

King, P. and Steiner, R. (1991) *The Freud–Klein Controversies 1941–45*. London: Routledge in association with the Institute of Psycho-Analysis, London.

Klein, M. (1935) *A Contribution to the Psychogenesis of Manic-Depressive States*, London: Hogarth.

Klein, M. (1946) Notes on some schizoid mechanisms, *International Journal of Psycho-*Analysis, 27: 99–110; republished (1952) in Melanie Klein, Paula Heimann, Susan Isaacs and Joan Riviere, *Developments in Psycho-Analysis*, London: Hogarth, pp. 292–320.

Klein, M. (1960) A note on depression in the schizophrenic, in M. Klein, *Envy and Gratitude and Other Works*, London: Hogarth.

Klein, M. (1997) The mutual influences in the development of ego and id, in M. Klein, *Envy and Gratitude and Other Works 1946–1963*, London: Vintage, Random House.

Klein, M. (1998a) A contribution to the psychogenesis of manic–depressive states, in M. Klein, *Love, Guilt and Reparation and Other Works 1921–1945*, London: Vintage, Random House.

Klein, M. (1998b) Mourning and its relation to manic–depressive states, in M. Klein, *Love, Guilt and Reparation and Other Works 1921–1945*. London: Vintage, Random House.

Kothari, M. and Mehta, L. (1998) The cloning bandwagon, *Issues in Medical Ethics*, 6(1): 17–19.

Kottler, J.A. and Englar-Carlson, M. (2010) *Learning Group Leadership: An Experiential Approach*, 2nd edition, London: Sage Publications.

Kramer, S. (2011) 'The dangers of this atmosphere': a Quaker connection in the Tavistock Clinic's development, *History of the Human Sciences*, 24(2): 82–102.

Kretzmann, N. and Stump, E. (2005) Aquinas, Thomas, in E. Craig (ed.) *The Shorter Routledge Encyclopedia of Philosophy*, London/New York: Routledge, pp. 30–48.

Lacan, Jacques (1947) La psychiatrique anglaise et la guerre, *L'évolution psychiatrique*, 27: 293–312.

Leibniz, G. (1679/1704 [1890]) *The Philosophical Works of Leibniz*, New Haven, CT: Tuttle, Morehouse and Taylor.

Lewin, K. (1935a) The conflict between Aristotelian and Galileian modes of thought in contemporary psychology, in K. Lewin (ed.) *A Dynamic Theory of Personality: Selected Papers*, New York/London: McGraw-Hill, pp. 1–42.

Lewin, K. (1935b) On the structure of the mind, in K. Lewin (ed.) *A Dynamic Theory of Personality: Selected Papers*, New York/London: McGraw-Hill, pp. 43–65.

Lewin, K. (1935c) Environmental Forces in child behaviour and development, in K. Lewin (ed.) *A Dynamic Theory of Personality: Selected Papers*, New York/London: McGraw-Hill, pp. 66–113.

Lewin, K. (1935d) Substitute activity and substitute value, in K. Lewin (ed.) *A Dynamic Theory of Personality: Selected Papers*, New York/London: McGraw-Hill, pp. 180–193.

Lewin, K. (1935e) Survey of the experimental investigations, in K. Lewin (ed.) *A Dynamic Theory of Personality: Selected Papers*, New York/London: McGraw-Hill, pp. 239–273.

Lewin, K. (1936 [1951]) Social-psychological differences between the United States and Germany, in G.W. Lewin (ed.) *Resolving Social Conflicts: Field Theory in Social Science*, Washington, DC: American Psychological Association, pp. 15–34.

Lewin, K. (1937 [1999]) Psychoanalysis and topological psychology, in M. Gold (ed.) *The Complete Social Scientist: A Kurt Lewin Reader*, Washington, DC: American Psychological Association, pp. 67–74.

Lewin, K. (1939 [1951]) Experiments in social space, in G.W. Lewin (ed.) *Resolving Social Conflicts: Field Theory in Social Science*, Washington, DC: American Psychological Association, pp. 59–67.

Lewin, K. (1943a) Forces behind food habits and methods of change, in *The Problem of Changing Food Habits: Report of the Committee on Food Habits 1941–1943*, Washington, DC: National Research Council, National Academy of Sciences, pp. 35–65.

Lewin, K. (1943b[1951]) Cultural reconstruction, in G.W. Lewin (ed.) *Resolving Social Conflicts: Field Theory in Social Science*, Washington, DC: American Psychological Association, pp. 35–39.

Lewin, K. (1944 [1951]) The solution of a chronic conflict in industry, in G.W. Lewin, (ed.) *Resolving Social Conflicts: Field Theory in Social Science*, Washington, DC: American Psychological Association, pp. 125–143.

Lewin, K. (1945 [1951]) Conduct, knowledge and acceptance of new values, in G.W. Lewin (ed.) *Resolving Social Conflicts: Field Theory in Social Science*, Washington, DC: American Psychological Association, pp. 56–70.

Lewin, K. (1947a) Frontiers in group dynamics: concept, method and reality in social science, *Human Relations*, 1(1): 5–41.

Lewin, K. (1947b) Frontiers in group dynamics: II. Channels of group life; social planning and action research, *Human Relations*, 1(2): 143–153.

Lewin, K. (1948 [1999]) Group decision and social change, in M. Gold (ed.) *The Complete Social Scientist: A Kurt Lewin Reader*, Washington, DC: American Psychological Association, pp. 330–341.

Lewin, K., Lippitt, R. and White, R.K. (1939) Patterns of aggressive behavior in experimentally created 'social climates', *Journal of Social Psychology*, 10(2): 271–299.

Lewis, M. (2000) Toward a development of psychopathology: models, definitions, and prediction, in A. Sameroff, M. Lewis and S. Miller (eds) *Handbook of Developmental Psychopathology*, 2nd edition, London: Kluwer Academic/Plenum Press, pp. 3–22.

Lewis, M. and Granic, I. (2000) *Emotion, Development, and Self-Organization: Dynamic*

Systems Approaches to Emotional Development, Cambridge: Cambridge University Press.

Lipgar, R.M. (1998) Beyond Bion's experiences in groups: group relations research and learning, in P. Bion Talamo, F. Borgogno and S.A. Merciai (eds) *Bion's Legacy to Groups*, London: Karnac Books, pp. 25–38.

Lokhorst, G.-J. (2011) Descartes and the pineal gland, in E.N. Zalta (ed.) *The Stanford Encyclopedia of Philosophy* (summer 2011 edition), online, available at: http://plato.stanford.edu/archives/sum2011/entries/pineal-gland.

Long, J.D. (2007) *A Vision for Hinduism: Beyond Hindu Nationalism*, London: Tauris.

Lopez-Corvo, R. (2005) *The Dictionary of the Work of Bion*, London: Karnac Books.

Lyth, O. (1980) Wilfred Ruprecht Bion (1897–1979) *International Journal of Psycho-Analysis*, 61: 269–273.

MacDonald, P.S. (2003) *History of the Concept of Mind: Speculations about Soul, Mind and Spirit from Homer to Hume*, Aldershot: Ashgate Publishing.

Mancia, M., Longhin, L. and Mancia, D. (2000) Kant's philosophy and its relationship with the thought of Bion and Money-Kyrle, *The International Journal of Psychoanalysis*, 81(6): 1197–1211.

Martin, P.A. (1960) On scierneuropsia, a previously unnamed psychogenic visual disturbance, *Journal of the American Psychoanalytic Association*, 8: 71–81.

Massicotte, W.J. (1994) A philosophical examination of recent clinical and theoretical psychoanalysis, PhD dissertation, Montreal: McGill University.

Massicotte, W.J. (1995) The surprising philosophical complexity of psychoanalysis (belatedly acknowledged), *Psychoanalysis and Contemporary Thought*, 18(1): 3–31.

Massicotte, W.J. (2005) Bion workshop, unpublished paper presented to the Canadian Psychoanalytic Society. AGM, Toronto.

Matthews, E. (1999) Bergson's concept of a person, in J. Mullarkey (ed.) *The New Bergson*, Manchester: Manchester University Press, pp. 118–134.

Mawson, C. (2011) *Bion Today*, London: Routledge.

McLarty, C. (1997) Poincaré: mathematics and logic and intuition, *Philosophia Mathematica* 5(2): 97–115.

Mead, M. (1947) The concept of culture and the psychosomatic approach, *Psychiatry*, 10(1): 57–76.

Meltzer, D. (1979 [1998]) *The Kleinian Development*, London: Karnac Books and the Harris Meltzer Trust.

Meltzer, D. (1985) *The Kleinian Development*, Strath Tay: Clunie Press.

Meltzer, D. (1986) *Studies in Extended Metapsychology: Clinical Applications of Bion's Ideas*, Strath Tay: Clunie Press.

Meltzer, D. (1981) Memorial meeting for Dr Wilfred Bion (1981), *International Review of Psychoanalysis*, 8: 3–14. Republished 1994 as '"The diameter of a circle" in the work of Wilfred Bion', in D. Meltzer, *Sincerity and Other Works*, ed. A. Hahn, London: Karnac Books, pp. 469–474.

Meyer, A. (1933) British influences in psychiatry and mental hygiene, *British Medical Journal*, 1(3777): 928–929.

Miller, E. (1998a) Are basic assumptions instinctive? in P. Bion Talamo, F. Borgogno and S.A. Merciai (eds) *Bion's Legacy to Groups*, London: Karnac Books, pp. 39–52.

Miller, E. (1998b) A note on the protomental system and 'groupishness': Bion's basic assumptions revisited, *Human Relations*, 51(12): 1495–1508.

Miller, J. (1983) Crowds and power: some English ideas on the status of primitive personality, *International Review of Psycho-Analysis*, 10: 253–264.

Money-Kyrle, R. (1936) The origins of love and hate, *International Journal of Psycho-Analysis*, 17: 137–138.

Moore, F.C.T. (2003) Bergson, in T. Baldwin (ed.) *The Cambridge History of Philosophy 1870–1945*, Cambridge: Cambridge University Press, pp. 67–73.

Morgan-Jones, R. (2010) *The Body of the Organisation and its Health*, London: Karnac Books.

Morgan-Jones, R. and Torres, N. (2010) Individual and collective suffering of organisational failures in containment: searching for a model to explore proto-mental dynamics, *Socio-Analysis*, 12(2010): 57–75.

Mullarkey, J. (1999) *The New Bergson*, Manchester: Manchester University Press.

Murray, H. (1990) The transformation of selection procedures: the War Office Selection Boards, in E. Trist and H. Murray (eds) *The Social Engagement of Social Science: Volume 1: The Socio-Psychological Perspective*, series: A Tavistock Anthology, Philadelphia, PA: University of Pennsylvania Press, pp. 45–67.

Nagel, T. (1979) *Mortal Questions*, Cambridge: Cambridge University Press.

Nandy, A. (1979) Ramanujan in England: an East–West collaboration in science, *Psychoanalytic Review*, 66(3): 423–442.

Nelson, E.E. and Panksepp, J. (1998) Brain substrates of infant–mother attachment: contributions of opioids, oxytocin, and norepinephrine, *Neuroscience Biobehavioral Research*, 22(3): 437–452.

Nemiah, J.C. (1987) Foreword, in G.J. Taylor (ed.) *Psychosomatic Medicine and Contemporary Psychoanalysis*, Madison, CT: International Universities Press, pp. xi–xiv.

O'Leary, M. (2010) *Revolutions of Geometry*, Hoboken, NJ: John Wiley and Sons.

O'Shaughnessy, E. (1995) 'Wilfred Bion: His Life and Work, 1897–1979', by Gérard Bléandonu, *International Journal of Psychoanalysis*, 76: 857–859.

O'Shaughnessy, E. (2005) Whose Bion? *International Journal of Psychoanalysis*, 86(6): 1523–1528.

Odin, S. (1982) *Process Metaphysics and Hua-Yen Buddhism*, Albany, NY: State University of New York Press.

Panksepp, J. (1999) Emotions as viewed by psychoanalysis and neuroscience: an exercise in consilience, *Journal of Neuro-Psychoanalysis*, 1(1): 15–38.

Panksepp, J. (2004) *Affective Neuroscience: The Foundations of Human and Animal Emotions*, Oxford: Oxford University Press.

Paton, H.J. (1927) *The Good Will: A Study in the Coherence Theory of Goodness*, London: Routledge.

Paton, H.J. (1931) The key to Kant's deduction of the categories, *Mind*, 40(159): 310–329.

Payne, S.M. (1952) Dr. John Rickman, *International Journal of Psycho-Analysis*, 33: 54–60.

Payne, S.M. (1957) 'Foreword', in J. Rickman, *Selected Contributions to Psycho-Analysis*, London: Hogarth Press and Institute of Psychoanalysis, pp. 9–16.

Pines, M. (1999) Forgotten pioneers: the unwritten history of the therapeutic community movement, *Therapeutic Communities*, 20(1): 23–42.

Pines, M. (2000) *Bion and Group Psychotherapy*, London: Jessica Kingsley.

Poincaré, H. (1907 [1914]) *Science and Method*, London: Thomas Nelson and Sons.

Popper, K. (1959) *The Logic of Scientific Discovery*, first English edition, London: Hutchinson and Co. (originally published in 1935).

Popper, K. (1977a) Materialism transcends itself, in K. Popper and J. Eccles (eds) *The Self and Its Brain*, New York: Springer International, pp. 3–35.

Popper, K. (1977b) Materialism criticized, in K. Popper and J. Eccles (eds) *The Self and Its Brain*, New York: Springer International, pp. 51–99.

Popper, K. and Eccles, J. (1977) *The Self and Its Brain*, New York: Springer International.

Prager, J. (1981) Moral integration and political inclusion: a comparison of Durkheim's and Weber's theories of democracy, *Social Forces*, 59(4): 918–950.

Prideaux, E. (1920) Mechanisms of hysteria, in H. Crichton-Miller (ed.) *Functional Disease: An Epitome of War Experience for the Practitioner*, Oxford: Oxford University Press, pp. 41–60.

Rapaport, D. (1953) On the psycho-analytic theory of affects, *International Journal of Psycho-Analysis*, 34: 177–198.

Rapaport, D. and Gill, M.M. (1959) The points of view and assumptions of metapsychology, *International Journal of Psycho-Analysis*, 40: 153–162.

Reid, C. (1993) *The Search for E.T. Bell, Also Known as John Taine*, Washington DC: The Mathematical Association of America.

Reiner, A. (2008) The language of the unconscious: poetry and psychoanalysis, *Psychoanalytic Review*, 95(4): 597–624.

Rescher, N. (2000) *Process Philosophy: A Survey of Basic Issues*, Pittsburgh, PA: University of Pittsburgh Press.

Rickman, J. (1938 [1957]) Need for a belief in God, in J. Rickman (1957) *Selected Contributions to Psychoanalysis*, London: Hogarth, pp. 384–390.

Rickman, J. (1938 [2003]) Does it take all kinds to make a world? in P. King (ed.) *No Ordinary Psychoanalyst: The Exceptional Contributions of John Rickman*, London: Karnac Books, pp. 159–183.

Rickman, J. (1950 [1957]) The factor of number in individual and group dynamics, in J. Rickman (1957) *Selected Contributions to Psychoanalysis*, London: Hogarth Press and Institute of Psychoanalysis, pp. 165–169.

Robinson, H. (2005) Materialism in the philosophy of mind, in E. Craig (ed.) *The Shorter Routledge Encyclopedia of Philosophy*, London/New York: Routledge, pp. 635–636.

Robinson, K. (2009) *Deleuze, Whitehead, Bergson: Rhizomatic Connections*, London: Palgrave Macmillan.

Rorty, R. (1979) *Philosophy and the Nature of the Mirror*, Princeton, NJ: Princeton University Press.

Roth, S. (2005) Dreams as the royal road to unconscious solutions, in the proceedings of the Russian–American Psychoanalytic Conference, 'Modern Psychoanalysis: What We Think about, How We Work, What We Want?' Moscow, 22–23 October, online, available in English at: www.spp.org.ru/page.php?id=99, and in Russian at: www.spp.org.ru/page.php?id= 145&PHPSESSID=54d31de9d342e.

Ryff, C.D. and Singer, B.H (2001) *Emotion, Social Relationships and Health*, New York: Oxford University Press.

Ryle, G. (1949) *The Concept of Mind*, London: Hutchinson.

Sameroff, A. (1975) Transactional models in early social relations, *Human Development*, 18(1/2): 65–79.

Sandler, J. (1997) *Freud's Models Of The Mind: An Introduction*, London: Karnac Books.

Sandler, P.C. (2003) Bion's war memories: a psychoanalytical commentary: living experiences and learning from them: some early roots of Bion's contributions to psychoanalysis, in R.M. Lipgar and M. Pines (eds) *Building on Bion: Roots*, London: Jessica Kingsley, pp. 59–84.

Sandler, P.C. (2004) Bion's work presented: A memoir of the future, some thoughts on its oblivion and dawn, Funzione Gamma 20, online, available at: http://www.funzionegamma.it/bions-work-presented-a-memoir-of-the-future-some-thoughts-on-its-oblivion-and-dawn.

Sandler, P.C. (2006) The origins of Bion's work, *International Journal of Psychoanalysis*, 87(1): 179–201.

Sandler, P.C. (2010) *The Language of Bion: A Dictionary of Concepts*, London: Karnac.

Sanfuentes, M. (2003) Group dynamics: a review, in R.M. Lipgar and M. Pines (eds) *Building on Bion: Roots*. London: Jessica Kingsley, pp. 118–131.

Sayers, J. (2002) Darling Francesca: Bion, love-letters and madness, *Journal of European Studies*, 32(125/126): 195–207.

Schafer, R. (1997) *Tradition and Change in Psychoanalysis*, Madison, CT: International Universities Press.

Schermer, V.L. (1985) Beyond Bion: the basic assumption states revisited, in M. Pines (ed.) *Bion and Group Psychotherapy*, London: Routledge and Kegan Paul, pp. 139–156.

Schermer, V.L. (2003) Building on 'O': Bion and epistemology, in R.M. Lipgar and M. Pines (eds) *Building on Bion: Roots*. London: Jessica Kingsley, pp. 226–253.

Schermer, V.L. and Pines, M. (1994) *Ring of Fire. Primitive Affects and Object Relations in Group Psychotherapy*, London/New York: Routledge.

Schlegel, F. (1799 [2003]) Letter about the novel, in J.M. Bernstein (ed.) *Classic and Romantic German Aesthetics*, Cambridge: Cambridge University Press.

Schopenhauer, A. (1844 [1969]) *The World as Will and Representation, Volume I*, New York: Dover Publications.

Schultz, J.H. (1932) 'Organneurosen' als psychotherapeutisches Problem, *Fortschritte Der Neurologie, Psychiatrie Und Ihrer Grenzgebiete*, 4: 337–360.

Scruton, R. (1982) *Kant*, Oxford: Oxford University Press.

Shaver, P.R. and Fraley, R.C. (2000) Attachment theory and caregiving, *Psychological Inquiry*, 11(2): 109–114.

Shimony, A. (1965) Quantum physics and the philosophy of Whitehead, in M. Black (ed.) *Philosophy in America*, London: Allen and Unwin, pp. 240–261.

Shimony, A. and Malin, S. (2006) Dialogue Abner Shimony–Shimon Malin, *Quantum Information Processing*, 5(4): 261–276.

Skrbina, D. (2005) *Panpsychism in the West*, London/Cambridge, MA: MIT Press.

Smith, C.M. (1978) Charles Darwin, the origin of consciousness, and panpsychism, *Journal of the History of Biology*, 11(2): 245–267.

Smith, D.L. (1999) *Freud's Philosophy of the Unconscious*, New York: Springer.

Smith, H. (1972) Wasson's *Soma*: a review article, *Journal of the American Academy of Religion*, 40(4): 480–499.

Sternberg, E.M. (2001) *The Balance Within: The Science Connecting Health and Emotions*, New York: W.H. Freeman and Company.

Stock, D. and Thelen, H.A. (1958) *Emotional Dynamics and Group Culture: Experimental Studies of Individual and Group Behaviour*, Washington, DC: National Training Laboratories.

Sulloway, F.J. (1979) *Freud, Biologist of the Mind: Beyond the Psychoanalytic Legend*, London: Burnett Books.

Sutherland, J.D. (1985) Bion revisited: group dynamics and group psychotherapy, in M. Pines (ed.) *Bion and Group Psychotherapy*, London: Routledge and Kegan Paul, pp. 47–86.

Suttie, I. (1924) The development and evolution of mind: biological v. psychosocial interpretations of the ontophylogenetic parallelism, *Journal of Neurology and Psychopathology*, 5(18): 133–145.

Suttie, I. (1935 [1960]) *The Origins of Love and Hate*, London: Routledge, Kegan and Paul.

Suzuki, D.T. (1957) *Mysticism: Christian and Buddhist*, New York: Harper and Brothers Publishers.

Symington, J. and Symington, N. (1996) *The Clinical Thinking of Wilfred Bion*, London: Routledge.

Tarski, A. (1956) *Introduction to Logic*, Oxford: Oxford University Press.

Taylor, G.J. (1987) *Psychosomatic Medicine and Contemporary Psychoanalysis*, Madison, CT: International Universities Press.

Thelen, H.A. (1985) Research with Bion's concepts, in M. Pines (ed.) *Bion and Group Psychotherapy*, London: Routledge and Kegan Paul, pp. 114–138.

Torres, N. (1999) The conversion of psychic and group significance into protomental signals, *II European Congress of Psychoanalytic Group Psychotherapy* (European Federation for Psychoanalytic Psychotherapy in the Public Sector). Barcelona.

Torres, N. (2000) Psycho-somatics as primitive conversion of meaning: empirical research on Bion's proto-mental matrix model, *Millennium Conference of the European Federation for Psychoanalytic Psychotherapy in the Public Sector*. Oxford.

Torres, N. (2003) Gregariousness and the mind: Wilfred Trotter and Wilfred Bion, in R.M. Lipgar and M. Pines (eds) *Building on Bion: Roots*, London: Jessica Kingsley, pp. 85–117.

Torres, N. (2008) Disorders of emotional containment and their somatic correlates: the proto-mental nature of addictions, self-harm and non-communicable diseases, unpublished PhD thesis, University of Essex: Centre for Psychoanalytic Studies, March.

Torres, N. (2010a) Protomentality, in R. Morgan-Jones, *The Body of the Organisation and its Health*, London: Karnac Books, pp. 53–80.

Torres, N. (2010b) Social stress related epidemic diseases: failures in emotional containment, in R. Morgan-Jones, *The Body of the Organisation and its Health.* London: Karnac Books, pp. 129–156.

Toynbee, A.J. (1935–1961) *A Study of History*, 2nd edition, London: Oxford University Press.

Trist, E. (1985) Working with Bion in the 1940s: the group decade, in M. Pines (ed.) *Bion and Group Psychotherapy*, London: Routledge and Kegan Paul, pp. 1–46.

Trist, E. (1993) Guilty of enthusiasm, in A.G. Bedeian (ed.) *Management Laureates, Volume 3*, Greenwich, CT: JAI Press, pp. 191–222.

Trist, E. and Murray, H. (1990a) *The Social Engagement of Social Science: Volume 1: The Socio-Psychological Perspective*, series: A Tavistock Anthology, London: Free Association Books.

Trist, E. and Murray, H. (1990b) A new social psychiatry: A World War II legacy, in E. Trist and H. Murray (eds) *The Social Engagement of Social Science: Volume 1:*

The Socio-Psychological Perspective, series: A Tavistock Anthology, London: Free Association Books, pp. 40–43.

Trist, E. and Murray, H. (1993) *The Social Engagement of Social Science: Volume 2: The Socio-Technical Perspective*, series: A Tavistock Anthology, London: Free Association Books.

Trist, E. and Murray, H. (1997) *The Social Engagement of Social Science: Volume 3: The Socio-Ecological Perspective*, series: A Tavistock Anthology, Philadelphia, PA: University of Pennsylvania Press.

Trotter, W. (1916) *Instincts of the Herd in Peace and War*, London: Unwin.

Trotter, W. (1932 [1941]) Art and science in medicine, in W. Trotter (1941) *The Collected Papers of Wilfred Trotter*, London: Geoffrey Cumberlege, Oxford University Press, pp. 85–101.

Trotter, W. (1939) Has the intellect a function? *The Lancet*, 233(6043): 1419–1422.

Vaillant, G.E. (1979) Health consequences of adaptation to life, *American Journal of Medicine*, 67(5): 732–734.

Vinden, F.H. (1977) The introduction of war office selection boards in the British army, in B. Bond. and I. Roy (eds) *War and Society Yearbook, Vol. 2*, London: Croon Helm, pp. 119–128.

Vonofakos, D. and Hinshelwood, R.D. (2012) Wilfred Bion's letters to John Rickman (1939–1951), *Psychoanalysis and History*, 14(1): 53–94.

Wallerstein, R.S. (1963) The problem of the assessment of change in psychotherapy, *International Journal of Psycho-Analysis*, 44: 31–41.

Ward, A. (2006) *Kant: The Three Critiques*, London: Polity Press.

Whitehead, A.N. (1911) *An Introduction to Mathematics*. London: Williams and Northgate.

Whitehead, A.N. (1920) *The Concept of Nature*, Cambridge: Cambridge University Press.

Whitehead, A.N. (1925 [1948]) *Science and the Modern World*, New York: Pelican Mentor Press.

Whitehead, A.N. (1929 [1978]) *Process and Reality: An Essay in Cosmology*, New York: The Free Press.

WHO (World Health Organization) (2000) *Noncommunicable Diseases and Mental Health: Key Areas of Work for the years 2000–2001*, online, available at: www.who.int/ncd/mip2000/documents/key_areas_en.pdf.

Wiener, P.P. (1973–1974) *Dictionary of the History of Ideas: Studies of Selected Pivotal Ideas*, New York: Charles Scribner's Sons.

Winnicott, D.W. (1967) Letter to Bion, 5 October, in F.R. Rodman (1987) *The Spontaneous Gesture*, Cambridge, MA: Harvard University Press.

Wisdom, J.O. (1952) A new model for the mind–body relationship, *British Journal for the Philosophy of Science*, 2(80: 295–301.

Wittkower, E. (1949) *A Psychiatrist Looks at Tuberculosis*, London: The National Association for the Prevention of Tuberculosis.

Woolf, Leonard (1969) *The Journey, Not the Arrival, Matters: An Autobiography of the Years 1939 to 1969*, London: Hogarth.

Wozniak, R.H. (1992) *Mind and Body: Rene Déscartes to William James*, Washington, DC: The National Library of Medicine and the American Psychological Association.

York III, G.K. and Steinberg, D.A. (2011) Hughlings Jackson's neurological ideas, *Brain*, 134(10): 3106–3113.

Index